KNOW YOUR
RELIGIONS
VOLUME 2

KNOW YOUR
RELIGIONS

VOLUME 2

A COMPARATIVE LOOK AT MORMONISM AND THE COMMUNITY OF CHRIST

Richard G. Moore

FOREWORD BY
William D. Russell, Ph.D.

Millennial Press

Millennial Press, Inc.
P.O. Box 1741
Orem, UT 84059

ISBN: 1-932597-67-0

Cover design and typesetting by Adam Riggs

DEDICATION

For Woody and Irene Mousley

TABLE OF CONTENTS

FOREWORD XI

INTRODUCTION 1

A BRIEF HISTORY OF COMMUNITY OF CHRIST 7

THE ONLY TRUE AND LIVING CHURCH UPON
THE FACE OF THE WHOLE EARTH AND THE QUESTION
OF SUCCESSION 33

CHURCH ORGANIZATION 47

LOOKING AT THE PAST: CHURCH HISTORY 53

THE PROPHET JOSEPH SMITH 61

PRIESTHOOD AND AUTHORITY 67

THE NATURE OF GOD 77

THE ORIGIN, NATURE, AND DESTINY OF HUMANITY 87

THE PLAN OF SALVATION 93

SCRIPTURES 107

SACRAMENTS AND ORDINANCES 123

TEMPLES...139

COMMANDMENTS...151

DISSIDENTS...159

CONCEPT OF ZION..169

FUTURE CHALLENGES OF COMMUNITY OF CHRIST 177

CONCLUSION..181

APPENDIX A: A STATEMENT OF BELIEF..185

APPENDIX B: SCRIPTURE IN THE COMMUNITY OF CHRIST............191

APPENDIX C: CHURCH HISTORY PRINCIPLES................................195

APPENDIX D: EXCERPTS FROM WE SHARE: IDENTITY,
MISSION, MESSAGE, AND BELIEFS..199

BIBLIOGRAPHY...217

ABOUT THE AUTHOR 231

ACKNOWLEDGMENTS

Thanks to Millennial Press for inviting me to write this volume of the *Know Your Religions* series. I am grateful to Dr. Alonzo L. Gaskill, Dr. Blair G. Van Dyke, and Lani Moore for reading the early drafts of this book and offering valuable suggestions that improved the manuscript. I offer special thanks to Community of Christ scholars and leaders who generously gave of their time and offered assistance during the research and writing process. I could not have written this book without their support and cooperation, and having their help made writing this work a very enjoyable experience for me. Thanks to Jenn Killpack, Community of Christ Public Relations, who answered my questions and sent me research materials, and to Ron E. Romig, Community of Christ Archivist, who provided pictures and other information for the book. I am indebted to Lachlan Mackay, Historic Sites Director for the Community of Christ, who tirelessly read the manuscript and offered insights, corrections, clarifications, and recommendations that were invaluable. Community of Christ World Church Secretary Andrew Shields was the first person from Community of Christ that I contacted, and he put me in touch with many very helpful people. In addition, Andrew read the manuscript, offered encouragement and suggestions, and answered a myriad of questions. I am also very appreciative of William D. Russell, Professor Emeritus of American History and Government, who wrote the foreword. He read what I thought was the final draft, found some errors, and offered suggestions that greatly improved the book. Everyone who offered assistance from Community of Christ was gracious, helpful, and incredibly pleasant. Thanks to all.

FOREWORD

This book is a welcome addition to the literature of Mormon studies because those of us in the Mormon tradition tend not to pay enough attention to other religions. This entire series of books is a great idea, and I commend Millennial Press for that. As to the comparison with the Community of Christ—which until April 6, 2001, was the Reorganized Church of Jesus Christ of Latter Day Saints (RLDS)—during the first century of the RLDS Church there were more than enough debates and writings by advocates of both churches, each lambasting the other to such an extent that a great deal of misinformation exists on both sides. Thankfully, the polemics have been far fewer in the last forty years or so, as close associations have developed between members of both churches. Family reunions of the descendants of Joseph and Emma Smith have been a valuable connection since there are descendants in both churches today. The general officers of both churches have also enjoyed personal interaction from time to time that is healthy for us all.

I am especially familiar with the close relations existing between historians of both churches and have been since 1971, when I was fortunate enough to join with our Church Historian Richard P. Howard, and with Mark McKiernan and Paul and Lyman Edwards (two brothers who are great-great-grandsons of Joseph the Martyr) at the Mormon History Association's annual meeting held at Brigham Young University in Provo, Utah. The immediate, warm friendships that developed with Leonard Arrington, Jim Allen, Tom Alexander, Davis Bitton, Maureen Beecher, Richard Poll, and many others created close ties that will never be broken. As I stated in my presidential address at the Mormon History Association meeting in Omaha, Nebraska, in 1983:

> In the Mormon History Association I have experienced love in the truest sense: love which is not conditioned upon belief in "correct" doctrine, or upon the practice of expected rituals, or upon actions which are above reproach. This kind of acceptance is often not found in those local wards or congregations where independent thinking and scholarship is not welcomed. And that is why, since 1971, I have made my annual pilgrimage to the Mormon History Association. It has been spiritually as well as intellectually renewing for me. That is why you are a group of people I have grown to love dearly. And this is why—though for most of you our ecclesiastical paths separated about 135 years ago—you my colleagues in the Mormon History Association, are truly my brothers and sisters.

Those of us in Community of Christ will welcome this book because, understandably, many members of a church about fifty times our size have never heard of us, know very little about us, or have only "information" that is distorted. Dr. Moore's task is made all the harder by the fact that the Community of Christ has changed so much over the past forty to fifty years and the fact that church leaders and world conferences do not take official positions on some important issues, especially not theological controversies like the virgin birth of Jesus. As a few examples, although opposition to the idea that Joseph Smith was a polygamist was central to our teachings for well over a century, today the Community of Christ does not take a position on whether the founding prophet did or did not engage in polygamy, nor do we take an official position on the historicity of the Book of Mormon. We leave these matters to the historians.

All churches evolve in their understanding of religious truth over time, but the Community of Christ has undergone radical change over the past forty or fifty years. It is not easy for an outsider to understand and characterize the contemporary position of a church that has evolved from being convinced it was the "one true church" to trying to be a faithful part of the larger body of Christ that is worldwide Christianity.

Professor Moore has read most of the important sources for understanding the contemporary Community of Christ and presents his information in a very fair manner. I did not detect any subtle LDS bias as I read the manuscript or any judgment of the Community of Christ's positions as lacking. Here is a source that readers can trust as honest and unbiased.

The organization of the chapters is well conceived, beginning with an introduction to the subject, followed by the Community of Christ teachings on the subject, then the LDS teachings on the subject, and finally concluding with a summary.

Four appendices add valuable information for all readers, whether LDS, Community of Christ, or those outside the Mormon tradition. First is a statement of belief drafted by a committee of general officers of the church and published in 1970, which replaced the "Epitome of Faith" (almost identical to the LDS "Articles of Faith" since both are based on Joseph Smith's Wentworth Letter) that the RLDS Church used for almost a century. Second is a recent (2003) statement about the nature of scripture as seen by Community of Christ, drafted by the church's Theology Task Force. Third is a very interesting statement of "Church History Principles" that was written by Community of Christ President Stephen M. Veazey in 2008 and stimulated by the awareness that a new three-volume history of the church, which is being prepared by Church Historian Mark Scherer, will be controversial for some church members. Fourth is a fourteen-page statement entitled, *We Share: Identity, Mission, Message and Beliefs* published by the Community of Christ in 2008.

These four appendices will be especially informative for LDS members and non-Mormons, but many Community of Christ members will be only vaguely familiar with the content of some of these documents.

Here we have another comparison between the two churches, but unlike the previous comparisons, this one is fair and not in the least bit polemical! Thanks to Richard G. Moore and to Millennial Press for this volume and for the series they are undertaking.

William D. Russell
Professor Emeritus of American History and Government
Graceland University

INTRODUCTION

This series of books, *Know Your Religions*, is an attempt to explain to Mormons the doctrines and religious beliefs of their non-Mormon brothers and sisters, not in a critical or competitive way, but in a simply comparative manner so as to increase knowledge and foster greater understanding. Stephen L. Richards said, "Greater knowledge brings more understanding, and with understanding prejudices disappear."[1]

For members of The Church of Jesus Christ of Latter-day Saints there is probably no greater need for understanding of any religion than there is for Community of Christ, formerly known as the Reorganized Church of Jesus Christ of Latter Day Saints.[2] Because of the common origin of the two churches and the rift that took place following the death of Joseph Smith Jr., the prophet of the Restoration, a relationship of suspicion and animosity existed for many years. Leaders and members of both groups have on occasion been harsh in their views, remarks, and writings about the "other" restoration church. Typically, each church saw the other as an apostate organization.

I am happy to report that in recent years a new spirit of open communication and cooperation has developed. The two churches have worked together on some historical site projects, archives have

---

1   Richards, *Where is Wisdom?* 119.
2   Thanks to Andrew Shields, Community of Christ World Church Secretary, for informing me that they refer to their organization as Community of Christ and not "the" Community of Christ. I have tried to do so throughout this work unless "the Community of Christ" is used in a quotation.

been opened to scholars from both churches, and friendships have been established. It is very common for Community of Christ historians and LDS historians to participate in the same conferences and share insights with each other.[3]

However, among the rank-and-file Latter-day Saints, there still exists much misunderstanding and misinformation about the origin, history, doctrine, and current status of Community of Christ.[4] Few Mormons have done any reading about the Reorganization and know very little about its beliefs. Latter-day Saints typically know that Community of Christ owns the Kirtland Temple, for years its prophet-presidents have been descendants of Joseph Smith, it has a temple that anybody can go into, and women in the church can hold the priesthood. Rumors have circulated about them "running out" of Joseph Smith descendants to lead the church, rejecting the Book of Mormon, and trying to sell the LDS Church the Kirtland Temple. Are any of these things true?

The purpose of this book is to briefly review the history of the Reorganization and consider the changes that have taken place over the years, especially those occurring since the 1960s. We will also examine the doctrines and beliefs of Community of Christ in comparison with those of The Church of Jesus Christ of Latter-day Saints.

For many years Community of Christ was known as the Reorganized Church of Jesus Christ of Latter Day Saints. It was very common in their literature for them to refer to themselves as Latter Day Saints. In April 2000 at its world conference, the church decided that "it would be known as the Community of Christ, although its legal

---

3   Both sides have noticed the changed relationship. In 2003, William D. Russell published an article in *Dialogue* magazine entitled, "The LDS Church and the Community of Christ: Clearer Differences, Closer Friends." To date, the Mormon History Association has had five Community of Christ historians serve as president of that organization.

4   I have been surprised by how many Latter-day Saints are not even aware of the name change from the Reorganized Church to Community of Christ. It is also not uncommon to hear a Mormon say something like, "Emma Smith started the reorganized church."

name would remain unchanged."[5] That transition officially took place on April 6, 2001.

I have found it necessary when quoting older Community of Christ sources or referring to the organization before it became Community of Christ to use the terms *Reorganized Church of Jesus Christ of Latter Day Saints, Reorganization, New Organization,* and *RLDS.* To avoid confusion, please note that RLDS sources sometimes refer to themselves as Latter Day Saints (notice that "Day" is capitalized and there is no hyphen between "Latter" and "Day"). I refer to The Church of Jesus Christ of Latter-day Saints by its formal name as well as the *LDS Church, Mormons, Utah church,* and *Latter-day Saints* (notice the hyphen).

In examining the beliefs of any religion, it is important to understand that there are official doctrines and then there are vast and varied beliefs of its members. Latter-day Saints certainly have differences of opinion when it comes to their religious beliefs. This is also true of Community of Christ. It has its conservatives, liberals, moderates, and fundamentalists. The purpose of this book is not to examine the various positions and personal interpretations of doctrine found in the lay membership of either religion. Rather, the intent is to compare official LDS doctrine to official Community of Christ doctrine.

Comparing the doctrines of the two churches has been somewhat challenging because it is not always easy to determine the official doctrine of Community of Christ. While LDS doctrine appears to be more clearly stated, perhaps even seen by some as dogmatic, Community of Christ has traditionally tried to avoid creedal statements and has sought to preserve openness when it comes to understanding the word of God.[6]

Community of Christ theologian in residence Anthony Chvala-Smith remarked that the Community of Christ, "with their diversity of theologies, do not presently appear to have a formal or institutional consensus about what ought to constitute the essential doctrines of the

---

5   Garr, Cannon, and Cowan, eds. *Encyclopedia of Latter-day Saint History,* "Reorganized Church of Jesus Christ of Latter Day Saints," 1002.

6   *Exploring the Faith,* 5.

church."[7] A published guide for members of Community of Christ includes this statement: "A belief that we cling to today may be reconsidered tomorrow, next month, or next year in the light of our new experience."[8]

This is not a recent phenomenon in the Reorganization. RLDS historian Richard P. Howard noted:

> There always has remained a certain tension between, on the one hand, those wanting definitive statements of religious dogma from church leadership to guide them in their stewardship of life and, on the other hand, those maintaining firmly their right of conscience to question every statement claiming any degree of religious authority, from whatever source.[9]

Howard did not see this tension as detrimental in any way, "but rather a sign of growth potential and an opportunity for a more enlightened dialogue among the membership."[10]

Even though the church has a prophet-president, revelation is more important than the revelator. It sees its theology not so much as "a task of the institutional church" or "the domain of a few academicians," but as something open to all church members.[11] President W. Grant McMurray suggested that members of Community of Christ should think of themselves not so much as a "people with a prophet" but as a "prophetic people."[12]

I have taken great care to represent Community of Christ doctrine correctly. I examined the official statements made by church leaders and the research and writings of their historians and scholars. I had personal contact and discussion with Community of Christ leaders and academicians, and selected members of Community of Christ read and critiqued each chapter of this book before publication.

---

7   Chvala-Smith, "A Trinitarian Approach to World Religions," in *Restoration Studies VIII*, 128.
8   *Walking with Jesus: A Member's Guide in the Community of Christ*, 27.
9   Howard, "The Reorganized Church in Illinois, 1852–82: Search for Identity," 71.
10   Ibid.
11   Larry Conrad and Paul Shupe, "An RLDS Reformation? Construing the Task of RLDS Theology," 102.
12   McMurray, "A Prophetic People," 226.

I'm not saying that every Community of Christ member will agree with what has been written. For that matter, I doubt that every member of The Church of Jesus Christ of Latter-day Saints will concur with each of my assessments of LDS doctrine. I am saying that I have tried to carefully portray each church fairly and correctly. I in no way represent either church and am responsible for any errors.

As I said in the beginning, I hope this book will increase knowledge and foster understanding between the members of these two restoration churches. Let us cling to the common ground of our faith in the Lord Jesus Christ and be more Christ-like in our dealings with each other and with all of God's children.

A Brief History
of Community of Christ

A COMMON BEGINNING

Both Community of Christ and The Church of Jesus Christ of Latter-day Saints trace their origin in this dispensation to the Prophet Joseph Smith. For several decades what are now two separate denominations shared a common history.

Joseph Smith Jr. was born in Vermont on December 23, 1805, the fourth child of Joseph Smith Sr. and Lucy Mack Smith. During the early years of his life, Joseph became caught up in the religious fervor—part of the Second Great Awakening—that was taking place in the area where he lived. Although a number of his immediate family members became involved with a particular Christian faith, Joseph was hesitant to join any specific denomination. In his own words:

> During this time of great excitement my mind was called up to serious reflection and great uneasiness; but though my feelings were deep and often poignant, still I kept aloof from all these parties, though I attended their several meetings as often as occasion would permit. . . . but so great were the confusion and strife among the different denominations, that it was impossible for a person young as I was, and so unacquainted with men and things,

to come to any certain conclusion who was right and who was wrong.[13]

Eventually, young Joseph Smith became aware of a passage of scripture in the New Testament that changed his life. James 1:5 reads: "If any of you lack wisdom, let him ask of God, that giveth to all men liberally and upbraideth not; and it shall be given him." At age fourteen, Joseph Smith decided to put that particular verse to the test and ask God which church he should join. Again, we return to Joseph's own account:

> It was on the morning of a beautiful, clear day, early in the spring of eighteen hundred and twenty. It was the first time in my life that I had made such an attempt, for amidst all my anxieties I had never as yet made the attempt to pray vocally. After I had retired to the place where I had previously designed to go, having looked around me, and finding myself alone, I kneeled down and began to offer up the desires of my heart to God.[14]

In a secluded grove of trees not far from his home in the Manchester-Palmyra area of New York, Joseph prayed and received the answer he sought in a theophany. In a pillar of light two personages appeared to the young man. One of the personages called Joseph by name and, pointing to the other personage, said, "This is My Beloved Son. Hear Him!"[15]

This experience of the young Joseph Smith eventually became known as the First Vision.[16] The information he received from that vision included the instruction to join none of the churches. He later

---

13   *History of the Reorganized Church of Jesus Christ of Latter Day Saints* 1:7–8, hereafter cited as *History RLDS*; *History of the Church* 1:3–4, hereafter cited as *HC*.

14   *History RLDS* 1:8–9; *HC* 1:5.

15   *History RLDS* 1:9; *HC* 1:5.

16   There are several differing versions of the First Vision, including accounts written in 1832, 1835, and 1838. The version that has been canonized by the LDS Church and is found in their Pearl of Great Price is the 1838 account. Community of Christ typically does not stress the 1838 account over any other versions, but it is more likely to use the 1832 account. Lachlan Mackay explained to me that when Community of Christ members had been converted to Joseph Smith's experience rather than having their own personal conversion, the introduction of differing accounts of the First Vision caused significant difficulty.

reported that after the vision ended "I found myself lying on my back, looking up into heaven." Joseph felt weak but soon recovered enough to go home, at which point he remarked to his mother that he had discovered for himself that the church she had joined was not true.[17]

Little is known about Joseph's life after the First Vision in 1820 until his next heavenly experience over three years later. In the fall of 1823, seventeen-year-old Joseph was worried that because "he had fallen into many foolish errors, and displayed the weakness of youth" perhaps his life had not been "consistent with that character which ought to be maintained by one who was called of God."[18] Feeling ashamed of his imperfections, Joseph sought forgiveness for his sins and weaknesses and perhaps even for another divine manifestation.

On the evening of September 21, 1823, Joseph retired to his bedroom for the night and prayed to God that he "might know his state and standing before him." A light appeared in Joseph's room and within that light Joseph saw an angelic minister who introduced himself as Moroni. Joseph was instructed by Moroni that God had a work for him to do, which included acquiring and translating an ancient record written on metal plates that were buried a short distance from his home.

The following day, Joseph Smith made his way to a hill near Manchester, New York. There, hidden under a rock of considerable size, he found a stone box containing the record of which Moroni had spoken. Moroni informed Joseph that he was not prepared to take the record at that time but must return to the hill each year on the same day until Joseph was fully prepared for the responsibility. Four years later Joseph did receive the plates and shortly thereafter began the translation process.

Amid persecutions and interruptions, but with the help of friends and family, Joseph completed the translation in June 1829. Less than

---

17   Joseph noted that prior to the First Vision his "father's family was proselyted to the Presbyterian faith, and four of them joined that church, namely, my mother, Lucy; my brothers Hyrum and Samuel Harrison; and my sister Sophronia." Joseph Smith— History 1:7; Pearl of Great Price, 48.

18   Joseph Smith—History 1:28; Pearl of Great Price, 51; a somewhat different version is found in *History RLDS* 1:12.

one year later the first edition of the published manuscript, known as the Book of Mormon, was ready for distribution.

With the publication of the Book of Mormon accomplished, the Lord instructed Joseph to officially organize the church. On April 6, 1830, at Fayette, New York, with a number of witnesses observing the proceedings, six men founded the Church of Christ. A number of others present were baptized that same day.

The fledgling organization grew quickly, and several branches of the church were formed. Some citizens in the communities where branches had been established were troubled by what they deemed a new and strange religion. Threats and persecution followed. Eventually, the Saints were forced to move to an area where they felt they could find some peace from persecution: Kirtland, Ohio.

The young church prospered in Ohio, more clearly establishing the organization's leadership and hierarchy, sending out missionaries to further the work, and building a temple. The doctrines of the restoration were expanded and clarified through revelation given to the Prophet Joseph Smith.

One of the revelations received during the Kirtland era specified Jackson County, Missouri, as the center place of the Zion that the Saints sought to establish. A number of church members were sent west to settle in that area. Soon, Kirtland, Ohio, and Independence, Missouri, became the two major centers of the church. However, persecution in Jackson County and disharmony and apostasy in the Kirtland area resulted in the abandonment of both gathering places. Out of necessity the Saints moved to Caldwell County, Missouri—a county created by the Missouri legislature for Mormon refugees who had lost their homes in Jackson County.

The Saints established the city of Far West, and many church members from Ohio gathered to that area with the Missouri Saints. The growth of membership in the Church of Jesus Christ of Latter Day Saints[19] and the influx of Saints to the Far West area again aroused the

---

19   The church created by Joseph Smith went through several name changes. Originally, it was called the Church of Christ. Later, it was known as The Church of Jesus Christ, the Church of the Latter Day Saints, and finally, through an April 1838 revelation given to the Prophet Joseph Smith at Far West, Missouri, it became known as The Church of Jesus Christ of Latter Day Saints. See "An Extract of Revelation," *Elders' Journal* 1 (August 1838): 52–53. See also Robert J. Woodford, *Historical Development*

suspicion and hatred of many Missourians. Persecution, violence, and skirmishes ensued, with both parties guilty of mob activities.

Missouri governor Lilburn W. Boggs evidently believed reports that it was the Mormons who were causing most of the problems. Boggs determined that Joseph Smith and other church leaders should be arrested and tried for crimes of treason against the state and that the Mormons should be driven from Missouri.

On the last day of October and first day of November 1838, a number of church leaders, including Joseph and Hyrum Smith, were turned over to state militia leaders as prisoners. They remained in Missouri prisons until they were released in the spring of 1839. In the meantime, Mormons were forced to leave their Missouri land and homes. They traveled eastward and crossed the Mississippi River into Illinois.

In Illinois the Saints purchased land in a town known as Commerce, where they created a thriving community that they renamed Nauvoo. Thousands of Saints gathered to Nauvoo and surrounding areas. They planned and were in the process of building a temple when antagonism and persecution from non-Mormons and dissenters from the church appeared again.

In June 1844 Joseph Smith, Hyrum Smith, and others were arrested and imprisoned in Carthage, Illinois, and on the 27th of June, an armed mob stormed Carthage Jail and killed Joseph and Hyrum Smith. To the Saints, the unthinkable had happened. They had lost the Prophet and his brother, the Patriarch. In the midst of mourning for the death of their beloved leaders, the questions of what would become of the church and who would lead must have weighed heavily upon the minds of the Saints.[20]

---

of the Doctrine and Covenants, 3:1506–7. The nickname "Mormons" was also attached to the Church as a form of derision based the Saints' belief in the Book of Mormon. Today, the church headquartered in Salt Lake City, Utah, goes by the official name of The Church of Jesus Christ of Latter-day Saints. Until April 2001, the church now headquartered in Independence, Missouri, went by the name: The Reorganized Church of Jesus Christ of Latter Day Saints. It is now officially known as Community of Christ.

20   Community of Christ historian Paul M. Edwards wrote, "Joseph failed to prepare the church for the time when he would no longer be able to lead. This meant that a vacuum would be filled by well-meaning but often unprepared claimants." Edwards, *Our Legacy of Faith: A Brief History of the Reorganized Church of Jesus Christ of Latter Day Saints,* 115. D. Michael Quinn's 1976 article "The Mormon Succession Crisis of 1844" suggests that Joseph Smith had actually "by word or by action established

Following the death of church leaders Joseph and Hyrum Smith, a number of individuals attempted to take the reins of the church in place of the fallen Prophet. What was reported to have been a unanimous vote at a meeting held in Nauvoo on August 8, 1844, in support of the Quorum of the Twelve Apostles clearly did not end the succession controversy.

The majority of the Saints accepted Brigham Young and the Quorum of the Twelve as the holders of the keys of the kingdom and authorized leaders to succeed Joseph Smith. Others followed various claimants to church leadership.

By April 1845, Sidney Rigdon had started his own church in Pittsburg, Pennsylvania. Apostle Lyman Wight abandoned Brigham Young and the rest of the Quorum of the Twelve to lead a splinter group to Texas. In the first few years after Joseph Smith died, James J. Strang was actually the most serious challenger to Brigham Young for church leadership. Membership estimates of the church begun by Strang at its high point range from 1,000 to 6,000—a very wide variance in estimation.[21] Whatever the actual number, Strang's organization did for a

---

precedents or authority for eight possible methods of succession." Quinn claims that most Latter Day Saints had "only the haziest concept of what should transpire in the leadership of the LDS Church if the founding prophet were to die." He went on to explain that for "the average Mormon the death of Joseph Smith, Jr., created a sometimes prolonged crisis in which it was necessary to decide which of the conflicting succession claimants was authorized by God." This crisis resulted in the fragmentation of the Church. Quinn, "The Mormon Succession Crisis of 1844," 187–88. Andrew F. Ehat argues that although Quinn "posed several theoretical methods of succession that either were outlined explicitly by or could be inferred from the teachings and revelations" of Joseph Smith, only five of the possibilities were feasible at the death of the Prophet. "Because none of Joseph's sons were old enough to have assumed the Presidency at the time of their father's death," that method "was unfeasible as an immediate option." Ehat, "Joseph Smith's Introduction of Temple Ordinances and the 1844 Mormon Succession Question," 6. James Whitehead remembered that "Hyrum was appointed his [Joseph Smith III] guardian till he should become of age." W. W. Blair, Journal, June 17, 1974 cited in Ehat, 251 n. 21.

21 Vickie Cleverly Speek, "From Strangites to Reorganized Latter Day Saints: Transformations in Midwestern Mormonism, 1856–79," in *Scattering of the Saints: Schism within Mormonism*, ed. Newell G Bringhurst and John C. Hamer, 142. The reliability of estimations made during the early years following the Restoration has always been suspect. An article in the May 15, 1845 *Times and Seasons* reported that the number of Church members was 200,000. Dean May estimates the total number of members at that time to be about 31,000—a substantial difference in estimations. Some reports put the number of people attending the April 1844 general conference where Joseph

time include former LDS Church leaders John E. Page, William Smith (Joseph's only surviving brother), William E. McLellin, John C. Bennet, and William E. Marks.

It is difficult to find reliable data concerning church population during the early years. It is also challenging to determine how many people went west with Brigham Young and how many chose not to follow Young and the Twelve. Approximations can vary substantially. In recent years scholars have tried to more carefully estimate the number of those who went west and those who stayed behind, typically settling somewhere in the Midwest. Scholars might differ on the percentage of church members going west and those remaining behind, but all would likely agree that the majority followed Brigham Young and the Twelve.[22]

As Community of Christ historian Paul M. Edwards wrote, "Probably hundreds of those faithful at Nauvoo were unaccepting of any of the leadership claims." Though some joined other churches, "many simply waited—often without knowing just what they were waiting

---

Smith gave the "King Follett Discourse" at 20,000. Others estimated the number attending that sermon to be about 8,000. Again, the difference between estimates is significant.

22 Dean L. May reported that although the majority went west with Brigham Young and the Twelve, those who remained behind may be a larger number than formerly believed. He suggested that perhaps as many as 40 percent of the Nauvoo Saints stayed behind after Brigham Young and his followers traveled west. At the time this information was published, May was the Director of the Center for Historical Population Studies at the University of Utah. Although his findings are educated estimates, they are still estimates and not based on documented numbers. Dean L. May, "A Demographic Portrait of the Mormons, 1830–1980," in *After 150 Years*, ed. Thomas G. Alexander and Jessie L. Embry, 39. Robert Bruce Flanders estimated that nearly one third of the total church membership remained behind. Flanders, *Nauvoo: Kingdom on the Mississippi*, 322. Several things must be considered. There were those who initially followed Brigham Young and then either stayed or returned to the Midwest. There were many who remained in the Midwest for some time before traveling west to the Great Basin to be with the Mormons. There is virtually no way to be sure exactly how many followed Brigham Young and how many chose to follow others claiming church leadership. As far as Nauvoo Saints remaining behind—very few would have remained in Nauvoo. Thomas L. Kane visited Nauvoo after the Saints had abandoned the city and referred to it as the "Deserted City." Kane described entering empty workshops and smithies and seeing "no work people anywhere. . . . I could have supposed the people hidden in the houses, but the doors were unfastened, and when at last I timidly entered them, I found ashes dead upon the earths." Quoted in Glen M. Leonard, *Nauvoo*, 619.

JOSEPH SMITH III
Courtesy Community of Christ Archives,
Independence, Missouri

for."[23] Some believed that the true successor to Joseph Smith should be his son, Joseph Smith III. Their rejection of Brigham Young and other claimants combined with the strong sense that the Prophet's son, Joseph Smith III, possessed the authentic claim to church leadership were important motivations for the Reorganization.[24]

Within a few years of the death of the Prophet Joseph Smith, the vast majority of the Saints left the Nauvoo area, either by choice or by force. Most followed Brigham Young and the Twelve, some joined other factions, and others did not unite with any organization. As one historian wrote, "The once tranquil society of beautiful Nauvoo was in turmoil as Saints were quickly scattered by winds of doctrine in 1845. . . . As former citizens fled to Wisconsin, Kentucky, Pennsylvania, and Texas, the strength once known in cohesive worship dwindled."[25]

Many former followers of Joseph Smith united with the various factions led by men such as Sidney Rigdon, James Strang, and William Smith, only to become disillusioned with these new churches, their leaders, and their doctrine. "The movement that became the Reorganized Church of Jesus Christ of Latter Day Saints," wrote Roger D. Launius, "arose in large part out of a schism within William Smith's faction in 1850."[26]

23   Edwards, *Our Legacy of Faith*, 125.
24   *History RLDS* 3:209.
25   Susan Easton Black, "Joseph Smith III and the 'Lost Sheep,'" in *Regional Studies in Latter-day Saint Church History: Illinois*, 56.
26   Roger D. Launius, *Joseph Smith III: Pragmatic Prophet*, 83.

THE REORGANIZATION

The two men who are given most credit for beginning the Reorganization are Jason W. Briggs and Zenos Gurley Sr. Briggs joined The Church of Jesus Christ of Latter-day Saints in 1841. After Joseph Smith was killed, Briggs first stayed with the majority of the Saints who followed Brigham Young and the Twelve. As the Saints moved west, Briggs left that group and united with James J. Strang's church. Following his time with Strang, Briggs became part of William Smith's group for a short period.

Briggs declared that his concern about who held the true authority led him to seek divine guidance. He said that the answer, which came to him in November 1851[27], was that a descendant of Joseph Smith should rightly preside over the restored church.

JASON W. BRIGGS
Courtesy Community of Christ Archives,
Independence, Missouri

Several moths later a copy of Brigg's revelation was delivered to Zenos Gurley Sr., who attested to having received a confirmation that Brigg's revelation was indeed true. The message was spread to several existing branches of Latter-day Saints who had not gone west with Brigham Young. A conference of these congregations met in the summer of 1852 to consider the revelation received by Jason Briggs. Historian and Community of Christ member Roger D. Launius wrote of this conference:

> It had no acknowledged head, no organization for which to transact business, no authority to act, and no business to transact. It was united only in its opposition to other Mormon factions,

---

27   Some Community of Christ members see Briggs' experience as being somewhat similar to the grove experience of Joseph Smith Jr.

ZENOS GURLEY
Courtesy Community of Christ Archives,
Independence, Missouri

in its acceptance of the Briggs document as divine revelation, in its belief that Mormonism as set forth in the Scriptures was correct, and in its affirmation that the proper successor to the prophetic office was growing to maturity in Nauvoo and would one day step forth to accept his calling.[28]

This New Organization of the Church of Jesus Christ of Latter Day Saints eventually selected apostles, including Briggs and Gurley, with Briggs as the presiding officer. In the years that followed, efforts were made by members of the New Organization to persuade Joseph Smith III to accept a role as leader of their church. For several years, young Joseph did not respond to any communication from the Reorganized Church.

In 1856 Edmund C. Briggs and Samuel H. Gurley, brothers of Jason Briggs and Zenos Gurley Sr., traveled to Nauvoo to speak with Joseph Smith III in person. Joseph told them he was not interested in their proposal that he become involved with the Reorganization.[29] Joseph Smith III would not accept the leadership role of the New Organization unless he felt he had been called by God.

After several years of what young Joseph considered to be humbling, preparation experiences, he agreed to take leadership of the organization readied for him by Reorganization founders Jason Briggs and Zenos Gurley Sr.

The church held a conference in Amboy, Illinois, in April 1860. On April 6, thirty years to the day that Joseph Smith Jr. organized what would become The Church of Jesus Christ of Latter-day Saints and nearly sixteen years after the death of his father, Joseph Smith III

---

28   Launius, *Joseph Smith III: Pragmatic Prophet*, 88.
29   Ibid., 101–4.

was unanimously accepted by the conference as the "prophet, seer, and revelator of the church of Jesus Christ, and the successor of his father" and was ordained "President of the High Priesthood of the Church by Bros. Z. H. Gurley and Wm. Marks."[30]

Although the Reorganization had been functioning to some degree since 1852, having Joseph Smith III accept the role of president of the church, plus the addition of his mother, Emma Smith[31], and his brothers, Alexander and David, provided strength and stability to the New Organization.

EMMA SMITH
Courtesy Community of Christ Archives,
Independence, Missouri

This was something many of those who had not been involved with the church since the Prophet Joseph died and those who had dissented from other factions had been waiting for.

---

30   April 6, 1860, conference minutes as quoted in Howard, *The Church Through the* Years 1:375. Information about the origin of the Reorganized Church of Jesus Christ of Latter Day Saints was obtained from the following sources: Bringhurst and Hamer, eds., *Scattering of the Saints: Schism within Mormonism*; Edwards, *Our Legacy of Faith*; Launius, *Joseph Smith III: Pragmatic Prophet*; Launius and Spillman, eds., *Let Contention Cease*; and Shields, *Divergent Paths of the Restoration.*

31   There has been some controversy as to whether Emma Smith ever officially joined the Reorganized Church, but those who disagree that Emma was a member of the RLDS Church are mistaken. Because the Reorganization was considered by its leaders and members to be the legitimate continuation of the church Joseph Smith Jr. organized, anyone who had been a member of the original church was not required to be rebaptized into the Reorganized Church. Some Latter-day Saints might argue that Emma never actually joined the Reorganization, but there is little question about her involvement with the RLDS Church. On the day that Joseph III was ordained as President of the Reorganization, a unanimous vote supported the motion that Emma Smith Bidamon, who was also present, "be received as a member of the Reorganization." Linda King Newell and Valeen Tippetts Avery, *Mormon Enigma: Emma Hale Smith*, 272. Joseph Smith III recorded, "Mother and I united with the church at that conference, as is known." Anderson, ed., *Joseph Smith III and the Restoration*, 115.

Those who were in attendance at the conference where Joseph Smith III became the president of the church heard him testify it was God's will that he accept the calling. "I came not here of myself, but by the influence of the Spirit," he declared. "For some time past I have received manifestations pointing to the position which I am about to assume. I wish to say that I have come here not to be dictated by any men or set of men. I have come in obedience to a power not my own, and shall be dictated by the power that sent me."[32]

It was a challenge for Joseph Smith III to unite and centralize a church composed of diverse individuals and congregations, especially when it had been created by many who had dissented from other groups. Several things were helpful to the unification process. First and foremost, he was the eldest son of the Prophet Joseph Smith. This provided those who had known and loved the Prophet a connection to the New Organization.

Second, there existed in the New Organization a belief that as a young boy Joseph III had received a special blessing from his father in the second floor council room of the Red Brick Store in Nauvoo. Some said they were present and remembered the Prophet pronouncing a blessing upon Joseph III promising that he would succeed his father in the leadership of the church.[33]

---

32   *History RLDS* 3:247–50.

33   D. Michael Quinn wrote: "Whether, in fact, Joseph Smith officially designated his son Joseph III to be his successor has been debated for more than a century. . . . Nevertheless, there is circumstantial evidence from the Nauvoo period indicating that Joseph Smith III was designated to be the successor to his father. Rumors about the matter were widespread enough to be included in an 1844 published history of Illinois." Quinn, "The Mormon Succession Crisis of 1844," 223–25. It appears that even some of the Saints who followed Brigham Young believed that the blessing pronounced upon Joseph Smith III may have been legitimate, but they were also convinced that the blessing became invalid because of their belief that all blessings are conditional upon worthiness and, in their view, Joseph III had forfeited his blessing because he had gone astray. An LDS source written well after the fact as a remembrance, and thus subject to questions concerning reliability, still represents the common LDS feeling about Joseph Smith III's claim to leadership. "Well do I remember," Mosiah Hancock wrote years after the incident was supposed to have taken place, "the Prophet's speech from the frame in front of his mansion—where he said, 'Brethren, I now roll this work onto the shoulders of the Twelve.'" Remarking on his father's loyalty to the Prophet Joseph, Hancock recalled saying to himself, "I trust that I will be as true to young Joseph, the Prophet's son, as my father is to his father." He told his father of his thoughts, at which his father replied, "No, Mosiah, for God has shown to brother Joseph that his son,

Finally, a strong, binding feeling among members of the New Organization was their belief that Brigham Young was a fraud and usurper
of authority. The primary objection to The Church of Jesus Christ of
Latter-day Saints under Brigham Young's direction was polygamy. In
his inaugural address as president of the Reorganized Church, Joseph
III said to those in the congregation:

> There is but one principle taught by the leaders of any faction
> of this people that I hold in utter abhorrence; that is a principle
> taught by Brigham Young and those believing in him. I have been
> told that my father taught such doctrines. I have never believed it
> and never can believe it. If such things were done, then I believe
> they were never done by divine authority. I believe my father was
> a good man, and a good man never could have promulgated such
> doctrines.[34]

Joseph Smith III did not believe that plural marriage had originated with his father. It appears likely that his mother had taught him
and his brothers that polygamy was something that Brigham Young
had introduced into the religion after the death of their father.[35] He
heard from others that his father was not involved with the practice
of plural marriage.[36] He was unaware that Joseph and a small group of

---

Joseph, will be the means of drawing many people away from this Church after him.
Brother Joseph gave us to understand that it was our duty to follow the Twelve." *Levi
and Mosiah Hancock Journals Excerpts*, 112–13.

34   Anderson, ed., *Joseph Smith III and the Restoration*, 163.

35   This is conjecture on my part. It may be that Emma never spoke about polygamy to
her sons until an interview Joseph and Alexander had with their mother just prior to
her death in 1979. It is possible that Joseph III and his brothers made the assumption
that polygamy was a product of Brigham Young's Mormonism.

36   A letter to Joseph Smith III from William B. Smith, brother of Joseph Smith Jr., found
in *History RLDS* 4:248–49 states, "I was in close council, more or less, with your
father; and never in all this familiar association with him, did I ever hear him hint or
say that he had received a polygamous revelation." In 1893, the only surviving sister of
Joseph Smith Jr. testified that she had never heard him mention the plural wife system
or order. She also certified that her brother had no wife except Emma. Ibid., 5:207. see
also "Aunt Katherine Salisbury's Testimony," Saints' Herald (May 6, 1893). With so
many family members telling him that his father had no involvement with plural marriage, it is no surprise that Joseph III did not believe polygamy was introduced to the
church by his father. There were, however, many people close to the Prophet Joseph
who said he did practice plural marriage. See Todd Compton, In Sacred Loneliness:
The Plural Wives of Joseph Smith, Salt Lake City: Signature Books, 1997.

individuals had secretly practiced polygamy, while publicly denying its existence.[37]

During his time as president of the Reorganized Church of Jesus Christ of Latter Day Saints, Joseph Smith III made every effort to clear his family's name and the name of the religion his father had founded from the stain he believed Brigham Young had caused. In an 1872 article written for *The Saints' Herald*, President Smith wrote: "The plain statement that Brigham Young is responsible for much of the evil and wrong the people of the Church of Jesus Christ of Latter Day Saints have suffered, may be and we believe is true."[38]

Known for his candor and sometimes blunt demeanor, Brigham Young expressed some equally strong feelings about young Joseph and the New Organization. Joseph reported to have heard that Brigham Young referred to him as an outlaw, apostate, and a spiritualist.[39] From their published sermons it appears that LDS leaders seldom attacked young Joseph, but some of their negative statements were directed at Emma Smith,[40] and some of these disparaging comments were made by Brigham Young.[41]

President Young was not always negative in his comments about Emma and appears to have had mixed feelings about the Smith family. There is no doubt that he was bothered that they had not stayed faith-

---

37   For example, in the March 15, 1843, issue of the *Times and Seasons*, it states: "We are charged with advocating a plurality of wives, and common property. Now this is as false as the many other ridiculous charges which are brought against us. No sect have a greater reverence for the laws of matrimony." *Times and Seasons* 4 (March 15, 1843): 143. See also *Times and Seasons* 3:763.

38   As found in *History RLDS* 3:690–91.

39   Anderson, ed., *Joseph Smith III and the Restoration*, 319–20.

40   For many years it was not uncommon to hear negative statements about Emma Smith from the general membership of The Church of Jesus Christ of Latter-day Saints. Part of this negative feeling toward Emma was a result of a few statements made by Brigham Young and other early Church leaders. There still exists a mistaken belief held by some Latter-day Saints that Emma Smith was the founder of what has become Community of Christ. In recent years, however, there has been much positive written, spoken, and portrayed in LDS media concerning Emma Smith. Indeed, she is beginning to take her place again in LDS history as an "elect lady."

41   It is probable that among Mormons the best-known statement made by Brigham Young about Emma is, "Joseph used to say that he would have her [Emma] hereafter, if he had to go to hell for her, and he will have to go to hell for her as sure as he ever gets her." Brigham Young, in *Journal of Discourses*, 17:159.

ful to the group of Saints he led. Young was likely angry with Emma for teaching her sons what he considered lies, yet he appeared always ready to welcome them back.

Brigham Young once said publicly, "What of Joseph Smith's family? What of his boys? I have prayed from the beginning for Sister Emma and for the whole family. There is not a man in this Church that has entertained better feelings towards them . . . and when they make their appearance before this people, full of his power, there are none but what will say-'Amen! we are ready to receive you.'"[42]

On another occasion Young declared, "The sympathies of the Latter-day Saints are with the family of the martyred prophet. I never saw a day in the world that I would not almost worship that woman, Emma Smith, if she would be a saint instead of being a devil. I feel so today. There is no good thing in a temporal point of view that I would withhold from her; anything that is in my power to do for her, I would willingly do with all my heart, and with an open hand."[43]

In the earliest days of the Reorganization it was almost as though the movement was defined more by what it was not than what it was. It was not Brigham Young's organization. Members were not polygamists. It was not the strange religion isolated in the Great Basin of the United States with secret temple rituals and unusual doctrines and beliefs. Great efforts were made by Joseph Smith III and the Reorganized Church to separate themselves from the Utah Mormons.

During his administration, Joseph Smith III focused on the LDS Church headquartered in Utah on two fronts: 1) ridding Mormonism of polygamy and 2) performing missionary work among Utah Mormons to save them from Brigham Young's tyranny and bring them back to the fold.[44]

---

42   Ibid., 8:69.

43   Young, *The Essential Brigham Young*, 188.

44   As years have passed, the animosity that the Reorganized Church of Jesus Christ of Latter Day Saints once felt for Brigham Young has mostly disappeared. Community of Christ historian Robert Flanders wrote, "How could Brigham Young, closest man to the Prophet, President of the Twelve, the Lion of the Lord, and a particular hero to the Church become anathema so quickly as he did after the death of Joseph Smith? . . . It is hard to understand the hatred of Young in the Reorganized Church on the face of his record alone. I suggest that he was a kind of scapegoat upon whom was heaped the accumulated and long-held fear and apprehension, doubt, and alienation that were

It was clear in his inaugural address that Joseph III was anti-polygamy and had a strong belief that his father had nothing to do with that "abhorrent" practice. Even before Joseph III joined the ranks of the Reorganization, it had already "rejected and condemned the practice of plural marriage."[45] If anything, young Joseph brought an even stronger feeling of condemnation for polygamy to the New Organization.[46]

In 1880 President Smith wrote a letter to Republican presidential candidate James A. Garfield. "I am not a politician," he wrote, "but I am engaged with others in what is called the 'Josephite or Anti-polygamic wing of the Mormon Church'; and am doing what I can to exorcise the Utah cancer from the fair feature of American civilization."[47]

Joseph Smith III became very politically involved with the national anti-polygamy movement. He even traveled to Washington to give a report to the Committee on Territories concerning the Utah church and how it became disobedient to the laws of the land after its split with the church his father had begun. In the years that followed, there was even a movement to have Joseph appointed as territorial governor of Utah, thinking he might be able to bridge the gap between the Mormons and the U. S. government. It is not known whether the possibility of Smith's appointment was ever seriously considered in Washington, but he would likely not have been interested in any event.[48]

---

unleashed in the hearts of many Saints by the death of the Prophet." Flanders, "Some Reflections on the Kingdom and Gathering in Early Mormon History," 159–60.

45   Launius, *Joseph Smith III: Pragmatic Prophet*, 190.

46   Community of Christ historian Roger D. Launius suggests that Joseph III's intense interest in proving his father's innocence concerning the beginnings of polygamy was twofold. First, he desired to clear his father's name and place the blame for polygamy on Brigham Young. Second, he had a "great concern about the welfare and viability of the Reorganized Church. . . . He believed that the church's uniqueness and reason for existence was more acceptable with a stance favoring his father's innocence of polygamy." Ibid., 203–4.

47   Joseph Smith III to James A. Garfield, June 18, 1880, as cited in Launius, *Joseph Smith III: Pragmatic Prophet*, 247.

48   Information about Joseph Smith III and his battle against polygamy was found in Launius, "Methods and Motives: Joseph Smith III's Opposition to Polygamy, 1860–1890,"; Launius, *Joseph Smith III: Pragmatic Prophet*, 247–72; and in *History RLDS* 4:368–69. In Joseph Smith III's memoirs he spoke of the possibility of being asked to serve as territorial governor of Utah: "The governorship of Utah was the position neither desirable nor practicable for me, in that my work lay entirely outside the field of politics, and that I had no ambition whatever for secular honors." *Saints' Herald*, February 11, 1936, 177, cited in Launius, *Joseph Smith III: Pragmatic Prophet*, 254–55.

When President Wilford Woodruff issued the Manifesto in 1890 it was the official beginning of the end of plural marriage practiced in The Church of Jesus Christ of Latter-day Saints. Joseph Smith III had been president of the Reorganized Church for thirty years and had worked tirelessly for those three decades to put an end to Mormon polygamy. In a sense, he may have felt that polygamy's demise justified his stand that it had not been a doctrine or practice in his father's church.

The Reorganized Church of Jesus Christ of Latter Day Saints sent its first missionaries to work among the Mormons in Utah in 1863. They initially met with moderate success in the Utah mission, going from no members in Utah in 1863 to over three hundred converts by spring 1864. A challenge published in Salt Lake City addressed to Brigham Young and the Twelve points out the message of these early RLDS missionaries was to prove that "Joseph Smith is the true successor of his father in the Presidency of the Church; that Utah is not the land of Zion, but the place where the rebellious saints who would not abide the commandments of God were driven to, from out of the land of Zion."[49]

One Community of Christ historian saw their message as three-pronged: 1) The true successor to Joseph Smith was Joseph Smith III, 2) "Brigham Young was an usurper of authority who ruled as a dictator without legal or spiritual authority," and 3) plural marriage was a false doctrine.[50]

Because of the initial success of RLDS missionaries, Joseph Smith III sent others to Utah, including his younger brothers, Alexander and David Hyrum. Finally, in 1876, the RLDS president decided to travel to Utah himself; the first of four trips he would make. The Smith brothers' missions to Utah were not as successful as they had hoped. They were typically treated well because they were the Prophet Joseph's sons, but they were not welcomed as Joseph III might have imagined, primarily because they saw themselves as liberators who had come to save Utah Mormons from Brigham Young's tyranny.

LDS Church leaders were well aware of the presence of Joseph's sons in their midst. Brigham Young had no intentions of allowing them

49   *History RLDS* 3:378.
50   Launius, *Joseph Smith III: Pragmatic Prophet*, 221.

to preach their message without refutation. In one meeting Brother Brigham said:

> There are a few here that knew Joseph Smith, the Prophet, and some of them are apostatizing from the work, which the Lord commanded him to found, to run after Young Joseph Smith, . . . Young Joseph Smith does not possess one particle of this priesthood. The Twelve Apostles and the other authorities of this Church would have been exceeding glad if the Prophet's family had come with us when we left Nauvoo for the valleys of these mountains. We would have made cradles for them if they had required them, and would have fed them on milk and honey. . . . She [Emma] has made her children inherit lies. To my certain knowledge Emma Smith is one of the damndest liars I know of on this earth; yet there is no good thing I would refuse to do for her, if she would only be a righteous woman; but she will continue in her wickedness. . . . If there are any Latter-day Saints who wish to be destroyed, run after that family, and I will promise you in the name of the God of Israel that you will be damned.[51]

Of that missionary era, Roger D. Launius wrote, "In spite of the work of Smith's hand-picked representatives, that of his brothers and himself, and the publications prepared for the Mormon audience, nothing seemed to demonstrate a satisfactory progress." Joseph Smith III began to realize that he had been incorrect in his belief that most Utah Mormons had been duped into following Brigham Young. Smith came to "understand that Young's followers for the most part accepted his leadership without misgivings" and found "that it was difficult to break the chains of bondage . . . when those chains did not truly exist."[52]

Joseph Smith III served as president of the Reorganized Church of Jesus Christ of Latter Day Saints from 1860 until his death in 1914. Beloved by his people, in his fifty plus years as the prophet, seer, and revelator of the RLDS Church, Joseph united a movement begun by dissenters. He created a unified church organization, established the power and leadership of the First Presidency, acquired the Kirtland Temple, published the "New Translation of the Bible," and successfully

51   Young, *Essential Brigham Young*, 188–89.
52   Launius, *Joseph Smith III: Pragmatic Prophet*, 238–39.

weathered an internal leadership crisis that resulted in Jason Briggs, one of the Reorganization's original founders, and Zenos Gurley Jr., apostle and son of the other founder of the New Organization, withdrawing from the Reorganization.[53] President Smith created a successful missionary program and witnessed the establishment of branches throughout the United States and in Canada, Australia, Great Britain, and parts of Europe. The RLDS Church founded Graceland College during President Smith's administration. It also built a sanitarium and hospital in Independence, Missouri.

Joseph Smith III did not want to leave the members of the RLDS Church in a state of confusion about who would lead following his death like many felt his father had. In the April 1906 general conference, he pronounced this revelation:

> Inasmuch as misunderstanding has occurred in regard to the meaning of a revelation hitherto given through my servant Joseph Smith in regard to who should be called to preside in case my servant should be taken away or fall by transgression, it is now declared that in case of the removal of my servant now presiding over the church by death or transgression, my servant Frederick M. Smith, if he remain faithful and steadfast, should be chosen, in accordance with the revelations which have been hitherto given to the church concerning the priesthood.[54]

---

53   Jason Briggs had been instrumental in the creation of the Reorganization. He served as the leader of the New Organization until Joseph Smith III accepted the position in 1860. Briggs was a member of the Council of Twelve. Briggs expressed some liberal theological ideas using a newspaper he founded, *The Messenger*, as "a vehicle for the presentation of his ideas about church history, doctrine, and policy." Launius, *Joseph Smith III: Pragmatic Prophet*, 274. Briggs questioned the infallibility of the Bible and other RLDS scripture. Even though it had been his revelation that proclaimed the leader of the church needed to be a descendant of the Prophet Joseph, he later complained that the Smith family had become a type of royal family, and there was danger of tyranny. Zenos Gurley Jr., another apostle and son of Brigg's cohort in establishing the New Organization, shared the same discomfort with the Reorganization as Briggs. Efforts were made to appease both of them, but eventually they were both stripped of their apostolic rank, and they withdrew from the Reorganization. A. R. Blair credits the charity of Joseph Smith III for keeping Briggs and Gurley in the church a decade longer than would have been possible without his efforts. For information on Briggs and Gurley see "Crisis in the Ranks," chapter twelve of *Joseph Smith III: Pragmatic Prophet*, and Edwards, *Our Legacy of Faith*, 154–59.

54   Community of Christ Doctrine and Covenants 127:8a–8b (1906).

In addition to the revelation mentioned above, Joseph Smith III prepared another clarification dealing with succession in 1912 called the "Letter of Instruction." This document made clear his intention that his son, Frederick M. Smith, was to succeed him. The document was also to be used in future situations of succession.[55]

Following the death of his father, Frederick M. Smith was ordained president of the RLDS Church in May 1915.[56] He would serve in this calling until his death in 1946. Fred M., as he was commonly known, was a well-educated man, receiving a PhD in sociology and organizational psychology. His own administrative style leaned towards centralization of authority.

Fred M.'s efforts to centralize power within the RLDS Church left some of the membership uncomfortable with either the balance of having personal spiritual guidance within the framework of the church or simply following the Prophet. Community of Christ historian Richard P. Howard wrote: "This period of our history, perhaps as much as any other, embodied the church's quest for a workable boundary between theocratic rule and common consent."[57]

During Frederick M. Smith's administration, the RLDS Church faced a power struggle between the First Presidency and the Council of the Twelve, something Fred M.'s father had also encountered. While the disagreement between its leaders went on, the RLDS Church was also experiencing financial problems. At a Joint Council[58] meeting held in 1924 to discuss what financial actions needed to be taken, the First Presidency insisted that they had a right to overrule any administrative decisions made by the Presiding Bishopric. At this point "the disagree-

---

55   Information concerning Joseph Smith III's presidency, accomplishments, final years, and church succession were taken from *History RLDS*; Anderson, ed. *Joseph Smith III and the Restoration*; Edwards, *Our Legacy of Faith*; Howard, *The Church Through the Years*; and Launius, *Joseph Smith III: Pragmatic Prophet*.

56   Frederick Madison Smith was chosen as the president of the Reorganized Church and High Priesthood by the general conference of April 1915. Because of illness, he was unable to attend the conference. His ordination to the office of president took place on May 5, 1915, in the Stone Church in Independence, Missouri. Community of Christ Doctrine and Covenants, 1958 edition, heading of section 132.

57   Howard, *The Church Through the Years* 2:221.

58   At that time the Joint Council included the First Presidency, Council of Twelve, and the Presiding Bishopric. It is known in today's Community of Christ as the Church Leadership Council and includes others in addition to those mentioned above.

ment between the president and the Twelve expanded to include the bishops."[59]

The atmosphere was tense at the 1925 general conference. Both sides of the issue of presidential control were clearly represented by the delegates present. President Smith was not a person who sidestepped problems, "and felt this issue had to be decided one way or the other."[60] After debate a vote was taken and the president's view was upheld by a 919 to 405 margin. "While the majority certainly favored the Presidency," wrote Paul Edwards, "there were a significant number unwilling to maintain their church membership under the circumstances. Just how many separated is not known, but the 1925 General Conference caused a serious breach and from it several separatist groups were eventually founded."[61]

President Frederick M. Smith passed away in March 1946. Several weeks later his younger brother Israel A. Smith was ordained president of the Reorganized Church of Jesus Christ of Latter Day Saints. He served until his tragic death in an automobile accident in June 1958. With foresight, Israel A. Smith had left instructions with other church leaders as to who would be his successor. The letter named William Wallace Smith, Israel's half-brother, as president of the church.

W. Wallace Smith was the son of Joseph Smith III and Ada Clark Smith, a woman Joseph III married following the death of his second wife.[62] It was during the years that W. Wallace Smith led the church that some very important progress and changes were made, including church growth worldwide and a redefining of the church's identity and mission.[63]

By the end of World War II, the RLDS Church, although there were several thousand members in branches outside of the United States, was still basically a North American church. President W. Wallace Smith felt the need to expand missionary efforts to a greater world

---

59   Edwards, *Our Legacy of Faith*, 215.
60   Ibid., 216.
61   Ibid., 217.
62   Joseph Smith III was widowed twice and married three times.
63   According to William D. Russell, it was not W. Wallace Smith, but others in the RLDS leadership who lead the focus on social issues. Personal communication with William D. Russell.

audience. Membership increased from 167,000 to more than 215,000 during his years as president. In 1960, the term "world church" was substituted for "general church" as a more appropriate title in light of the church's new worldwide emphasis.[64]

In addition to the increased missionary effort, the message of the Reorganization was reinterpreted. W. Wallace Smith saw two limiting attitudes that had previously defined the Reorganization. First, the RLDS Church had always felt the need to clearly separate itself from The Church of Jesus Christ of Latter-day Saints and its beliefs about polygamy, temples, and godhood. Second, the "gathering of Israel" as it had been viewed in the early church no longer seemed applicable to a modern world church. As Paul M. Edwards explained: The members of the Joint Council felt "that the church needed to identify its objectives in light of who and what it was, not in reaction to an institutional history."[65]

During the 1960s, W. Wallace Smith began encouraging the Reorganized Church to focus more on modern social issues. The *Saints' Herald* published a series of articles considering "specific problems in society: inequality, welfare, civil rights, science, and a multitude of other topics drawing the church into the larger debate taking place in America."[66] Church leaders were trying to reorient their membership to consider their religion not as something bound to the past, but as a dynamic, worldwide institution making efforts to solve modern problems.

This shift in paradigm included necessary theological reformation. Liberal thinkers in the Reorganization "emerged to engage in the steady dismantling of what had been a traditional Reorganized Church theological consensus" wrote Roger D. Launius. "That consensus," he continued, "had been built on the tensions between the desire to remain faithful to the stories, symbols, and events of early Mormonism,

---

64   Information about this era of RLDS History was taken from Edwards, *Our Legacy of Faith* and Howard, *The Church Through the Years*.

65   Edwards, *Our Legacy of Faith*, 259–60.

66   Launius, "Coming of Age? The Reorganized Church of Jesus Christ of Latter Day Saints in the 1960s," 34.

on the one hand, and the yearning for respectability among and hence openness to Protestantism, on the other."[67]

As Reorganized Church leaders became more liberal, they took a more ecumenical approach to theology. The result of this has been "aspects of Reorganization belief held in common with other Christians have been given comparatively more emphasis and those aspects of church thought which are unique have been given less emphasis."[68] Not all of the members of the Reorganized Church felt that these moves away from traditionalism were inspired. This has caused a "deepening theological division within the ranks of the Reorganized Church of Jesus Christ of Latter Day Saints."[69]

The 1978 world conference marked the end of W. Wallace Smith's nearly twenty-year term as president. Unlike previous church presidents who served in that position until death, W. Wallace Smith retired from being president. His son, Wallace B. Smith, was ordained as the new president of the RLDS Church, and W. Wallace Smith became "president emeritus."[70]

President Wallace B. Smith took the church into the 1980s with a program entitled "Faith to Grow." The program "was designed to invest congregations with a new sense of purpose, of self-worth, and to extend themselves with a new emphasis on evangelism."[71] The church began a new era of rapid expansion, especially into Third World countries. Leaders and members of the church saw themselves as part of the larger world and not so much as "the" chosen people.

Two major events during the 1980s dramatically changed the Reorganized Church of Jesus Christ of Latter Day Saints. At the April 1984 world conference, President Wallace B. Smith presented what would become Doctrine and Covenants section 156, which opened the way for women of the church to receive the priesthood. Section 156

---

67   Ibid., 39. See also Blair, A. R., "Reorganized Church of Jesus Christ of Latter Day Saints: Moderate Mormonism," in *The Restoration Movement: Essays in Mormon History*, 207–30.

68   Russell, "The Fundamentalist Schism, 1958–Present," in *Let Contention Cease*, Launis and Spillman, eds., 125.

69   Ibid.

70   Edwards, *Our Legacy of Faith*, 277–78.

71   Ibid., 278.

also called the Saints to prepare to build a temple in Independence, Missouri. According to the revelation found in section 156, this temple was to "be dedicated to the pursuit of peace. It shall be for reconciliation and for healing of the spirit. It shall also be for a strengthening of faith and preparation for witness."[72]

The ordaining of women to the priesthood was a controversial decision within the RLDS Church. Although the majority of the RLDS members were supportive of the action, there were many who saw this "as the latest in a long history of 'unacceptable changes' in the church, [and] chose to separate themselves from the larger movement."[73]

Ground breaking for the temple took place in 1990. Four years later, at the 1994 world conference, the temple was dedicated, completing the project that Joseph Smith Jr. had originally made known to the Saints in 1831. It was a dream come true for the Reorganized Saints.

In 1995 President Wallace B. Smith announced that he planned to retire and indicated that W. Grant McMurray was to be his successor. That action took place at the 1996 world conference. W. Grant McMurray became the first non-Smith family member to preside over the church, thus ending a nearly 170-year tradition since Joseph Smith organized the church in 1830.

In 2000 a plan was announced to change the name of the church to something that would more adequately represent the new direction of the church's theology and mission to the world.[74] On April 6, 2001,

---

72   Community of Christ Doctrine and Covenants 156:5a–5b. More information about temples is found in chapter twelve of this book.

73   Edwards, *Our Legacy of Faith*, 282. It has been reported that "roughly one-fourth of our active members left the church as a result of Section 156 of Community of Christ Doctrine and Covenants, which makes women eligible for priesthood ordination." Russell, "The LDS Church and Community of Christ: Clearer Differences, Closer Friends," 187.

74   After the 1992 world conference was held, a committee was created to discuss the possibility of a new name for the RLDS Church and to give suggestions to the First Presidency. One of the names submitted was Community of Christ. At a Church Leadership Council retreat held in Colorado in 1994, a new mission statement for the Church was agreed upon. The new mission statement was, "We proclaim Jesus Christ and promote communities of joy, love, and peace." This new focus on community likely led to the new name for the church: Community of Christ. Russell, "The Last Smith Presidents and the Transformation of the RLDS Church," 77–79.

the name change became official and what had been the Reorganized Church of Jesus Christ of Latter Day Saints became Community of Christ.

W. Grant McMurray resigned from Community of Christ leadership effective November 29, 2004. The remaining members of the First Presidency stayed in their positions of leadership and presided over Community of Christ until the summer of 2005. At a special conference held in June 2005, Stephen M. Veazey was ordained to the office of prophet-president of Community of Christ. Under President Veazey's direction the approximately 250,000-member Community of Christ continues to pursue its mission to proclaim Jesus Christ and promote communities of joy, hope, love, and peace.[75]

THE CHANGING FACES OF THE RESTORATION

Both Community of Christ and The Church of Jesus Christ of Latter-day Saints have evolved in doctrine and theology since their joint beginning in 1830. This is understandable because both churches believe in living prophets, modern revelation, and an open canon. Both religions recognize the statement made by Joseph Smith in a letter to John Wentworth: "We believe all the God has revealed, all that he does now reveal, and we believe that he will yet reveal many great and important things pertaining to the kingdom of God."[76]

While some similarities and common beliefs remain, it might be surprising to some how different the two churches have become. One Community of Christ scholar noted: "Between about 1880 and the 1960s, the theological differences between our two churches changed very little, except for the mainline LDS abandonment of polygamy in the 1890s." He went on to say that Community of Christ began to shift in the 1960s from being a sect trying to preserve the "Kirtland version" of Mormonism to "becoming a denomination more in the mainstream

---

75   Information was obtained from the official Community of Christ website.

76   *Articles of Faith of The Church of Jesus Christ of Latter-day Saints*, number 9, in the Pearl of Great Price, 60; known in Community of Christ as the "Epitome of Faith," *History RLDS* 2:570.

of American Protestantism."[77] Former prophet-president of Community of Christ, W. Grant McMurray noted, "When you think about it, the Mormon Church and the R.L.D.S. Church share about a 14-year history in the early 19th century . . . and since then, we've developed on very different tracks."[78]

77   Russell, "The LDS Church and the Community of Christ: Clearer Differences, Closer Friends," *Dialogue* (Winter 2003), 185

78   Niebuhr, "New Leader for Church That Share Mormon Roots," *New York Times,* May 12, 1996, 16.

The Only True and Living Church Upon the Face of the Whole Earth and the Question of Succession

In the early history of the LDS Church and the RLDS Church, the concept of the restoration of the kingdom of God to the earth played a primary role in doctrine and missionary efforts. Both groups believed in the Great Apostasy—that the authority found in the ancient New Testament Church of Jesus Christ had been lost following the death of the original Twelve Apostles. Error had crept into the doctrine; saving ordinances were no longer valid and became corrupted.

Joseph Smith Jr. was viewed as the Prophet of the Restoration, receiving divine authority through heavenly messengers and restoring to the earth "plain and precious" doctrines, ordinances, and authority that had not been on the earth for over fifteen hundred years. Both The Church of Jesus Christ of Latter-day Saints and the Reorganized Church of Jesus Christ of Latter Day Saints saw themselves as Christ's restored church, the only true church on the face of the earth. They viewed all other religions, including each other, as having some truth, but lacking the necessary authority and truth to save their followers. This belief stemmed from statements made by Joseph Smith, including an account of the First Vision when Jesus replied to Joseph's question as to which church he should join that he "must join none of them, for they were all wrong."[79]

---

79   Joseph Smith—History 1:19, Pearl of Great Price, 49; *History RLDS* 1:9. This statement comes from Joseph Smith's 1838 history. Clearly, the concept that all churches had gone astray was taught by Joseph Smith prior to 1838. The 1832 account of

Authority from God was of vital importance to the Restoration. Both churches believed that a Great Apostasy had occurred in the years following the resurrection of Jesus Christ and that the authority of Christ's true church had been lost from the earth. The LDS and RLDS churches believed that God's authority had been restored to the earth and each maintained that the proper authority was passed down through its leaders and that the other had lost that authority.

The LDS Church and the RLDS Church saw their founder, Joseph Smith Jr., as an inspired man through whom God restored His authority and gospel truths to the earth. However, the two restoration churches view Joseph Smith quite differently today.

Both churches believe in modern revelation and in living prophets; however, neither church would make the claim that prophets are infallible. Both would admit that prophets are mortal men with inherent mortal weakness, but that each prophet is called to the sacred mission of acting as the mouthpiece of God.

COMMUNITY OF CHRIST

Community of Christ still believes in the Restoration through the Prophet Joseph Smith, but in recent years it has begun to see the Great Apostasy and the Restoration in a different light. A common understanding "among Reorganized Latter Day Saints [was] that what happened in 1830 with Joseph Smith was the restoration of a particular organization and institutional entity which existed at one time as the original Church of Christ."[80]

Today, Community of Christ sees the early Christian church in the first century following the death of Jesus with an extremely "limited organizational structure and institutional formality."[81] Former Community of Christ prophet-president W. Grant McMurray said, "We must

---

the First Vision describes how the religions of the day had turned aside from the gospel, don't truly keep the commandments, and "draw near to me with their lips while their hearts are far from me." Welch, ed., *Opening the Heavens*, 7. According to Joseph Smith's own story, he knew in 1820 that he was not to join any of the existing Christian religions. The need for a restoration because of the Great Apostasy was likely taught during the very early years of the movement.

80   *Position Papers*, 93.
81   Ibid., 91.

disabuse ourselves of the notion that the first-century Christian church was somehow restored in its fullness . . . that our nineteenth century church conformed even remotely to that of the first century."[82]

With no particular original organization, practices, or established set of doctrines, there could be no Great Apostasy in the manner once envisioned by the Reorganization.[83] The authority could not be lost because Jesus Christ is the authority. According to Community of Christ scholars, to view whatever apostasy did take place as a complete and total loss of authority "is to say in effect that the event of the Incarnation has been nullified, which is contrary to the very understanding of the Incarnation as the central saving event for all time and all men."[84]

The Restoration, as viewed by the modern Community of Christ, would be that Jesus Christ did work through the Prophet Joseph Smith and "that the Holy Spirit is at work in our lives, validating our deepest struggles and our highest joy as existence in Christ. This is what we mean by the fulness of the gospel."[85] Because of the shift in their point of view "these days you will not hear the concepts of apostasy and restoration mentioned as often in church meetings as they were in the past."[86] The dynamic nature of Christ's church demonstrates that "the apostasy and the restoration were not events that happened one time in history but rather are processes continually at work among us."[87]

As far as Community of Christ and authority is concerned, a member of the First Presidency explained that "an unfortunate and erroneous concept about the nature of authority is that only one organized

---

82   McMurray, "'Something Lost, Something Gained': Restoration History and Culture Seen from 'Both Sides Now,'" 52–53.

83   Community of Christ scholars have generally concluded that "it is not historically accurate to say that Jesus established a church during his earthly ministry, with various priesthood offices and sacraments." Russell, "The LDS Church and the Community of Christ: Clearer Differences, Closer Friends," 188–89. With no actual "church" established by Jesus, there could be no Great Apostasy or Restoration as viewed by the LDS Church.

84   *Position Papers*, 97. The Incarnation is God entering the world in Jesus Christ.

85   "The Identity of the Church," as cited in Booth, "Recent Shifts in Restoration Thought," in *Restoration Studies I*, 172.

86   Russell, "The LDS Church and the Community of Christ: Clearer Differences, Closer Friends," 189.

87   "The Identity of the Church," as cited in Booth, "Recent Shifts in Restoration Thought," in *Restoration Studies I*, 172.

JOSEPH SMITH, JR.
Courtesy Community of Christ Archives,
Independence, Missouri

church institution at a time may have authority to represent God." Community of Christ recognizes its authority and declares that it has a divine purpose in the world, but "when we make this assertion it does not necessarily follow that no other person or institution has spiritual authority." God works through many persons and groups through the Holy Spirit, enhancing rather than diminishing the authority of the church. The First Presidency member concludes that "our faith in the majesty and power of that revelation would be diminished immeasurably if we perceived the ongoing authoritative ministry of Jesus Christ as being confined to our day and sect."[88]

Community of Christ see themselves as part of the body of Christ—the great community of Christianity. One Community of Christ historian referred to "the unannounced shift from its claim to be the 'true remnant church' of Joseph Smith, Jr. to becoming a 'missional church' based in the life of Christ." He went on to say that the claims of being the only true church have "been replaced by a theological ecumenism that values all religions, believing each to be of inestimable worth."[89]

Lineal succession in the presidency was a major concern for the Reorganized Church for many years. Very early in the history of the Reorganization a resolution was passed "that the successor of Joseph Smith, Jun., as the Presiding High Priest, in the Melchisedec Priest-

---

88   *Presidential Papers*, 3rd ed., 33.
89   Mark A. Scherer, "Answering Questions No Longer Asked," 31. It is also interesting to note that in the same article Scherer states: "This leads some to conclude that we are not the church of Joseph Smith, Jr., and I agree with that assessment. More accurately, I believe the Community of Christ reflects the best qualities of Emma Hale Smith— courage, perseverance, commitment, peacemaking, and non-judgmental compassion. We are 'Emma's church.'"

hood, must of necessity be the seed of Joseph Smith, Jun."[90] Community of Christ believes that Joseph Smith III was chosen by God and meant to lead the church after the death of his father. For generations it followed the pattern of ordaining a descendant of Joseph Smith Jr. to the office of prophet-president. Succession through the line of Joseph Smith Jr. was by tradition more than requirement, although most members of the Reorganized Church expected a descendant of the Prophet Joseph to preside over the church, and it came to be viewed by many as a necessity.[91]

---

90   Early Reorganization Minutes (commonly referred to as Book A) June 12, 1852, as quoted in McMurray, "'True Son of a True Father': Joseph Smith III and the Succession Question," in *Restoration Studies I*, 135.

91   For example, in his 1958 publication, *Succession in Presidency and Authority*, Russell F. Ralston outlined what he considered God's laws of succession. These included:

God's law of succession, given for direction of his people in latter days, is clear. Briefly it is this: the successor to the prophet will be (a) appointed by the prophet, (b) sustained by revelation, (c) chosen by the people, and (d) ordained as President of the High Priesthood. God promised that Joseph Smith's blessing of prophetic leadership would be placed on the head of his posterity after him that through him and his seed the kindred of the earth will be blessed. None of the leaders of the Church in Utah have been of the seed of Joseph Smith and thus do not come within the promise of God. The Reorganized Church has always been blessed with the prophetic leadership of the 'seed' of the prophet martyr. (Ralston, as quoted in *Fundamental Differences between the LDS and RLDS Churches*, 15.)

Joseph Smith III's "A Letter of Instruction" was not as adamant that a descendant of Joseph Smith, Jr. become prophet-president of the Church. He wrote:

Following the legendary teaching of the eldership and the precedent established in the reorganizing of the church, based upon the revelations which were accepted and on record at the death of Joseph and Hyrum Smith, the eldest living son of the president of the high priesthood acting as president of the church would be eligible under the considerations named in question. *Unless such action was contravened by revelation directing otherwise, such son should be chosen.* This would be in harmony and consistent with the precedents of history and the legendary teaching referred to. Do the revelations point out with sufficient clearness that such a son is appointed by revelation as the proper one to be chosen and sustained as successor to his father, his father having died in office while being sustained by the faith, confidence, and prayers of the church? *Yes, unless such action upon the part of the church is prevented by revelation directing otherwise* [Emphasis added].

Based upon Joseph Smith III's instructions, the eldest son of the president of the church was eligible to succeed his father unless revelation was given to the church directing otherwise. "A Letter of Instruction" was originally published in *The Saints' Herald*, March 13, 1912. For a copy of "A Letter of Instruction" by Joseph Smith III, see the official website of Community of Christ: www.cofchrist.org/history/letter-of-instruction.asp

Joseph Smith III did not see that being a descendant of Joseph Smith Jr. was a requirement for the prophet-president of the church. He explained:

> I claim to be his successor by lineal right, and by his blessing, and lastly by the right of selection and appointment. It is not necessarily a birthright to be the President of the Church. It comes by virtue of fitness and qualification, I may say, good behavior and the choice of the people, recognizing a call or a right. . . . The existence of the Reorganized Church does not depend on my lineal successorship as I understand it.[92]

Another tradition was that each subsequent prophet-president was to be appointed by the existing prophet-president prior to his death. William D. Russell wrote:

> We of the Community of Christ tradition have always said that our priesthood, from the deacon to the prophet-president, are called by God. Through most of our history, three additional expectations have governed the office of Church president: (1) the president has been a lineal descendant of Joseph Smith Jr.; (2) he served until his death; and (3) he named his successor.[93]

The practice of the prophet-president serving in that calling until death changed in 1978 when W. Wallace Smith appointed his son, Wallace B. Smith, to serve as prophet-president of the church and then retired at the age of seventy-seven. In like manner, Wallace B. Smith retired from the position of prophet-president in 1996 at the age of sixty-seven.

Another custom changed at the 1996 world conference when Wallace B. Smith named W. Grant McMurray to be the new prophet-president of the church. McMurray was the first non-Smith to serve in that position, thus ending the practice of the church being led by the lineal descent of Joseph Smith Jr.

---

92   Taken from Joseph Smith III's testimony at the Temple Lot case as quoted in McMurray, "'True Son of a True Father': Joseph Smith III and the Succession Question," in *Restoration Studies I*, 142.

93   Russell, "Grant McMurray and the Succession Crisis in the Community of Christ," 27–28.

W. Grant McMurray resigned from Community of Christ leadership in 2004, without naming his successor. The remaining members of the First Presidency directed the church until a special conference was held in the summer of 2005. In the months between McMurray's resignation and the special conference, Community of Christ faced the challenge of selecting a prophet-president who had not been chosen by the current president of the church, altering a long-standing tradition. This is a Community of Christ author's description of the events that followed:

> The two-member First Presidency announced a process of "discernment" attempting to ascertain the will of God as to who should lead the Church. The Council of Twelve, in consultation with the First Presidency and the leaders of the other major Church quorums, and inviting the response of all members, led this process, which relied heavily on Joseph Smith III's 1912 "Letter of Instruction," dealing with the issue of succession in the presidency. Sunday, February 27, 2005, was designated as a special day of prayer and preparation throughout the Church. The Twelve reported that, after an extended period of prayer and fasting culminating in a March 2 meeting, "God graced our efforts and gave to each of us a testimony that Stephen M. Veazey is called to lead the Church as prophet-president."[94]

All three traditions of the original Reorganization have changed. It is no longer viewed as necessary that the prophet-president be a descendant of Joseph Smith, the prophet-president need not remain in that position of leadership until he dies, and the custom of the previous prophet selecting the next prophet is no longer seen as required. The current or future presidents of Community of Christ might revert back to the earlier traditions, but it seems unlikely.

During the first century of Community of Christ history, when it was known as the Reorganized Church of Jesus Christ of Latter Day Saints, members' opinions of Joseph Smith Jr. ranged from "near deified" to fallen prophet. Most respected Joseph as the founding prophet

---

94   Ibid., 40–41.

of the Restoration but believed that his time in Nauvoo was a dark period, when incorrect doctrines and practices were introduced.[95]

There were attempts to defend the Prophet Joseph, either denying he had anything to do with the unusual teachings or suggesting that he had been manipulated by some of the strong personalities in church leadership that surrounded him. Community of Christ author A. R. Blair suggests that a dramatic and controversial remaking of Joseph Smith Jr. took place. While the RLDS Church "never sought to dehumanize him by elevating him beyond human fault," there was an attempt "to apply some whitewash to him if not some gilding."[96]

There are still differences in opinion among today's Community of Christ members concerning Joseph Smith Jr. Because prophets are seen as humans with weaknesses, Joseph Smith Jr. can be respected as a prophet and for his role in the Restoration, and yet he can still be viewed as a very flawed individual. Roger Launius gave his opinion that many Community of Christ members still accept Joseph as a prophet, but "their view of his prophetic role in the Church is severely limited when compared to the view of the LDS Church and perhaps early RLDS views."[97]

Community of Christ is a theocratic democracy. There is a prophet-president who has been called and appointed to direct the church by rev-

---

95   See Flanders, "Dream and Nightmare: Nauvoo Revisited," in *The Restoration Movement: Essays in Mormon History*, eds. McKiernan, Blair, and Edwards, 141–66.

96   Blair, "Reorganized Church of Jesus Christ of Latter Day Saints: Moderate Mormonism," in *The Restoration Movement: Essays in Mormon History*, 223. Some early Saints were aware of Joseph's involvement with polygamy, but firmly believed that he saw the error of his ways, repented, and was trying to put a stop to polygamy at the time of his death. The first editor of the *Saints' Herald* wrote: "Joseph Smith repented of his connection with this doctrine [polygamy], and said that it was of the devil. He caused the revelations on that subject to be burned, and when he voluntarily came to Nauvoo . . . he said that he was going to Carthage to die. . . . By his conduct at that time he proved the sincerity of his repentance. . . . If Abraham and Jacob, by repentance, can obtain salvation and exaltation, so can Joseph Smith." Quoted in Blair, "Reorganized Church of Jesus Christ of Latter Day Saints: Moderate Mormonism," in *The Restoration Movement: Essays in Mormon History*, 223.

97   Launius, "Is Joseph Smith Relevant to the Community of Christ?" 61. Launius also wrote that Community of Christ views Joseph Smith as more human than he is in the LDS tradition. "As to the many doctrinal idiosyncrasies that emerged from the mind of Joseph Smith, those are sometimes viewed as the ramblings of a misguided fanatic. That he became increasingly egocentric and power hungry is a given for virtually all Community of Christ members." Ibid. The author doubts that Launius can speak with confidence about all of Community of Christ members.

elation from the Spirit. However, revelation is considered "a collective responsibility of the entire body of Christ."[98] This is not to say that revelation for the church can be received by any of its members. The First Presidency is still "the authority that interprets the scripture and law of the church."[99] However, a member of Community of Christ would likely have more say in the creation of policies than would an LDS counterpart.[100]

The law of common consent within Community of Christ involves sending delegates to world conferences "where open debates, using parliamentary procedures, lead to policy formulation."[101] Statements pronounced by the prophet-president as revelation are viewed as such, but as former Community of Christ president W. Grant McMurray put it, "Seeking to discern God's will for us in our own time . . . is a shared task of religious inquiry, not a duty of one person locked in a closet."[102]

---

98   Taken from a prayer offered at a special conference held in 2005 by Don Compier, dean of Community of Christ seminary, as cited in Russell, "Grant McMurray and the Succession Crisis in the Community of Christ," 42.

99   *Saints' Herald,* June 2007, under "Conditions for Membership," 40.

100   A good example of this is the question of whether converts coming into Community of Christ need to be rebaptized if they have already been previously baptized in a different Christian church. The world conference requested "the First Presidency to examine the issue of rebaptism in the context of the worldwide mission of the Community of Christ," and to prayerfully receive God's will for instructions relevant to this issue. Community of Christ leadership has asked church members to join in the discernment and discussion process on this issue. Ibid.

101   Alder and Edwards, "Common Beginnings, Divergent Beliefs," 19.

102   McMurray, "A 'Goodly Heritage' in a Time of Transformation: History and Identity in the Community of Christ," 66. Community of Christ view on revelation and scripture plays an important part in the process of canonization. Scripture and modern revelation is recognized as vitally important but imperfect in the sense that it is a human attempt to verbalize divine will. In that light, when President Veazey received the revelation that would become section 163 of the Doctrine and Covenants, he prayerfully and intellectually struggled with the writing of the words of counsel. He sought the inspiration of counselors, and received feedback from caucuses and quorums after it had been presented. He then released "the document for formal consideration and action." The church-at-large engaged in discernment about the eventual standing of the document. It was accepted as revelation and approved for inclusion in the Doctrine and Covenants. Veazey, "Doctrine and Covenants 163: My Testimony," *Herald* (July 2007): 12–14. A testimony to Community of Christ's continuing belief in modern revelation is found in the fifty additional revelations that have been added to their Doctrine and Covenants since the beginning of the presidency of Joseph Smith III. In today's LDS Church, a revelation is unanimously approved by the First Presidency and Quorum of Twelve Apostles and then presented to the body of the Church at general conference for a sustaining vote before it is canonized.

In April 2009, President Stephen M. Veazey invited the whole church to engage with the leadership in a prayerful discernment about the issue of rebaptism as a condition for church membership. He said, "We believe this approach is in harmony with Doctrine and Covenants 162:2c."[103] That particular verse in Community of Christ Doctrine and Covenants states that "as a prophetic people you are called, under direction of the spiritual authorities and with the common consent of the people, to discern the divine will for your own time and in the places where you serve."[104]

The changes that have occurred in Community of Christ have been greatly influenced by increased scriptural scholarship, the application of professional historical methodologies in a closer scrutiny of its origin and history, and its ministering efforts into many countries of the world. In the 1960s, the RLDS Church recognized that some characteristics from its earlier days were inhibiting its ministering efforts and growth outside of North America. First, was the assumption that it had to establish clear differences between the RLDS Church and the LDS Church. Second, it realized that its becoming a world church was hindered by the early concept of "gathering" that was no longer applicable.[105]

Apostle Clifford Cole identified the challenges faced when taking the gospel to non-Christian cultures. He said that non-Christian people were not interested in how the RLDS Church was different from other Christians, but they wanted to know what RLDS members, as Christians, believed.[106] The church began to shift in its emphasis from what made them distinctive to discovering a better way to minister to people of all cultures. In some cases, it found that the Joseph Smith story, the teaching of "one true church," the Book of Mormon[107], and even the church's name—the Reorganized Church of Jesus Christ of Latter Day Saints—got in the way of effectively delivering the message of Jesus Christ. All these things were an impetus for change in

---

103 Veazey, "A Defining Moment," Address to the Church given April 5, 2009.

104 Community of Christ Doctrine and Covenants 162:2c (2004).

105 Edwards, *Our Legacy of Faith*, 259.

106 Ibid., 260.

107 The story of the coming forth and translation of the Book of Mormon was not seen as an effective method for teaching the message of Jesus Christ as was the Bible. Community of Christ has used the Bible as the focus of its teachings.

the RLDS Church and caused leaders and members to reevaluate the mission of the church.

LATTER-DAY SAINTS

Today, the LDS Church retains essentially the same views of apostasy and restoration as it did when it was originally founded. It affirms that a Great Apostasy did take place and that doctrines were altered and authority lost. It maintains that Joseph Smith did restore Christ's true church to the earth and that The Church of Jesus Christ of Latter-day Saints is the "only true and living church upon the face of the whole earth."[108]

The Church of Jesus Christ of Latter-day Saints would likely come closer to a belief that the prophet speaks directly for God than the modern Community of Christ. In the LDS view, the president of the church may have his human failings, but when he speaks as a prophet, what he is saying is the mind and will of God.

Obedience to the prophet is considered a matter of faith within Mormonism. Elder Henry B. Eyring of the Quorum of the Twelve said:

> When a prophet speaks, those with little faith may think that they hear only a wise man giving good advice. Then if his counsel seems comfortable and reasonable, squaring with what they want to do, they take it. If it does not, they consider it either faulty advice or they see their circumstances as justifying their being an exception to the counsel. Those without faith may think that they hear only men seeking to exert influence for some selfish motive.[109]

A common belief within The Church of Jesus Christ of Latter-day Saints is that God will never allow the living prophet to lead the church astray.[110] Latter-day Saints see Joseph Smith Jr. and each succeeding

---

108 LDS Doctrine and Covenants 1:30 (1831).
109 Eyring, "Finding Safety in Council," 24.
110 LDS Doctrine and Covenants, Official Declaration 1, 292 (1890). The following excerpt is taken from an address given by President Wilford Woodruff: "The Lord will never permit me or any other man who stands as President of this Church to lead you astray. It is not in the program. It is not in the mind of God. If I were to attempt

president of their church as God's chosen prophet, who guides the people as instructed by the Lord. There may be some debate among some Latter-day Saints concerning statements made by prophets, but those who find themselves out of harmony with the prophet usually discover they are out of the mainstream of Mormonism.[111]

The Church of Jesus Christ of Latter-day Saints believes that Joseph Smith Jr. was given the authority to lead Christ's restored church by heavenly messengers and that he held the keys and rights to pass that authority to others. It holds to the belief that when a man is called to be an apostle, he is given all the keys necessary for him to lead the church, but those keys remain dormant until the time comes when he is called to be the president.

When a president of the LDS Church dies, the First Presidency is automatically dissolved, and the counselors return to their places of seniority in the Twelve. The mantle of church leadership is passed to the Quorum of the Twelve, with the president of the Twelve presiding. The Quorum of the Twelve has essentially become the presidency of the church and now must decide whether to reorganize the First Presidency or to preside for a time as a quorum.[112]

---

that, the Lord would remove me out of my place, and so He will any other man who attempts to lead the children of men astray from the Oracles of God and from their duty."

111 Tanner, "The Debate is Over," 2. In this message from the First Presidency, N. Eldon Tanner quoted General Young Women President Elaine Cannon who said, "When the Prophet speaks, . . . the debate is over." President Tanner agreed that those who fight against the counsel of the living prophet are simply fighting against the will of God.

112 A letter entitled "Succession in the Presidency of The Church of Jesus Christ of Latter-day Saints" was sent to all Church Educational System personnel in January 2008 following the passing of President Gordon B. Hinckley. It stated that "when the president of The Church of Jesus Christ of Latter-day Saints passes away, the following events take place:

The First Presidency is automatically dissolved.

The two counselors in the First Presidency revert to their places of seniority in the Quorum of the Twelve Apostles. Seniority is determined by the date on which a person was ordained to the Twelve, not by age.

The Quorum of the Twelve Apostles, now numbering 14 and headed by the senior apostle, assumes Church leadership.

The senior apostle presides at a meeting of the Quorum of the Twelve to consider two alternative propositions.

Should the First Presidency be reorganized at this time?

Should the Church continue to function with the Quorum of the Twelve presiding?

In its early history, the LDS Church was presided over for some years by the Quorum of the Twelve. Since the passing of Wilford Woodruff, the First Presidency has been reorganized within a few days of each prophet's death, with the senior apostle being sustained as prophet, seer, and revelator.

SUMMARY

Initially, both the LDS Church and Community of Christ believed in the restoration of Christ's true church to the earth through the Prophet Joseph Smith. Today, Community of Christ has moved away from the claim to be the only true church. Rather, it sees itself as part of Christ's great community of Christians on the earth. The LDS Church continues to see itself as the restoration of the church founded by Jesus Christ in the meridian of time and as the only religion recognized by God as His church.

Both religions believe that Joseph Smith was a prophet of God, and modern prophets lead each of the two churches today. Although led by a prophet-president, Community of Christ membership may have more of a voice in the decision-making process than their counterparts in the LDS Church. Community of Christ is a theocratic democracy. The LDS Church believes that the living prophet is God's spokesman, and members are counseled to follow the prophet.

Authority played an important role in the early history of both churches. The Reorganization initially saw itself as the continuation of the church founded by Joseph Smith Jr. because of scriptural precedents[113], the blessing given to Joseph Smith III by his father, and the

---

After discussion, a formal motion is made and accepted by the Quorum of the Twelve Apostles.

If a motion to reorganize the First Presidency is passed, the Quorum of the Twelve unanimously selects the new president of the Church."

113   "Several observations need to be made with reference to the period 1852–60. First, support for the concept of lineal succession was developed around scriptural precedents rather than accounts of designations or ordinations by the prophet. These latter reports, although extant since 1844, played a negligible role in the literature and missionary outreach of the church during this time frame." McMurray, "'True Son of a True Father': Joseph Smith III and the Succession Question," in *Restoration Studies I*, 135.

lineal succession it had from Joseph Smith for many years. Today, it no longer sees lineal authority as a vital concern.

Following the death of Joseph Smith Jr., the LDS Church followed a pattern of leadership based on the Quorum of the Twelve being a second presidency of the church. The member of the Twelve who has served in the Quorum for the longest time is next in line to serve as president of the church following the death of the prophet.

CHURCH ORGANIZATION

Community of Christ and the LDS Church began as one entity and, therefore, have many similarities in the organization and leadership positions of their two churches. However, as the years have passed since Joseph Smith Jr.'s death and the division took place, some differences have developed.

COMMUNITY OF CHRIST

In Community of Christ "the First Presidency is the leading quorum of the church and presides over the whole church."[114] The First Presidency consists of the prophet-president and two counselors.[115] The second presidency of the church is the Council of Twelve, and is composed of twelve apostles. This council is primarily responsible for the church's missionary efforts.

The three members of the Presiding Bishopric of Community of Christ, a bishop and two counselors, are the chief financial officers of

114 *Priesthood Manual,* 2004 ed., 24.

115 When Stephen M. Veazey was presented to the 2005 conference to be the new prophet-president, two delegates "objected to the fact that 'seer and revelator' had been left out of the statement by the Twelve recommending Veazey to be 'president of the high priesthood, prophet and president of the church.' . . . Apostle Dale E. Luffman, presiding over the meeting, suggested that the word 'prophet' pretty well covers 'seer and revelator' also, then later noted that 'seer' and 'revelator' connote 'images of magic and folklore' that, he suggested, no longer serve us well." Russell, "Grant McMurray and the Succession Crisis in the Community of Christ," 44.

CURRENT COUNCIL OF TWELVE
Courtesy Community of Christ Archives, Independence, Missouri, Photograph by Dennis Piepergerdes

the church. It is their responsibility to administer the temporal affairs
of the church.

The three members of the First Presidency, the Council of the Twelve
Apostles, the three members of the Presiding Bishopric, the President
of the High Priests Quorum, the Presiding Evangelist, the Senior President of the Seventy, the Director of International Headquarters, the
Director of Human Resources, and the World Church Secretary comprise the leadership body of Community of Christ known as the World
Church Leadership Council.[116]

The office of seventy is "a specialized function of the eldership"
whose calling is to work in specific missionary responsibilities. When
released from the assignment of seventy, a person's priesthood office
is that of elder. The seventies represent the church throughout the
world and are organized into seven quorums, with each quorum being
presided over by a president. "Together, the seven quorum presidents
compose the Council of Presidents of Seventy. One of their number

---

116   Community of Christ, *Church Administrator's Handbook,* 2005 ed., 25–26 lists some
of the members of the World Church Leadership Council. Andrew Shields, World
Church Secretary, informed me of the members who have been added to that council
since the publication of the 2004 *Priesthood Manual.*

is chosen to preside over the council and is known as the senior president of the Seventy."[117]

In addition to the Council of the Presidents of Seventy and the Quorums of Seventy, other leadership functions in Community of Christ are vested in the Quorum of High Priests, the Order of Bishops, and the Order of Evangelists.[118]

There is a Standing High Council (which is not found in the LDS Church) that assists the First Presidency by giving advice on judicial matters and in areas of church policy. This council does not interpret scripture or make church laws and policies, but it is there to advise the First Presidency, which is responsible for church policy.[119]

CURRENT FIRST PRESIDENCY (L-R, COUNSELOR DAVID D. SCHAAL, PRESIDENT STEPHEN M. VEAZEY, COUNSELOR BECKY L. SAVAGE)
Courtesy Community of Christ Archives, Independence, Missouri, Photograph by Dennis Piepergerdes

Congregations in Community of Christ are similar to wards in the LDS Church. Congregations, "the fundamental unit of the church's administrative, ministerial, and missional life," are communities of disciples that meet "preferably at least weekly, to engage in worship, education, fellowship, and other preparation for mission."[120]

Congregations are led by a pastor, a calling similar to that of a bishop in the LDS Church. Pastors can be male or female, but they must be priesthood holders, ideally a high priest or elder. Pastors may

---

117   *Priesthood Manual,* 2004 ed., 25.

118   Community of Christ, *Church Administrator's Handbook,* 2005 ed., 5. In Community of Christ, evangelists were formerly known as patriarchs. Joseph Smith Jr. taught, "An Evangelist is a Patriarch." Smith, *Teachings of the Prophet Joseph Smith,* 151. "It is the duty of the Twelve, in all large branches of the church, to ordain evangelical ministers, as they shall be designated unto them by revelation." Community of Christ Doctrine and Covenants 104:17; LDS Doctrine and Covenants 107:39. See also *History RLDS* 2:570 and the sixth article of faith. The LDS Church continues to use the term "patriarch" rather than evangelist.

119   *Priesthood Manual,* 2004 ed., 24.

120   Community of Christ, *Church Administrator's Handbook,* 2005 ed., 8.

serve more than one year but are elected by the congregation they serve, one year at a time. In certain situations two or more pastors may be elected to serve one congregation. Pastors can also appoint counselors to serve as members of the congregational pastorate.[121] There are suggested organizational structures and positions, but each congregation is free to develop the organization that best meets its needs and situation.[122]

The office of bishop exists in both the LDS Church and Community of Christ. In Community of Christ "the office of bishop is a specialized expression of high priest ministry, in which personal gifts meet ministry needs in a specific time and place."[123] Called and ordained by the First Presidency, bishops "through appointment or contractual agreement with the church, may serve as single-line administrators for a mission center," work with mission center presidents as mission center financial officers, serve as world church ministers, or any number of other assignments.[124]

The Order of Bishops was officially organized in 1913. This order is a church quorum that "nurtures and supports the ministry of bishop." In today's Community of Christ "both men and women serve as high priest ministers ordained to the office of bishop. They serve the church as both paid and self-sustaining ministers in their mission centers."[125]

Community of Christ congregations are grouped together into larger church units called mission centers, similar to stakes in the LDS Church organization. Mission centers are presided over by a mission center president (similar to an LDS stake president) appointed by the world church, and sustained annually by the mission center conference. Mission center presidents report to the field apostle, a member of the Council of Twelve, assigned to that field. A field is a group of

---

121 Ibid., 8–9.
122 Ibid., 13.
123 Cramm, Stassi, "Bishops: Ministers of Generosity," in *PA 231*, compiled by the Presiding Bishopric, 21.
124 Ibid., 21–23.
125 Ibid., 49

mission centers established and changed from time to time by the First Presidency.[126]

LATTER-DAY SAINTS

The LDS Church organization is led by the First Presidency and the Quorum of the Twelve Apostles, the second presidency of the church. Other leadership groups include the Presidency and Quorums of the Seventy, the Presiding Bishopric, and general auxiliary leaders.[127]

Where there is a sufficient number of members, geographical areas are divided into stakes and wards, led by stake presidents and bishops. Districts and branches, led by district presidents and branch presidents, are established in areas where there are not enough members to organize a stake. An LDS stake is led by a high priest who is called by those in authority above him to be the stake president. The stake president is assisted by two counselors and twelve men who compose the stake high council.

In the LDS Church, a bishop is the ecclesiastical leader of a ward. Neither stake presidents nor bishops receive any remuneration for their service as ecclesiastical leaders. Stake presidents typically serve for a period of about nine years and bishops for about five years. Each ward has an elders quorum, presided over by an elders quorum president. High priests belong to a stake quorum presided over by the stake president. On the ward level, high priest groups are under the direction of a high priest group leader. There are also priests, teachers, and deacons quorums in each ward.

SUMMARY

There are organizational similarities between the two churches, including a First Presidency, Quorum of the Twelve, and Presiding Bishopric. There are also similar titles in priesthood offices, such as high priest, elder, priest, teacher, and deacon. Beyond the names, some

---

126   Community of Christ, *Church Administrator's Handbook,* 2005 ed., 8, 13, 15–16, 20.

127   General auxiliary leaders do not exist in Community of Christ. In the LDS Church, these would include general presidencies of the Relief Society, Sunday School, Young Women's organization, Young Men's organization, and Primary.

substantial differences have developed over the years. Each church has leadership positions not found in the other organization.[128]

---

128   In a personal correspondence, William D. Russell wrote: "I think a key difference in priesthood is that LDS boys and men proceed up a ladder, so to speak, from deacon to teacher to priest to elder, typically at a certain age. Those in the Community of Christ are called only when a specific ecclesiastical officer feels a certain woman or man is called by God to a specific office, e.g. priest. The typical elder has had only one previous call: most often priest, less often deacon, and rarely teacher. Sometimes the first call is elder. This makes it much more difficult for the ecclesiastical officer, usually the pastor, to determine (1) is God calling a person to the priesthood? (2) If so, what office?" I will note here that even though Russell sees young men in the LDS Church as progressing "up a ladder" in offices of the priesthood, it is definitely not an automatic progression. Each young man is to be thoroughly interviewed by his bishop regarding his readiness and worthiness before being called to a priesthood office.

LOOKING AT THE PAST: CHURCH HISTORY

Community of Christ and the LDS Church both have a strong sense of their roots. Both churches have historians and church history sites. In more recent years, there has been much cooperation between the two organizations in doing historical research and preserving historical records and landmarks. While opinions of individual historians within either organization can vary greatly, it is the churches' official, or at least mainstream, view of church history that we will try to focus on.

COMMUNITY OF CHRIST

There is no "official position" of Community of Christ in matters of church history today. Community of Christ historian Mark A. Scherer wrote, "Although this has not always been the case, members (and their historians) are free from the strictures that confuse matters of faith with sound historical methodology. Simply stated: 'Our history is not our theology.'"[129] It is because of this freedom, Scherer believes, "a member of the Community of Christ can ask tough historical questions without fear of being considered 'weak in the faith.'"[130]

Roger Launius noted that for over one hundred years the Reorganization remained "faithful to the stories, symbols, and events of early

---

129   Scherer, "Answering Questions No Longer Asked," 28.
130   Ibid.

Mormonism, on the one hand, even as it sought respectability among Christians of other denominations."[131] In the last quarter of the twentieth century, a theological reformation took place in Community of Christ, resulting "in the virtual abandonment of most of the vestiges of Mormonism that informed the movement for a century and in their replacement by more mainline Christian conceptions."[132]

Former Community of Christ president W. Grant McMurray agrees that history should not be confused with theology, suggesting that if such were the case "a faith crisis is awaiting us in someone's attic, only an archival document away." He was not suggesting that history should be ignored, but appreciation of church history "does not mean slavishly adhering to the past." Church history should be seen for what it really is: "A rich and profound story of imperfect people bumbling their way through life, trying to be faithful, yearning for truth. Just like us."[133]

Community of Christ historian Richard P. Howard asked, "Why should the church seek to relive the past, as if there were no present or future, as if the early Saints somehow demanded a replication of their history by later generations?" He then spoke of the balance between drawing courage and compassion from the church's history, while moving forward by following continuing revelation. Community of Christ can, at best, "offer the world the vision of a people living on the boundary between history and revelation, with one foot in the past, and the other moving in faith into the future."[134]

In 1970 the First Presidency of the Reorganized Church wrote a foreword to the book *Exploring the Faith*, which included this statement: "Historical and traditional points of view needed to be expanded in view of contemporary religious experience and scholarship."[135]

An example of this changing view of RLDS history is the issue of polygamy. The Reorganization has always taken a firm position against polygamy. It was one of, if not *the* major issue of difference with the

---

131   Launius, "Is Joseph Smith Relevant?" 61.
132   Ibid., 62.
133   McMurray, "'Something Lost, Something Gained': Restoration History and Culture Seen from 'Both Sides Now,'" 52.
134   Howard, "The Emerging RLDS Identity," in *Restoration Studies III*, 46.
135   *Exploring the Faith*, 5.

LDS Church from the very beginning. William D. Russell wrote, "One reason for RLDS success in rallying dissident Mormons in the Midwest from the 1850s onward was the fact that we were the only significant Mormon splinter group which did not embrace polygamy."[136]

In Joseph Smith III's first sermon as president of the New Organization, he stated that he held polygamy in "utter abhorrence." He blamed Brigham Young for the very existence of polygamy and said that even though he had heard that his father taught such doctrines, "I have never believed it and never can believe it. . . . I believe my father was a good man, and a good man never could have promulgated such doctrines."[137]

For over one hundred years the Reorganized Church rejected the idea that Joseph Smith Jr. had anything to do with the practice of plural marriage. During the last quarter of the twentieth century, RLDS historians and others "probed deeper into the origins of plural marriage, demonstrating beyond reasonable doubt the Mormon prophet's central role in developing the doctrine during the Nauvoo experience and offering frameworks for understanding it."[138]

In 2006 President W. Grant McMurray stated "I don't think we will ever know the extent of Joseph Smith's involvement in the introduction and practice of polygamy. However, no credible historian is arguing today that he had no involvement whatsoever."[139] Community of Christ historian Mark A. Scherer wrote, "In the past, polygamy has been viewed [by the RLDS] in the historical context as a controversial belief associated with the newly emerging Nauvoo Temple theology. But today let us view polygamy as an issue of human worth, peace and justice, and ministerial abuse."[140] McMurray has suggested that Community of Christ "need only to say the Reorganization has

---

136   Russell, "The LDS Church and the Community of Christ: Clearer Differences, Closer Friends," 178.
137   *History RLDS* 3:248.
138   Launius, "Methods and Motives: Joseph Smith III's Opposition to Polygamy, 1860–90," 105.
139   McMurray, "'Something Lost, Something Gained': Restoration History and Culture Seen from 'Both Sides Now,'" 53.
140   Scherer, quoted by Russell, "The LDS Church and the Community of Christ: Clearer Differences, Closer Friends," 179.

never accepted it and waste not one further word in defense of our position."[141]

Current Community of Christ President Stephen M. Veazey wrote that since becoming the president of church he has "engaged in an extensive study of our story," including an exploration of "books and articles from a wide spectrum of scholars, authors, and publishers, ranging from the faithful to the skeptical and in between." His conclusion was that "truth has nothing to fear from scrutiny."[142]

President Veazey suggested that an "apologetic" approach to the history of Community of Christ, in which the church is always presented in a favorable light, "is not sufficient for the journey ahead" because that approach "does not evidence the integrity that must be fundamental to our witness and ministry." The First Presidency of Community of Christ "decided it would be timely to provide a set of 'Church History Principles' to help guide the church's reflections and discussions."[143] Highlights from these principles include the following:

1. Continuing exploration of our history is part of identity formation.
2. History informs but does not dictate our faith and beliefs.
3. The church encourages honest, responsible historical scholarship.
4. The study of church history is a continuing journey.

---

141   McMurray, "'Something Lost, Something Gained': Restoration History and Culture Seen from 'Both Sides Now,'" 53. Community of Christ Fundamentalists still defend Joseph Smith Jr. and continue to blame Brigham Young and others for the introduction of plural marriage into the various restoration churches following the death of the Prophet Joseph. Although this primary division between the LDS and Community of Christ churches has disappeared, it is ironic that anyone found practicing polygamy today in the LDS Church will be excommunicated and the LDS Church does not allow for baptism of people practicing polygamy in cultures where polygamy is legal, while Community of Christ policy allows for the baptism of men practicing polygamy in Third World countries, as long as they promise not to take additional wives. Russell, "The LDS Church and the Community of Christ: Clearer Differences, Closer Friends," 179.
142   Veazey, "Perspectives on Church History," 10.
143   Ibid.

5. Seeing both the faithfulness and human flaws in our history makes it more believable and realistic, not less.

6. The responsible study of church history involves learning, repentance, and transformation.

7. The church has a long-standing tradition that it does not legislate or mandate positions on matters of church history.

8. We need to create a respectful culture of dialogue about matters of history.

9. Our faith is grounded in God's revelation in Jesus Christ and the continuing guidance of the Holy Spirit.[144]

Community of Christ considers its history to be a sacred story, which is "part of a much larger sacred story that is rooted in Christian history." Members proclaim that "within this larger history, Community of Christ has a particular story that is inspiring, colorful, and increasingly international."[145] Their church history is important to them, not in determining what they are, but to see God's hand in their development.

> The story of the church is one of unusual faith, vision, and creativity in response to God's call. We can clearly see God's Spirit active in every chapter of our faith story. What began with a teenager seeking God in prayer in the early 1800s continues today. God gives each generation insights, experiences, and challenges for divine purposes.[146]

The history or faith story of Community of Christ is much more than the earliest years of the Restoration that took place during the life of Joseph Smith Jr. It has a long history separate from the LDS Church that helped it develop into what it has become today. President Veazey

---

144   Ibid., 11–12. The complete text of "Church History Principles" is included in appendix C of this book.
145   Community of Christ, *We Share Identity, Mission, Message, and Beliefs*, 7.
146   Ibid.

reminded the church that "the longer part of our history by far is the story of the Reorganization." He proclaimed:

> That history makes up over 150 years of our heritage. It is the story of Jason Briggs whose account of his experience with the Spirit in response to prayer about the future of the church became the rallying point for the "scattered Saints." It is the story of the faith, courage, and tenacity of Emma Smith. Without her we would not be here. It is also the story of the pivotal response of Joseph Smith III to the leadings of the Spirit in his young life.[147]

LATTER-DAY SAINTS

The LDS Church's "official view" of church history is to focus on the positive aspects of it and the hand of God in it. Certainly LDS Church leaders cannot dictate what Mormon historians research and write. However, some scholars have put their membership in the LDS Church in jeopardy by writing things that the leadership deemed as apostasy and harmful to growth and development of the church.

Clearly, LDS leaders would like Mormon historians to write things that are not only true but also faith promoting. Speaking to a group of LDS educators, Elder Boyd K. Packer of the Church's Quorum of the Twelve gave these four cautions:

1. There is no such thing as an accurate, objective history of the Church without consideration of the spiritual powers that attend this work.

2. There is a temptation for the writer or the teacher of Church history to want to tell everything, whether it is worthy or faith promoting or not.

3. In an effort to be objective, impartial, and scholarly, a writer or a teacher may unwittingly be giving equal time to the adversary.

4. The final caution concerns the idea that so long as something is already in print, so long as it is available

---

147   Veazey, "A Defining Moment," Address to the Church given on April 5, 2009.

from another source, there is nothing out of order in using it in writing or speaking or teaching.[148]

Speaking about a Mormon historian who had lectured on a former president of the LDS Church and shown him in an unfavorable light, Elder Packer remarked, "What that historian did with the reputation of the President of the Church was not worth doing. He seemed determined to convince everyone that the *prophet* was a *man*. We knew that already." Elder Packer suggested that it would have been much more worthwhile for the historian "to have convinced us that the *man* was a *prophet*, a fact quite as true as the fact that he was a man."[149]

With this type of strong urging from some of the Brethren, Latter-day Saints, for the most part, view their church's history with reverence and admiration, often referring to the strong faith of the early Mormon pioneers. As President Joseph F. Smith admonished the Saints in the April 1904 general conference:

> The hand of the Lord may not be visible to all. There may be many who can not discern the workings of God's will in the progress and development of this great latter-day work, but there are those who see in every hour and in every moment of the existence of the Church, from its beginning until now, the overruling, almighty hand of Him who sent His Only Begotten Son.[150]

SUMMARY

As stated in the beginning of this chapter, the history of the church has been important to both churches for many years. Although historians from both churches continue to research areas of their history, basic philosophical differences about the past have appeared. Community of Christ continues to be very interested in their history, but the principles set forth by the First Presidency "provide the guidelines needed to treasure our history, but not be totally defined by it." As stated by President Veazey: "While affirming the essential role of historical study,

---

148   Packer, "The Mantle is Far, Far Greater Than the Intellect," 262–71.
149   Ibid., 264–65.
150   Joseph F. Smith, in *LDS Conference Reports 1904*, 2.

the principles ["Church History Principles"] state that history does not have the final word on matters of faith and unfolding direction in the church today."[151]

Perhaps the LDS Church does not treasure its history any more than Community of Christ. However, it does appear to have a stronger connection to its history. It would be safe to say that it reveres the founding fathers more and draw strength for today by looking at the past. The history of the LDS Church is a motivating factor for many Mormons in their efforts to follow the Brethren.

151   Veazey, "A Defining Moment," Address to the Church given on April 5, 2009.

THE PROPHET JOSEPH SMITH

The Church of Jesus Christ of Latter-day Saints and Community of Christ both recognize Joseph Smith Jr. as the founder of their churches and the Prophet of the Restoration Movement. There is no doubt that the early members of both organizations held the Prophet Joseph in high esteem. Shortly after Joseph was killed, future LDS president John Taylor wrote "Joseph Smith, the Prophet and Seer of the Lord, has done more, save Jesus only, for the salvation of men in this world, than any other man that ever lived in it."[152]

COMMUNITY OF CHRIST

Early Reorganization views of Joseph Smith Jr. are evident in that on June 12, 1852, a resolution was made "that the successor of Joseph Smith, Jun., as the Presiding High Priest, in the Melchisedec Priesthood, must of necessity be the seed of Joseph Smith, Jun."[153] Although the New Organization claimed to be the legitimate continuation of the original restoration church founded by Joseph Smith Jr. in its earliest beginnings, its claim was strengthened by Joseph Smith III's acceptance of church leadership. In 1960, Russell F. Ralston noted that the

---

152 LDS Doctrine and Covenants 135:3 (1844).

153 Early Reorganization Minutes (commonly referred to as Book A) June 12, 1852, as quoted in McMurray, "'True Son of a True Father': Joseph Smith III and the Succession Question," in *Restoration Studies I*, 135.

Reorganization had "always been blessed with the prophetic leadership of the 'seed' of the prophet martyr."[154]

Few would deny that Joseph Smith Jr. was a fascinating and unusual character in American history. Robert Flanders commented that Joseph's life, in many ways, fulfilled the great American Dream. "He was a self-made man, rising from poverty to power, from semi-literacy to knowledge of both worldly and heavenly mysteries, from anonymity to fame, from being nobody to being somebody."[155] Smith's rise from obscurity to being considered famous or infamous around the world is a fulfillment of an angelic statement made to seventeen-year-old Joseph Smith, saying his "name should be had for good and evil among all nations, kindreds, and tongues, or that it should be both good and evil spoken of among all people."[156]

Joseph Smith Jr. was venerated by the Reorganized Church of Jesus Christ of Latter Day Saints for many years. Robert Flanders went so far as to say "to generations of faithful followers he was a demi-god."[157] However, there were some doctrines that Joseph was said to have taught that were troubling to the Reorganization. For years these teachings were denied, dismissed as Utah Mormon lies, rejected, or simply ignored.

In recent years, Community of Christ historians and scholars have come to accept that Joseph Smith "promulgated a series of unique ideas on eternity, the multiplicity of gods, the possibility of progression to godhood, celestial and plural marriage, baptism for the dead, and other ideas associated with Mormon temple endowments." New historical findings have resulted in Community of Christ walking "a fine line in interpreting the legacy of Joseph Smith."[158]

---

154   Ralston, *Fundamental Differences Between the LDS and RLDS Churches*, 15. Russell F. Ralston was a prominent missionary Seventy who spent a lot of time in Salt Lake City in the 1950s and became an Apostle in the RLDS Church in 1964. This need to be "blessed by the 'seed' of the prophet martyr" is certainly not the mainstream Community of Christ thinking today. Thanks to William D. Russell for his insight on Russell F. Ralston.

155   Flanders, "Dream and Nightmare: Nauvoo Revisited," in *The Restoration Movement: Essays in Mormon History*, eds. McKiernan, Blair, and Edwards, 141.

156   *History RLDS* 1:12–13; Joseph Smith—History 1:33, in the Pearl of Great Price.

157   Flanders, "Dream and Nightmare: Nauvoo Revisited," in *The Restoration Movement: Essays in Mormon History*, eds. McKiernan, Blair, and Edwards, 141.

158   Launius, "Is Joseph Smith Relevant to the Community of Christ?" 61.

Probably the most troubling issue that Community of Christ has had to deal with was Joseph Smith's involvement with polygamy—a possibility that it had strongly rejected for years.

Community of Christ's recognition that the doctrine of plural marriage, at least in part, can be traced to Joseph Smith Jr., along with other issues and concerns, has required a reinterpretation of Joseph Smith as a prophet.

"Joseph Smith, Jr. has enjoyed a place in this religious tradition [Community of Christ] strikingly different from that he has attained among the Utah-based Latter-day Saints," wrote Roger D. Launius. He went on to say that, "without question, he is much less revered and less legendary" in Community of Christ "than among the Latter-day Saints, for whom Joseph Smith is significant, not just for his life but for his religious innovations."[159]

Today's Community of Christ honors and acknowledges the accomplishments of Joseph Smith Jr., but it also recognizes that he was a flawed human being. In 2003, speaking to the Mormon Historical Association, Grant McMurray, then president of Community of Christ, said that he believed Joseph Smith "was brilliant and visionary, probably a religious genius, certainly the founder of the most significant indigenous religious movement to be birthed on American soil." He also said he believed Joseph Smith to be "deeply flawed, with profound human weaknesses, inconsistencies, and shortcomings."[160]

In his 2006 article entitled "Is Joseph Smith Relevant to the Community of Christ?" Roger D. Launius contended "that Joseph Smith's activities represented a conflicting set of ideals for those identified with the Community of Christ."[161] He recognized that his views on Joseph Smith may not be the same as those of many in Community of Christ:

> I suspect that many members still view [Joseph Smith's] early
> structuring of the Church and its basic doctrines as prophetic.
> Even so, their view of his prophetic role in the Church is severely

159   Ibid., 58.
160   McMurray, "A 'Goodly Heritage' in a Time of Transformation: History and Identity in the Community of Christ," 65–66.
161   Launius, "Is Joseph Smith Relevant to the Community of Christ?" 59.

limited when compared to the view of the LDS Church and perhaps to early RLDS views. By distancing itself from many of his
actions and selectively emphasizing his prophetic role, the Community of Christ views him as more human than he is in the LDS
tradition. His Nauvoo innovations are an "embarrassment," but
many still view him as a figure of significance in the formation of
the Church.[162]

Launius referred to the broad-based reformation that took place in
the Reorganization in the latter part of the twentieth century, "which
resulted in the virtual abandonment of most of the vestiges of Mormonism." He concluded that "in the process of that reformation, the
character of Joseph Smith has become an embarrassment" and that
Joseph "is often viewed as a skeleton in the closet of the Community
of Christ."[163]

It is difficult to determine how prevalent this feeling is within the
general membership of Community of Christ. It is certainly not the
official position of Community of Christ. It is, however, fair to say
that there has been a shift in recent years to focus less on Joseph Smith.
Community of Christ Theologian-in-Residence Tony Chvala-Smith
made it clear that "the Community of Christ no longer treats the Joseph Smith story as the normative lens through which it interprets
the Christian message."[164] Andrew Bolton, the former Community of
Christ Coordinator for Peace and Justice and now an Apostle, put it
this way, "We used to see Jesus through the eyes of Joseph; now we see
Joseph through the eyes of Jesus."[165]

Perhaps one of the best explanations of Community of Christ's
relationship to Joseph Smith today is a statement made by one of its
scholars. He wrote, "We as members of the Community of Christ lift
up the teachings of a Carpenter from Nazareth and not a Prophet from
Palmyra." He went on to say that this was not stated to demean the
contribution of Joseph Smith, a great man and founder of the Restora-

---

162   Ibid., 61.
163   Ibid., 62.
164   Quoted in Russell, "The LDS Church and the Community of Christ: Clearer Differ-
       ences, Closer Friends," 189.
165   Ibid.

tion Movement. Rather, "we in the Community of Christ prefer to go to the primary source rather than secondary source" for our doctrine and teachings.[166]

LATTER-DAY SAINTS

Today, the LDS Church maintains a firm belief in and strong loyalty to Joseph Smith and his role as prophet of the Restoration. In 2005, the two-hundredth anniversary of the birth of Joseph Smith, Elder Richard G. Scott declared that Joseph Smith was "an extraordinary spirit prepared before the foundation of the earth," who would "become the greatest prophet sent to earth."[167] Joseph Smith remains highly revered as the prophet of the Restoration among the membership of The Church of Jesus Christ of Latter-day Saints.

SUMMARY

Joseph Smith Jr. is recognized as the founder of both Community of Christ and The Church of Jesus Christ of Latter-day Saints. The early Saints of both churches recognized him as a prophet of God.

The LDS Church continues to revere the accomplishments and revelations of Joseph Smith Jr. It acknowledges that he was an imperfect man, capable of mistakes. However, members accept his teachings as revelatory and the word of God. They worship God and believe that they can come closer to God by following the ancient and latter-day prophets. The First latter-day prophet was Joseph Smith, Jr.

Community of Christ is also appreciative of Joseph's prophetic abilities and honors him as its founder. As the religion has developed, it has distanced itself somewhat from Joseph Smith Jr. and some of his teachings because they see them at odds with the teachings of the Bible. The church views Joseph Smith's contribution to the Restoration as great but try to see beyond the flawed messenger and sometimes flawed message to the divine truths that come from God.

---

166 Personal e-mail from Mark Scherer to Alonzo Gaskill. Used with permission of Mark Scherer.
167 Scott, "Truth Restored," 80.

PRIESTHOOD AND AUTHORITY

During the process of translating the Book of Mormon in 1829, Joseph Smith Jr. and his scribe, Oliver Cowdery, began pondering their need to be baptized and were concerned that no church on earth possessed the authority from God to properly perform baptisms. According to the "The History of Joseph Smith" as published in the church's Nauvoo newspaper, *Times and Seasons*:

> We on a certain day went into the woods to pray and inquire of the Lord respecting baptism for the remission of sins, as we found mentioned in the translation of the plates. While we were thus employed, praying, and calling upon the Lord, a messenger from heaven descended in a cloud of light, and having laid his hands upon us, he ordained us, saying unto us, "Upon you my fellow servants in the name of Messiah, I confer the priesthood of Aaron.[168]

Joseph reported that the heavenly messenger who conferred the lesser or Aaronic Priesthood upon him and Oliver was John the Baptist. John informed Joseph and Oliver that he was acting under the direction of Peter, James, and John, who were to restore the higher or Melchizedek Priesthood at a future date. A short time later, that ordination also took place.[169]

---

168 *Times and Seasons* 3 (August 1, 1842): 865; *History RLDS* 1:34–35; *HC* 1:39.

169 While there is no specific recorded date for the restoration of the Melchizedek Priesthood, Larry C. Porter's research has narrowed down the time when it likely took place.

The early Saints viewed receiving the priesthood from heavenly messengers as a major part of the restoration of Christ's church to the earth. They believed that although many of the doctrinal truths about gospel of Jesus Christ may have remained intact, the loss of authority to act in His name resulted in the Great Apostasy. Christ's true church was lost to the inhabitants of the earth. This is the reason why when Joseph Smith prayed to know which church he should join, the Savior informed him that he "must join none of them, for they were all wrong."[170]

COMMUNITY OF CHRIST

Priesthood power or authority was seen by both churches as absolutely necessary to their claims of being Christ's true church. This became a major source of contention between the two organizations for many years. Each church argued that it was the official church restored by Joseph Smith Jr. and therefore the possessor of priesthood authority.

The Reorganization stood by its conviction that Joseph Smith Jr. had blessed his son to be the prophet-president of the church in his stead.[171] It also based its belief on revelations received by founders of the New Organization concerning the posterity of Joseph Smith and its right to lead. The June 12, 1852, resolution that the Prophet Joseph's successor "must of necessity be the seed of Joseph Smith, Jun."[172] resulted in the very common belief within the Reorganization that it was absolutely required that a descendant of Joseph Smith Jr. lead the church.

He wrote that "the restoration of the Melchizedek Priesthood apparently occurred between 15 May 1829 and 1 June 1829, but definitely during a May-June time-frame at the outside." Porter, "The Priesthood Restored," in *Studies in Scripture: The Pearl of Great Price*, 400–401.

170 *History RLDS* 1:9; Joseph Smith—History 1:19.

171 D. Michael Quinn wrote: "there is evidence that Joseph Smith, Jr. hoped that his sons might eventually preside over the Church. . . . Whether, in fact, Joseph Smith officially designated his son Joseph III to be his successor has been debated for more than a century." Quinn, "The Mormon Succession Crisis of 1844," 223. Lachlan Mackay stated, "The belief that Joseph intended his sons to be future church leaders was widespread among churches of the dispersion, including the post-Nauvoo LDS church." Personal communication to the author.

172 Early Reorganization Minutes (commonly referred to as Book A) June 12, 1852, as quoted in McMurray, "'True Son of a True Father': Joseph Smith III and the Succession Question," in *Restoration Studies I*, 135.

One Reorganized Church writer argued that "none of the leaders of the Church in Utah have been of the seed of Joseph and thus do not come within the promise of God."[173] According to Joseph Smith III, it was never an absolute necessity that Joseph's seed lead the church. His "A Letter of Instruction" makes it clear that the Church president should be a descendant of Joseph Smith Jr., "

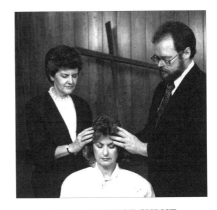

**COMMUNITY OF CHRIST
PRIESTHOOD HOLDERS
PERFORMING AN ORDINANCE**
Courtesy Community of Christ Archives,
Independence, Missouri

The RLDS Church recognized the initial priesthood authority of the original Twelve of this dispensation, but it was convinced that only as a united body was the power and authority of the Twelve equal to the First Presidency.[175] The Reorganization saw Brigham Young as a usurper of power and a deceiver of the Saints.[176]

---

173   Ralston, *Fundamental Differences Between the LDS and RLDS Churches*, 15.

174   "A Letter of Instruction" was originally published in the *Saints' Herald*, March 13, 1912. For a copy of "A Letter of Instruction" by Joseph Smith III, see the official website of Community of Christ: www.cofchrist.org/history/letter-of-instruction.asp

175   Ibid. At the first conference of the Reorganization held in 1852, it passed this resolution: "Resolved, that, as the office of First Presidency of the Church grows out of the authority of the Presiding High Priest, in the high priesthood, no person can legally lay claim to the office of First President of the Church without a previous ordination to the Presidency of the High Priesthood." *History RLDS* 3:209–10. They saw Brigham Young's ordination to president of the church and his reorganization of the First Presidency as invalid and a usurpation of authority.

176   One researcher wrote that the RLDS Church pointed to a verse in the Doctrine and Covenants which reads "none else shall be appointed unto this gift except it be through him [Joseph Smith, Jr.]." Community of Christ Doctrine and Covenants 43:2a; LDS Doctrine and Covenants 43:4 (1831). He concluded that RLDS leadership believed it was Joseph III, not Brigham Young, who had been selected by Joseph Smith Jr. as the rightful leader of the church. "In other words, Brigham Young was a fraud who had used the Church's weakness in a time of vulnerability and confusion to usurp its leadership." Boegle, "Mormons Divided: The Emergence of Two Mormon Churches Following the Death of Joseph Smith," 29–39.

The Reorganization also believed that, because the Nauvoo Temple was not completed, the church was rejected by God.[177] This conclusion was based on the following verses from the Doctrine and Covenants:

> But I command you, all ye my saints, to build a house unto me; and I grant unto you a sufficient time to build a house unto me; and during this time your baptisms shall be acceptable unto me. But behold, at the end of this appointment your baptisms for your dead shall not be acceptable unto me; and if you do not these things at the end of the appointment ye shall be rejected as a church, with your dead, saith the Lord your God.[178]

The Reorganization saw Brigham Young's actions of taking over the church and, eventually, reorganizing the First Presidency as transgressing the laws of God. According to another revelation received by the Prophet Joseph, so many men have their "hearts set upon the things of this world, and aspire to the honors of men, that they do not learn this one lesson—that the rights of the priesthood are inseparably connected with the powers of heaven." Priesthood may be conferred upon a man, but if he seeks to hide his sins, gratify his pride and vain ambition, or exercise control over the children of men, "in any degree of unrighteousness, behold, the heav-

---

177   Whether the Nauvoo Temple was completed or not has been a source of contention between what is now Community of Christ and the LDS Church for many years. The Reorganization contends that the exterior of the temple was finished, but the interior was never completed. The LDS Church's stand is that the Nauvoo Temple was completed or "sufficiently finished" to be dedicated and for temple ordinances to be performed. It is likely that some of the interior was not completed. However, it is also true that portions of the temple were dedicated as they were completed and those rooms were used for temple ordinances. The entire structure was dedicated by Elder Orson Hyde publicly on May 1, 1846. This difference of opinion as to whether the Nauvoo Temple was not "completely" finished or was "sufficiently" finished does not appear to be discussed that much anymore by either church.

178   Community of Christ Doctrine and Covenants, 1958 edition, 107:10f–11a; LDS Doctrine and Covenants 124:31–32 (1841). This section was first included in the 1844 edition of the Doctrine and Covenants. This section was placed in the appendix of the Community of Christ Doctrine and Covenants (along with some other sections) by action of the world conference held in 1970 because of the doctrine of baptism for the dead, which is not accepted by the Reorganized Church. At the 1990 world conference, the appendix was removed from the Community of Christ Doctrine and Covenants, which meant that section 107 was removed completely from RLDS scripture. The doctrine of baptism for the dead will be covered in another chapter.

ens withdraw themselves; the Spirit of the Lord is grieved; and when it is withdrawn, Amen to the priesthood or the authority of that man."[179]

Early RLDS members saw Brigham Young as a man who was ambitious, controlling, and corrupt in his views of doctrine, specifically that of plural marriage. They would not dispute that he once held the priesthood and priesthood keys, but they felt that God had withdrawn that power and authority from him. In their view, the LDS Church could not have the power or authority of the priesthood.

Over one hundred years after the organization of the Reorganized Church, a question was submitted to the Reorganization's official periodical about whether it recognized the Utah priesthood. The response was "we do not recall any instance wherein the Reorganized Church has acknowledged or accepted any priesthood authority springing from ordinations performed under the auspices of the factional organization set up in Utah." Recent scholarship has shown otherwise.[180]

In recent years, Community of Christ has begun to see priesthood in a different light. It no longer considers it to be an authority that had been removed from the earth and, therefore, had to be restored by Joseph Smith. Members do not believe that they are "the only bearers or possessors of authoritative ministry."[181] They no longer see themselves as *the* true church, but as an important part of the body of Christ, with

179   *Times and Seasons* 1 (July 1840): 131–32; LDS Doctrine and Covenants 121:35–37 (1839). The Community of Christ Doctrine and Covenants does not contain this particular section. Those who had been members of the Church under Joseph Smith and who later joined the Reorganization might have been familiar with this revelation if they had read it in the *Times and Seasons* published in Nauvoo.

180   *Question Time* 1:350. Thanks to Lachlan Mackay of Community of Christ for pointing out information about Joseph Smith III and his consideration of the possibility that other restoration churches might have authority. Lachlan wrote: "Although they [the authors of *Question Time*] didn't recall it, [Joseph Smith III] had acknowledged that other Latter Day Saint tradition churches might have authority. See Joseph Smith III to W.E. Winkworth, 11 Feb 1911: 'The church accepts the idea that there may be in each and every portion into which the church was divided at the death of Joseph and Hyrum Smith, individuals who held and may now hold legitimate priesthood. This includes the church in Utah. We are willing to concede that there may be individuals in that body who have not forfeited fully their priesthood.'" Personal communication to the author.

181   Booth, "Changing Concepts of Priesthood Authority," in *Restoration Studies VI*, 101.

all parts comprising the true church. They are an integral part of the community of Jesus Christ.[182]

Priesthood authority is now viewed as callings within the ministry. God calls an individual to specific responsibilities according to that person's particular gifts and abilities. It is the concept of a universal priesthood, rather than "the traditional notion of a specialized priest-hood who have been granted unique spiritual gifts, and consequently special authority, to minister for Christ."[183]

Those in administrative positions in Community of Christ assess congregational needs, choose a person to meet those needs, and seek confirmation from God that this person is the one to be called to a specific function. Worthiness is determined, and the person is called to that position and ordained to the necessary priesthood. Priesthood is a calling to service in the ministry of Christ.[184]

There are various presiding and sacramental priesthood offices within Community of Christ.[185] In 1984, President Wallace B. Smith presented

---

182 "In the Restoration movement we sometimes speak of the priesthood as having been 'restored' at the time the church was founded. This emerged from a belief in that time that the churches had gone astray and that the power of ministry had been lost. While the extent to which that is true may be argued, it is our faith that something sacred and authoritative happened when our church was founded. We continue to embrace the spirit of that experience now. It is not about rejecting other churches or their ministries. Instead, the key principle is our belief that God blesses us in our ministry when we faithfully respond and serve. The effectiveness of our priesthood is never based on some historic event from another era but on the spiritual vitality we exhibit in our own time." Community of Christ, *Priesthood Manual,* 2004 ed., 12.

183 Booth, "Changing Concepts of Priesthood Authority," in *Restoration Studies VI,* 103.

184 The 2004 edition of Community of Christ's *Priesthood Manual* contains these statements on priesthood:
    Roles in society are undergoing changes and new understandings. This is also true of priesthood. Today we recognize that many functions once thought to be only the province of priesthood can be performed by various persons, whether ordained or unordained. . . . It is primarily in administering the ordinances and sacraments of the church and in some presiding functions that those in the priesthood have exclusive roles that cannot be performed in the church by anyone else. More important than the question of what one can or can't do is the question of what one *feels called* to do and is willing to accept responsibility for in the life of the church. (*Priesthood Manual,* 2004 ed., 11).

185 Any person who has been baptized and confirmed in the Church has received the "office of member." A person who "holds the office of member may perform any function of the church, other than presiding and sacramental roles that are the responsibility of specific priesthood offices." *Priesthood Manual,* 2004 ed., 21. This comment does need some clarification. Only a Community of Christ member who has been ordained to

a revelation to the world conference that clarified the meaning and scope of priesthood service. The following is an excerpt of that revelation:

> Hear, O my people, regarding my holy priesthood. The power of this priesthood was placed in your midst from the earliest days of the rise of this work for the blessing and salvation of humanity. There have been priesthood members over the years, however, who have misunderstood the purpose of their calling. Succumbing to pride, some have used it for personal aggrandizement. Others, through disinterest or lack of diligence, have failed to magnify their calling or have become inactive. When this has happened, the church has experienced a loss of spiritual power, and the entire priesthood structure has been diminished. . . . I have heard the prayers of many, including my servant the prophet, as they have sought to know my will in regard to the question of who shall be called to share the burdens and responsibilities of priesthood in my church. I say to you now, as I have said in the past, that *all are called according to the gifts which have been given them. This applies to priesthood as well as to any other aspects of the work. Therefore, do not wonder that some women of the church are being called to priesthood responsibilities.*[186]

Since the mid-1980s, women in Community of Christ have been able to have priesthood conferred upon them and be ordained to offices within both Aaronic and Melchisedec priesthoods.[187] As of this writing, there are currently four women serving as apostles in the Twelve and a female counselor to the prophet-president in the First Presidency.[188]

---

the priesthood can perform a presiding or sacramental role in the Church. This means that a person who is not specifically ordained to the priesthood cannot do things such as perform baptisms, confirmations, baby blessings, marriages, or bless and pass the sacrament of the Lord's supper. A person with the "office of member" can use his or her talents and skills to do anything in the Church that does not require a specifically ordained priesthood office.

186   Community of Christ Doctrine and Covenants 156:7–9c (1984); emphasis added.

187   The revelation was presented to the Church (Community of Christ) in 1984, and women began to be ordained the following year.

188   At this writing, women have held every priesthood office in the Community of Christ except prophet-president.

There is no set age to receive the priesthood in Community of Christ. It is based more on the spiritual maturity and giftedness of the individual. Some people have received the priesthood in their later teens, but it is not typical for young people to receive the priesthood.

LATTER-DAY SAINTS

The LDS Church believed that it had the proper authority because priesthood keys were passed from Joseph Smith Jr. to the Quorum of the Twelve. The Twelve formed "a quorum, equal in authority and power to the three presidents."[189] At the time of Joseph Smith's death, Brigham Young was president of the Twelve, "which Twelve hold the keys to open up the authority of my kingdom."[190]

As for the LDS Church's current view of the Reorganization or any other group that claimed authority through Joseph Smith Jr., it maintains its stand that no church other than The Church of Jesus Christ of Latter-day Saints possesses the authority from God known as priesthood. Mormons would not disagree that many who joined the Reorganization had received the priesthood when Joseph Smith Jr. led the church. They simply assert that priesthood without keys cannot function or be passed on to another. In their view, the keys of the priesthood were and are found only in the LDS Church.

In the LDS Church, only males can hold the priesthood. A male must be at least twelve-years-old to hold the Aaronic Priesthood. To receive the Melchizedek Priesthood a man must be at least eighteen years of age. It should also be noted that men of black African descent were not allowed to hold priesthood in the LDS Church until 1978.[191] In 1865 a revelation given to Joseph Smith III authorized people of black

---

189   LDS Doctrine and Covenants 107:24 (1835). Lachlan Mackay of Community of Christ shared this insight: "This section [Doctrine and Covenants 107] was also used to support William Marks as Joseph's successor. It goes on to say that the Presidents of Seventy, the Standing High Councils, are also equal in authority to the Twelve, who are equal in authority to the Presidency. It also discusses the need for the Twelve and Seventy to make unanimous decisions (verse 27) and would likely be why early Community of Christ members believed the Twelve needed to act unanimously after Joseph's death". Personal communication with the author.

190   LDS Doctrine and Covenants 124:128 (1841).

191   "Although at least two black men—Elijah Abel and Walker Lewis—were ordained during Joseph Smith's lifetime, sometime in the 1840s Church leaders announced that

African descent to hold the priesthood in the Reorganized Church. Both churches allowed blacks membership from the very beginning.[192]

SUMMARY

The idea that, because of the loss of authority, the true church of God was not on the earth since the Great Apostasy until its restoration through the Prophet Joseph Smith was a fundamental belief of the early restoration Saints. That same concept was maintained by the Reorganized Church for many years but is seen somewhat differently in the modern Community of Christ. It remains the belief of the LDS Church today.

---

blacks could not hold the priesthood." Garr, Cannon, and Cowan, eds., *Encyclopedia of Latter-Day Saint History*, 107.

192 Community of Christ Doctrine and Covenants 116 (1865): 1c states: "Therefore it is expedient in me that you ordain priests unto me, of every race who receive the teachings of my law, and become heirs according to the promise." In verse four of that same section, it says, "Be not hasty in ordaining men of the Negro race to offices in my church, . . . nevertheless, I will that all may be saved, but every man in his own order, and there are some who are chosen instruments to be ministers to their own race."

THE NATURE OF GOD

There is no more basic belief in Community of Christ and in The Church of Jesus Christ of Latter-day Saints than their belief in the existence of God. The LDS Church's first article of faith reads: "We believe in God, the Eternal Father, and in His Son, Jesus Christ, and in the Holy Ghost."[193] The Articles of Faith, written by Joseph Smith, were known in the Reorganized Church as the Epitome of Faith and were accepted for over one hundred years.[194]

Both restoration churches believe in God, Jesus Christ, and the Holy Spirit. Both accept Jesus Christ as the Son of God. Both are firm in their conviction that Jesus atoned for the sins of all humanity and that He was crucified, He died, and He was resurrected. Both groups believe that the Holy Spirit can influence mortals to come unto Christ and empower those who do become committed to the Savior with gifts of the Spirit.

Both churches are resolute in their belief in God. There is, however, no more fundamental doctrinal difference between the two churches than their understanding of the nature of God.

---

193   Articles of Faith, found in Pearl of Great Price, 60.
194   Community of Christ never did reject the Epitome of Faith. Over the years they have revised and continue to develop a more adequate statement of beliefs through receiving further light on doctrine.

COMMUNITY OF CHRIST

After close examination of the Epitome of Faith (Articles of Faith), Community of Christ "recognized that a more adequate statement of the beliefs of the church should be developed."[195] A Committee on Basic Beliefs was formed and the committee created "A Statement of Belief."[196] The first four paragraphs of this document deal with the nature of God. Paragraph One states, "We believe in God the eternal Father, source and center of all truth, who is almighty, infinite, and unchanging, in whom and through whom all things exist and have their being."[197] Paragraph Two affirms Community of Christ's belief in "Jesus Christ, the Only Begotten Son of God . . . who is God in the flesh . . . who is mediator between God and man."[198] Paragraphs Three and Four testify of Community of Christ's belief in the Holy Spirit and his role in empowering men who are committed to Christ.[199]

Since the groundbreaking *Exploring the Faith* was published in 1970, there have been further insights and development in Community of Christ theology, so that *Exploring the Faith* is not as accurate rendering of the church's current doctrine on the nature of God as more recent publications. The 2009 publication of *We Share: Identity, Mission, Message, and Beliefs* is the most current and authoritative document dealing with basic Community of Christ beliefs.

GOD

Community of Christ adheres to the more mainstream Christian definition of God: the Trinity. "We believe in one living God who meets us in the testimony of Israel, is revealed in Jesus Christ, and moves through all creation as the Holy Spirit. We affirm the Trinity—God who is a community of three persons."[200] The three members of the Trinity are one in substance but separate and distinct in their personhood. Community of Christ would agree with the Athanasian Creed

---

195   *Exploring the Faith*, 5.
196   "A Statement of Belief" was published in *Exploring the Faith*, 10–15. It is included in its entirety as appendix A in this book.
197   *Exploring the Faith*, 16.
198   Ibid., 30.
199   Ibid., 52, 62.
200   *We Share*, 14.

that the Father is God, the Son is God, and the Holy Spirit is God, yet they are not three gods, but one God.[201]

While Community of Christ is firmly grounded in the doctrine of the Trinity today, this has not always been the case. One scholar acknowledged "there seems to have been some discussion in the birth of the Reorganized movement around several theological topics, and total agreement on these issues is not always found."[202] One of these issues was the nature of the Godhead.

The "Questions and Answers" section of a March 1898 issue of the *Saints' Herald* included this question: "Will you kindly state through the *Herald*, the faith of the church on the Godhead. Whether there is one or two personages?"[203] The response was that although the church had "not taken formulated ground by conference action that we are aware of," the church's position could be stated "about as follows:— There are in the Godhead proper, two personages; God, the Father; Christ the Son; the Father and the Son; or God the Father, and God the Son."[204]

Even though this response was published in the church's own periodical, the *Saints' Herald*, it appears that Joseph Smith III was more

---

201   Cited in Chvala-Smith, "A Trinitarian Approach to World Religions," in *Restoration Studies VIII*, 128.

202   Hatch, "History of the Godhead in the Community of Christ," in *Restoration Studies IX*, 119.

203   Cited in Hatch, "History of the Godhead in the Community of Christ," in *Restoration Studies IX*, 121. This would also coincide with the *Lectures on Faith* published in 1835, which stated: "There are two personages who constitute the great, matchless, governing, and supreme power over all things, by whom all things were created and made, that are created and made, whether visible or invisible, whither in heaven, on earth, or in the earth, under the earth, or throughout the immensity of space. They are the Father and the Son." *Lectures on Faith* 5:2. Some people see Joseph Smith's concept of God evolving over the years, changing from "one God" in the early years of the Restoration to three separate beings in the Godhead by the Nauvoo period. Others believe that he was consistent from the beginning. In an address attributed to Joseph Smith given shortly before his death, he is reported to have said: "I have always declared God to be a distinct personage, Jesus Christ a separate and distinct personage from God the Father, and that the Holy Ghost was a distinct personage and a Spirit: and these three constitute three distinct personages and three Gods." Smith, *Teachings of the Prophet Joseph Smith*, 370. Since evidence for both sides of the argument exists, it becomes an individual matter of faith.

204   Hatch, "History of the Godhead in the Community of Christ," in *Restoration Studies IX*, 121.

inclined to believe in one God. By the end of his presidency the issue of the Godhead appears to have been resolved by the adoption of the "more traditional understanding of God" or belief in the trinity.[205]

Some Community of Christ members wonder how it is that the LDS Church does not believe in the Trinity, citing verses from the Book of Mormon as evidence supporting that doctrine. Abinadi proclaims:

> I would that you should understand that God himself shall come down among the children of men and shall redeem his people. And because he dwells in flesh, he shall be called the Son of God; and having subjected the flesh to the will of the Father, being the Father and the Son—the Father because he was conceived by the power of God, and the Son because of the flesh; thus becoming the Father and Son—they are one God, the very eternal Father of heaven and of earth.[206]

Later, in the Book of Ether, the Brother of Jared sees the Lord and hears His voice: "Behold, I am he who was prepared from the foundation of the world to redeem my people. Behold, I am Jesus Christ. I am the Father and the Son."[207]

: Today's Community of Christ doctrine concerning God is the doctrine of the Trinity. When they refer to God, "they mean a divinity understood as an all-encompassing absolute. God exists as one being, a unifying dimension to man's universe."[208] They testify that "all things that exist owe their being to God: mystery beyond understanding and love beyond imagination."[209]

PLURALITY OF GODS

Between the two churches, an issue dealing with the nature of God that is much more divisive than the debate between Trinity and three distinct personages in the Godhead has to do with the plurality of Gods. Joseph Smith Jr. taught the concept of theosis; that God was

---

205   Ibid.
206   Community of Christ Book of Mormon, Mosiah 8:28–29; LDS Book of Mormon, Mosiah 15:1–4.
207   Community of Christ Book of Mormon, Ether 1:77; LDS Book of Mormon, Ether 3:14.
208   Alder and Edwards, "Common Beginnings, Divergent Beliefs," 22.
209   *We Share*, 14. It should also be noted that Community of Christ members do not see God as primarily male. The same is true of the Holy Spirit in Community of Christ doctrine.

once a man who became a God; and that His children can become like Him.[210]

Community of Christ scholar Stephen Hatch noted that "the idea of multiple Gods and man's exaltation to God are theological beliefs the Community of Christ has staunchly opposed." Yet, his research "suggests that the matter was not as clearly decided as might be suspected."[211] In the minutes taken from joint meetings of the First Presidency and the Twelve, it was noted that church leaders had discussed, among various theological topics, the plurality of Gods.[212] An excerpt of one such discussion is recorded:

President Smith (Joseph Smith III) proposed a question for discussion as follows. Are there a plurality of Gods? E. Blair spoke in the affirmative . . . Resolved that we believe the doctrine of plurality of Gods is scriptural. Resolved that when the doctrine of plurality of Gods is taught it should be done with prudence. President Smith said we should not be justified in making the faith of individuals on this matter a test of fellowship.[213]

In Stephen Hatch's article, "History of the Godhead in the Community of Christ," he concluded that "although it may be painful for some in the Community of Christ to acknowledge, in the church of 1865 plurality of Gods was a theological viewpoint supported by some of its leaders."[214] It does appear that Joseph Smith III maintained a belief in one God throughout his life and the belief in plurality of Gods as a viable RLDS church doctrine seems to have disappeared by last part of Smith's presidency.[215]

---

210   Some Community of Christ members would question whether Joseph Smith taught theosis. They believe that the King Follett Discourse (April 7, 1844) and the Sermon in the Grove (June 16, 1844) attributed to Joseph Smith are not reliable sources.

211   Hatch, "History of the Godhead in the Community of Christ," in *Restoration Studies IX*, 119.

212   This discussion was held very early in Reorganization's history, and plurality of gods was rejected by most in the RLDS Church during Joseph Smith III's presidency.

213   Ibid., 120.

214   Ibid.

215   "Instead of a major debate over the issue, it simply faded away as a more orthodox Christian view of God, that of the Trinity, became the primary belief of the movement. By 1890 the plurality of gods was referred to as a 'doctrine of man.'" Edwards, *Our Legacy of Faith*, 161.

JESUS CHRIST

It is evident by the names of both churches, Community of Christ and The Church of Jesus Christ of Latter-day Saints, that they share a common belief that Jesus Christ is the Lord, Savior, and Redeemer. Both groups would agree that it is faith in the Lord that brings salvation for "there is no other name given under heaven save it be this Jesus Christ, of which I have spoken, whereby man can be saved."[216] Both churches would agree that it is by the grace of Christ that we are saved.

Perhaps the most significant difference in the belief in Jesus Christ expressed by both groups is the Community of Christ's view that Jesus is part of the Trinity, while the LDS Church sees Jesus not only as a literal son of God, but a being entirely separate from the Father in substance.[217]

Community of Christ doctrine concerning Jesus states: "We believe in Jesus Christ, the Son of the living God, the Word made flesh, the Savior of the world, fully human and fully divine. Through Jesus' life and ministry, death and resurrection, God reconciles the world and breaks down the walls that divide. Christ is our peace."[218]

HOLY SPIRIT

Both restoration churches believe in the Holy Spirit or Holy Ghost. Again, Community of Christ sees the Holy Spirit as part of the Trinity. And again, the LDS Church sees the Holy Ghost as a member of the Godhead but a separate and distinct personage from the Father and the Son.

Community of Christ doctrine includes the Holy Spirit in the Trinity with the Father and the Son. The Spirit "is the living presence and the personal power of God that works in our individual lives to achieve" the purposes of God. When Jesus Christ, the physical incarna-

---

216   Community of Christ Book of Mormon, 2 Nephi 11:38; LDS Book of Mormon, 2 Nephi 25:20: In the Community of Christ Book of Mormon it reads "there is no other name given." A minor difference is found in the LDS edition of the Book of Mormon which reads "there is none other name given."

217   A doctrine of the LDS Church is that we are all spirit children of our Heavenly Father, and that Jesus, as the firstborn spirit child of God, is our elder brother.

218   *We Share*, 14.

tion of God, left the earth, it was the Holy Ghost or Holy Spirit that came to "make real in our lives the person and witness of Jesus."[219]

We Share includes the following statement about the Holy Spirit:

> We believe in the Holy Spirit, Giver of Life, holy Wisdom, true God. The Spirit moves through and sustains creation; endows the church for mission; frees the world from sin, injustice, and death; and transforms disciples. Wherever we find love, joy, peace, patience, kindness, generosity, faithfulness, gentleness, or self-control, there the Holy Spirit is working.[220]

LATTER-DAY SAINTS

The LDS Church believes that there are three separate and distinct members of the Godhead: Father, Son, and Holy Ghost. God the Father is literally the Father of Jesus Christ. Latter-day Saints believe that "the Father has a body of flesh and bones as tangible as man's; the Son also; but the Holy Ghost has not a body of flesh and bones, but is a personage of Spirit."[221]

Some Latter-day Saints wonder how Community of Christ, which originated with Joseph Smith and the First Vision, could possibly believe in the Trinity. In response, Community of Christ scholars would point out that there are a number of accounts of the First Vision and the accounts differ. The earliest known recorded version refers only to the appearance of Jesus and does not mention another personage.

They would also argue that there is a great difference between the actual encounter with the divine and a mortal's feeble attempt to describe that encounter. This is not to say that the First Vision did not take place. They are simply saying that we must "not equate Joseph Smith's later reconstructions and interpretations of the First Vision with the First Vision itself."[222]

It appears that most Community of Christ members believe in the historicity of the First Vision but would see it in a different light than

---

219   Information on the Holy Spirit and quotes came from *Exploring the Faith*, 52–60.
220   *We Share*, 14.
221   LDS Doctrine and Covenants 130:22 (1843).
222   Howard, "Joseph Smith's First Vision: The RLDS Tradition," 28.

the LDS Church. Steven L. Shields expressed it this way: "The First Vision was Joseph Smith Jr.'s personal conversion experience, and was not foundational for the development of the Latter Day Saint Church."[223] The *Church Members Manual* minimally describes the First Vision: "While praying alone in the woods near his home about the year 1820, this teenager had an amazing vision that changed his life."[224]

In addition to the LDS belief that there are three distinct and separate individuals in the Godhead, is a doctrine Joseph Smith taught that stated God the Father "once was a man like one of us and that God Himself, the Father of us all, once dwelled on an earth the same as Jesus Christ himself did in the flesh and like us."[225] Joseph Smith also stated, "You have got to learn how to make yourselves Gods,"[226] which led to the LDS couplet attributed to Lorenzo Snow: "As man now is, God once was; As God now is, man may be."[227]

The LDS Church sees itself as a Christian church. The official name of the church is The Church of Jesus Christ of Latter-day Saints. Latter-day Saint leaders and members testify of Jesus Christ as Lord and Savior. Again, a significant difference between the LDS Church and Community of Christ is that LDS doctrine proclaims that Jesus is the literal Son of God, a separate personage from His Father. Jesus and God are one in that They are perfectly united in all They do for the benefit of humanity.

The Church of Jesus Christ of Latter-day Saints would agree with many Community of Christ views concerning the purposes and mission of the Holy Ghost. Latter-day Saints see the Holy Ghost as a revelator who makes the will of God known to His children. The Holy Ghost is a comforter, bringing peace and guidance to those who can feel his influence.

Again, a primary difference between the Community of Christ and the LDS Church is the LDS view of the Holy Ghost himself. LDS doc-

223   Shields, "The Latter Day Saints and the Restoration: An Exploration of Some Basic Themes," in *Restoration Studies VII*, 120.
224   RLDS, *Church Members Manual*, 9.
225   Joseph Smith Jr., "The King Follett Discourse," as found in Larson, "The King Follett Discourse: a Newly Amalgamated Text," 201.
226   Ibid.
227   Ludlow, ed., *Latter-day Prophets Speak*, 72.

trine states that the Holy Ghost is a personage of spirit—a man with a spirit body, who is a member of the Godhead, but who is separate and distinct from the Father and the Son.

SUMMARY

Both churches believe in the God, Jesus Christ, and the Holy Ghost. Both accept Jesus Christ as Lord and Savior. Both affirm the influence of the Holy Spirit as a source of bringing fallen humans back to God and revealing God's will to those who seek Him.

The actual nature of God is what is contested between the two churches. The LDS Church believes that there are three distinctive individuals who comprise the Godhead. The Father and the Son have bodies of flesh and bone; the Holy Ghost has a spirit body.

Community of Christ follows the traditional Christian belief that God, Jesus Christ, and the Holy Spirit constitute the Trinity. The foundational belief of Community of Christ concerning God, Jesus, and the Holy Spirit is "God's revelation in Jesus Christ and continuing presence through the Holy Spirit, as proclaimed by scripture, is the foundation of our faith, identity, mission, message, and beliefs."[228]

---

228 *We Share*, 10.

THE ORIGIN, NATURE, AND DESTINY OF HUMANITY

The origin, nature, and destiny of humanity are of major importance to both Community of Christ and the LDS Church. Interestingly, the two restoration religions have very different views concerning humanity and its origin, nature, and ultimate destiny.

COMMUNITY OF CHRIST

According to Community of Christ, "God did not create man from intelligence because they do not consider intelligence either an environment or a co-eternal substance with God."[229] Douglas D. Alder and Paul M. Edwards contrast and compare Community of Christ beliefs and the LDS doctrines of human origin:

> The Reorganized Latter Day Saints follow the more traditional view that God is "necessary" and man "contingent." . . . God could not, *not* have been—God *was* from the beginning. Man was not necessary; therefore, he did not exist from the beginning. The LDS agree that God was necessary, but they add that man's existence is also necessary. They cannot conceive of the nonexistence of either God or man. It is impossible for either God or man to come into being, or to cease to be. Things do not come

---

229 Alder and Edwards, "Common Beginnings, Divergent Beliefs," 24. This is interesting in light of section 90, verse 5 of Community of Christ version of the Doctrine and Covenants (1833), which states that "Man was also in the beginning with God. Intelligence, or the light of truth, was not created, neither indeed can be."

from nothing, nor do they become nothing. Man's spirit lives before birth, and this spirit unites with the body through the birth process. The real point of distinction between the RLDS and the LDS is not the question of the necessary existence of God, but in the Mormon belief in the necessary existence of each individual human agent.[230]

As to the origin of humanity, Community of Christ would be similar to Protestants in its doctrine. People exist because God willed it so. Each individual "had nothing to say in the matter; he could not have chosen to be, or not to be."[231]

A basic view of Protestantism is that humanity is essentially bad. The position of the LDS Church is that people are basically good. Concerning the nature of humans, Community of Christ scholar Paul M. Edwards has suggested that Community of Christ's view of humanity is somewhere between the Latter-day Saints and Protestants.[232] This, however, is not consistent with the more recent and official statements from Community of Christ. From the *We Share* booklet comes this statement: "As an expression of Divine love, God created the heavens and the earth and *all that is in them, and called them 'good.'*"[233] Human beings, as creations of God, were and are called "good" by their Creator.

---

230   Ibid., 23. This view of man not existing prior to being created by God and placed upon the earth may be a more recent development in Community of Christ doctrine. Volume one of *Question Time* is a compilation of questions and answers published in the *Saints' Herald* from 1949 to 1953. The answers are opinions of the authors that were then published in the official RLDS magazine. They would represent a common belief at that time, but not necessarily the official position or doctrine of the Church. In discussing the premortal existence of man, based on verses found in the Bible, Book of Mormon, and Doctrine and Covenants, it states "The gist of this teaching is that the spirit which houses the intelligence of man is made by God, but intelligence is eternal. Bringing both together, God effected the spiritual creation in the eternal world before the creation of the earth." James E. Bishop, in *Question Time* 1:41. In the same book, Charles Fry wrote of "man's spiritual creation before he was in the flesh" and notes that "all knowledge of the spirit life is withheld on coming into the flesh." Ibid., 42. It is not clear what the official doctrine of the RLDS Church concerning the premortal life of man was at that time. Today's Community of Christ would agree with mainstream Christianity in saying that there was no premortal existence of mankind.

231   Edwards, "Persistences That Differ: Comments on the Doctrine of Man," 44.

232   Ibid., 46.

233   *We Share*, 14; emphasis added.

The concept of original sin within Community of Christ theology is somewhat vague, but the official statement that "God created us to be agents of love and goodness" demonstrates a much more positive view of humanity than the Protestant view of original sin, which says that humans are somehow tainted by the transgression of their original parents.[234]

Community of Christ believes that "every human being is created in the image of God," and, without exception, is of great worth. It teaches that "God has blessed humankind with the gift of agency: the ability to choose whom or what we will serve within the circumstances of our lives." Even though we were created by God "to be agents of love and goodness," people misuse that agency and "take the gifts of creation and self and turn them against God's purposes with tragic results."[235]

God has provided humankind with the gift of freedom. This freedom enables people to either approach God or to draw away from God. The LDS Church would agree with this assessment of agency. When people use their agency unwisely, it causes a "condition of separation and alienation from God and one another." Sin is this universal condition that requires "divine grace that alone reconciles us with God and one another."[236]

Community of Christ does believe in the negative effects of sin upon the human family. From "A Statement of Belief" comes this declaration:

> In following the dictates of pride and in declaring his independence from God, man loses power to fulfill the purpose of his creation and becomes the servant of sin, whereby he is divided within himself and estranged from God and his fellows. This condition, experienced by our ancestors who first came to a knowl-

---

234   Ibid. In 1980, Edwards stated: "There is little doubt that in written and delivered statements man is viewed very pessimistically. The whole concept of original sin would be supported by the vast majority of church members." Edwards, "Persistences That Differ: Comments on the Doctrine of Man," 46. This might be evidence of the developing doctrine within Community of Christ or it might point out the differences between a common belief among the majority of church members and official doctrine of Community of Christ or both.

235   *We Share*, 14.

236   Ibid.

edge of good and evil, is shared by all who are granted the gift of accountability.[237]

The Basic Beliefs Committee of Community of Christ also viewed humanity as being endowed with the power of discernment "by which God draws man near to Him." An essential belief is that "it is given to men to know God."[238] In our fallen condition we can exercise our agency through the power of discernment to come unto Christ and find peace. The following comes from *We Share*:

> The gospel is the good news of salvation through Jesus Christ: forgiveness of sin, and healing from separation, brokenness, and the power of violence and death. This healing is for individuals, human societies, and all of creation. This new life is the loving gift of God's grace that becomes ours through faith and repentance.[239]

As far as Community of Christ's view of the ultimate destiny of humanity is concerned:

> Our eternal destiny is determined by God according to divine wisdom and love and according to our response to God's call to us. God's judgment is just and is based on the kind of people we have become in relation to the potential of our lives.[240]

Community of Christ believes that while individuals can grow spiritually and develop Christ-like characteristics, humans are not like

---

237 *Exploring the Faith*, 90.
238 Ibid., 93.
239 *We Share*, 14.
240 *Walking with Jesus*, 90. The LDS Church would also agree that we will be judged based on the kind of people we have become, but it would no doubt suggest that because we are God's children, our potential is greater than what Community of Christ believes. William D. Russell gives his opinion that Community of Christ does not appear to be as interested in life after death as they used to be. He wrote, "Today there seems to be very little concern about life after death in the Community of Christ. Many don't have the foggiest idea what happens after death—or before birth, for that matter. We just try to muddle through this life without messing up any more than we have to." It was his observation that the LDS Church continues to maintain a strong emphasis on life after death. Russell, "The LDS Church and the Community of Christ: Clearer Differences, Closer Friends," 189.

God and can never become like God. People are created; God is uncreated. God is unique—there is no one else like or beside God.

LATTER-DAY SAINTS

The LDS Church sees humans not merely as creations of God, but as, literally, spirit children of God the Father. LDS doctrine views God as an exalted man—a person with a resurrected physical body housing God's spirit. Community of Christ theology "accepts the more traditional position that God does not have a material being" therefore distinguishing "between the creation of man and God."[241] Early LDS apostle Parley P. Pratt taught that "Gods, angels, and men are all of one species, one race, one great family."[242]

Mormon doctrine would define "original sin" as the transgression of Adam and Eve in the Garden of Even; the action that caused the fall to mortality. Latter-day Saints do not view infants as being born in sin. Rather, they see them as innocents born into a fallen world. While the common Christian view is that man is essentially bad, Latter-day Saints see man as being basically good.

The LDS Church's conviction that mankind is the literal offspring of God is the basis for its belief that man can eventually become like God. This is another contrast between the two churches. The LDS Church believes that the ultimate destiny of those who follow Christ will be to return to God's presence, become like God, and be "joint-heirs with Christ"[243] and all that the "Father hath shall be given unto him."[244]

SUMMARY

The Church of Jesus Christ of Latter-day Saints and Community of Christ agree that humanity exists in a fallen condition on the earth today. But, everyone has agency and the ability to be guided by the Lord, follow Christ, and become spiritual beings.

241 Alder and Edwards, "Common Beginnings, Divergent Beliefs," 24.
242 Pratt, *Key to the Science of Theology*, 21.
243 Romans 8:17
244 LDS Doctrine and Covenants 84:38 (1832); Community of Christ Doctrine and Covenants 83:6f (1832).

The two restoration churches differ in their views of the origin of humanity and their ultimate destiny. Community of Christ sees humans as creations of God, entities that did not exist until God willed their being. The Latter-day Saint view of humans is that they are premortal spirit children of God, who is their Heavenly Father. He created their spirit bodies, which house an eternal intelligence that has always existed.

The destiny of humanity in Community of Christ doctrine is to draw closer to God and receive an eternal destiny according to God's love, wisdom, and perfect judgment. Human destiny, however, is not to become like God. The LDS Church believes the purpose and destiny of God's children is to become like God, if they follow the commandments and pattern given by Jesus Christ.

The Plan of Salvation

God revealed to Moses the purpose for creating the earth and placing people upon it: "For this is my work and my glory, to bring to pass the immortality, and eternal life of man."[245] Clearly, in God's infinite wisdom, things are done with a plan and a purpose.

In more recent Community of Christ publications, there is no specific mention of a "plan" of salvation. It is referred to as "God's vision of reconciliation, salvation, wholeness, justice, and peace expressed in the scriptural definition of shalom."[246] The salvation of humanity through Jesus Christ is still a major foundational belief of Community of Christ. Under the "Basic Beliefs of Community of Christ" in *We Share: Identity, Mission, Message, and Beliefs* is this statement on salvation:

> The gospel is the good news of salvation through Jesus Christ: forgiveness of sin, and healing from separation, brokenness, and the power of violence and death. This healing is for individuals, human societies, and all of creation. This new life is the loving gift of God's grace that becomes ours through faith and repentance. Baptism is how we initially express our commitment to lifelong discipleship. As we yield our lives to Christ in baptism we enter Christian community (the body of Christ) and have the promise of salvation. We experience salvation through Jesus Christ, but

---

245 Community of Christ Doctrine and Covenants 22:23b (1830); Pearl of Great Price, Moses 1:39.

246 *We Share*, 3.

affirm that God's grace has no bounds, and God's love is greater than we can know.[247]

The Church of Jesus Christ of Latter-day Saints believes that God has a plan of salvation designed for humanity before the foundation of the world. This plan includes the creation of the earth and the Fall of Adam, but it centers on the Atonement of Jesus Christ. Both churches would agree that the Atonement of Christ is the centerpiece of God's plan.

COMMUNITY OF CHRIST

Community of Christ views mortal life as a time to choose to serve God, to overcome the world, and to fulfill the purpose of human creation. People are to use the gifts God has given them to serve others and to do what they can to make this world a better place. One of the Basic Beliefs reads:

> Every human being is created in the image of God. In Jesus Christ, God took on the limits of human flesh and culture, and is known through them. We therefore affirm without exception the worth of every human being. We also affirm that God has blessed humankind with the gift of agency: the ability to choose whom or what we will serve within the circumstances of our lives.[248]

Both churches view the purpose of earth life as an opportunity for individuals to become all that God intends for them to become. Community of Christ believes that all of its members are called to serve God, but they are "called as different members of the body, to live out our faithfulness in different ways."[249] God bestows gifts and opportunities to serve Him.

One of Community of Christ's enduring principles is "all are called" by Jesus Christ to follow Him and become "disciples who share his life and ministry."[250] Community of Christ members are to "respond faith-

---

247   *We Share*, 14–15.
248   Ibid., 14.
249   Personal communication with Community of Christ World Church Secretary Andrew Shields.
250   *We Share*, 11.

fully, with the help of the Holy Spirit, to [their] best understanding of God's call.[251] The presiding officers with authority in the church, through the discernment of the Holy Spirit, "are prompted through wisdom and revelation to call and ordain people to specific priesthood ministries."[252]

Both Community of Christ and The Church of Jesus Christ of Latter-day Saints would affirm that "the worth souls is great in the sight of God."[253] A verse in the Book of Mormon reads: "Adam fell, that men might be; and men are, that they might have joy."[254] One of Community of Christ's Enduring Principles is the "Worth of All Persons." They believe that "God views all people as having inestimable and equal worth" and they "seek to uphold and restore the worth of all people individually and in community, challenging unjust systems that diminish human worth."[255]

The Book of Mormon teaches that the Fall of Adam brought about changes that made it possible for children to be born into a mortal situation. "Were it not for our transgression," said Eve, "we never should have had seed."[256] Lehi also taught that if there hadn't been a fall, Adam and Eve "would have had no children."[257]

One of the most basic tenets of Community of Christ is that Jesus Christ died and was resurrected, overcoming physical death and opening the way for all people to be resurrected. "The resurrection of the crucified Jesus reveals God's glory and our future. Christ's resurrection

---

251   Ibid. Their view concerning what they can become, however, is that the creation cannot possibly become like the Creator. Community of Christ theology does not include the possibility of people becoming like God. It also rejects the doctrine of plurality of Gods. They believe that there is one God and that there will always be one God.

252   *Walking with Jesus*, 87.

253   Community of Christ Doctrine and Covenants 16:3c (1829); LDS Doctrine and Covenants 18:10 (1829).

254   Community of Christ Book of Mormon, 2 Nephi 1:115; LDS Book of Mormon, 2 Nephi 2:25. The punctuation of the Community of Christ Book of Mormon was used.

255   *We Share*, 10–11.

256   Holy Scriptures, Inspired Version, Genesis 4:11; Pearl of Great Price, Moses 5:11.

257   Community of Christ Book of Mormon, 2 Nephi 1:113; LDS Book of Mormon, 2 Nephi 2:23.

is a revelation of God's promise of new life for all humanity and all creation."[258]

What people do while in this mortal life matters. Humanity has been given the ability to choose to follow God's will or to selfishly ignore His will. Community of Christ teaches that we will stand before God and be judged according to what we do during our lives.[259] There is no "question about whether or not men must be responsible for the things they do in the flesh. *They must!*"[260]

Community of Christ believes that both spiritual and physical deaths were introduced into the world as consequences of the Fall of Adam. It also believes that the Atonement of Jesus Christ negates these consequences. Life after physical death is part of the theology of Community of Christ.

There would be agreement between the two restoration churches that the work of salvation goes on after mortal life has ended. Joseph Smith referred to a spiritual experience that happened in January 1836 at a First Presidency meeting held in the Kirtland Temple. He said that the heavens were opened upon them and he heard the voice of the Lord saying:

> All who have died without a knowledge of this gospel, who would have received it if they had been permitted to tarry, shall be heirs of the celestial kingdom of God; also all that shall die henceforth without of knowledge of it, who would have received it with all their hearts, shall be heir of that kingdom.[261]

Both churches would concur that the opportunity to hear and accept the gospel of Jesus Christ exists beyond this mortal realm. Progress and learning can still take place. This means that every person is provided the opportunity to accept the gospel of Jesus Christ, either in this life or the life to come. This is clearly taught in *Exploring the Faith*: "Every soul has a chance to hear the gospel unfettered by the hedge of national or cultural or racial or religious bias."[262] Because of the grace

---

258   *Walking With Jesus*, 90.
259   Shields, *Latter Day Saint Beliefs*, 60.
260   *Exploring the Faith*, 107.
261   *History RLDS* 2:16; LDS Doctrine and Covenants 137:7–8 (1836).
262   *Exploring the Faith*, 107.

of Jesus Christ, "education and salvation are not options terminated by death."[263]

There is much common ground concerning the plan of salvation where Community of Christ and the LDS Church would agree. Despite the substantial similarities in many of the plan of salvation beliefs, the two restoration churches do see aspects of the plan of God very differently.

Community of Christ does not believe in the eternal nature of humanity, meaning humankind's existence prior to mortality. Members believe that God created previously non-existent humankind. They hold true that God has always existed, but they do not believe in the premortal existence of people.

As far as the creation of the earth is concerned, Community of Christ is "comfortable in the assertion that God created everything from nothing."[264] "In a very real manner," Community of Christ "does not deal with the mechanics of, or question the nature of, creation. They have preferred rather to describe the responsibilities of what is called man."[265]

All people face adversity during their mortal probation. Some difficulties are simply part of living in a fallen world. Some are a result of transgressing the laws of God. If a mortal becomes the servant of sin,

---

263   Ibid.
264   Alder and Edwards, "Common Beginnings, Divergent Beliefs," 24. From the King Follett Discourse, which the Latter-day Saints attribute to Joseph Smith, comes this statement:
"Doesn't the Bible say He created the world?" And they infer, from the word create, that it must have been made out of nothing. Now, the word create came from the word *baurau*, which does not mean to create out of nothing; it means to organize; the same as a man would organize materials and build a ship. Hence we infer that God had materials to organize the world out of chaos—chaotic matter, which is element, and in which dwells all the glory. Element had an existence from the time He had. The pure principles of element are principles which can never be destroyed; they may be organized and reorganized, but not destroyed. They had no beginning and can have no end." (Smith, *Teachings of the Prophet Joseph Smith*, 354.)
Community of Christ over the years has questioned the legitimacy of the King Follett Discourse. For some time they have doubted that it came from Joseph Smith. Now, some believe that Joseph Smith did actually give the sermon but was mistaken in his doctrine.
265   Edwards, "Persistences That Differ: Comments on the Doctrine of Man," 45.

"he is divided within himself and estranged from God."[266] Why did the Basic Beliefs Committee make no statement about the devil? The World Conference of Community of Christ has not dealt with the concept of the devil, so there is no official statement about the existence of Satan.

With no official declaration and no consensus of the belief of Community of Christ members, opinions about Satan's existence range from one end of the spectrum to the other. There are "those who believe that Satan is a person, that he actually led a rebellion in heaven and was cast out from the presence of God." Others "believe that the devil is not a person but the personification of evil."[267]

Based on a number of verses found in the Bible and the Book of Mormon, Community of Christ teaches that when a person dies, he or she is "taken home to that God who gave them life."[268] The spirits of all people at the time of their death "come directly under the Lord's direction and are appointed their place of abode while waiting the time of their resurrection."[269] The righteous enter into paradise or heaven to await their resurrection, while the wicked that are redeemable are cast into prison and the wicked that are not redeemable are cast into outer darkness or hell.[270]

The Basic Beliefs Committee stated: "We join all Christians in the belief that Jesus Christ arose from the tomb and that he lives."[271] They also added, "All the joy and hope of man is based on the reality of the resurrection."[272] Taking its beliefs on the nature of resurrection and the

266 *Exploring the Faith*, 11.
267 *Question Time* 3:361–62. No statements about the devil were made by the Basic Beliefs Committee.
268 Community of Christ Book of Mormon , Alma 19:43; LDS Book of Mormon, Alma 40:11.
269 *Question Time* 1:428.
270 Ibid., 432. The two classes of wicked are explained in this manner: "The redeemable are those who lived under sin in this world and were unrepentant, and are consequently not fitted for the kingdom of God. The fullness of the gospel did not reach them here so that they neither accepted nor rejected it, yet their sin is not unpardonable since it is not against full light and knowledge. . . . The irredeemable are the willfully wicked who have heard the gospel and rejected it against their own conscience and their own knowledge, so that the Spirit of God which had striven with them gave them up and left them in utter darkness. Their sin is unforgivable." Ibid., 432–33.
271 *Exploring the Faith*, 217.
272 Ibid., 221.

resurrected body from the writings of the Apostle Paul, Community of
Christ declares four basic points about resurrection:

1. The body which man lays down in death will not
   be the same body that comes forth in the resurrection. . . . the body given by God will be transformed
   but recognizable.
2. The body which goes to the grave is mortal and per-
   ishable. The new body will be immortal and imper-
   ishable.
3. The mortal or natural body is raised a spiritual body.
4. The resurrected body shall be like the body of the
   Lord Jesus Christ.[273]

A more recent Community of Christ pronouncement on resurrection and eternal life states:

> Christ is risen! Thus we believe that God is God of life, not
> of death. By faith we share in eternal life even now. In Christ,
> God's love finally will overcome all that demeans and degrades the
> creation, even death itself. Easter also gives us hope that the tragic
> suffering and death of victims, throughout history, is not the last
> word. We believe the Holy Spirit will transform all creation to
> share in the glory of God.[274]

Community of Christ theology asserts that eternal judgment is
"kind" because "it is not *a* judgment; it is *God's* judgment."[275] From one
paragraph of "A Statement of Belief" comes this declaration: "Through
the judgment of God the eternal destiny of men is determined according to divine wisdom and love and according to their response to God's
call to them."[276]

Community of Christ proclaims that "the living God whom we
serve is a God of justice and mercy." It affirms that Jesus Christ is the
judge of the living and the dead, and it stresses the importance of making inspired judgments here in mortality. "God cares about how we

---

273   Ibid., 222
274   *We Share*, 16.
275   *Exploring the Faith*, 229.
276   Ibid., 231.

treat our neighbors and enemies and how we make use of creation's gifts. It matters supremely to God how we welcome the poor, the stranger, the sick, the imprisoned, and the rejected."[277]

Based on the revelation known as "The Vision" received by Joseph Smith and Sidney Rigdon on February 16, 1832, Community of Christ has a somewhat different view of heaven and hell than the common Christian conception of life after death. This "vision revealed a spectrum of conditions for people in the after-life, dependent upon choices and behaviors during their earthly life."[278]

Community of Christ's view of heaven is much more complex than the mainstream Christian view of heaven and includes three levels. The first level, or celestial glory, is for "those who embrace and participate in God's spiritual nature." The second level of heaven, or terrestrial glory, is for "those who accept God's material expression as exists in the Son." The third level of heaven, or telestial glory, is for "those who respond to the ministry of the Holy Spirit" to the degree of the measure they accept.[279]

In Robert Gunderson's article, "Toward Defining the Source of True Mormon Doctrine," Gunderson describes the Community of Christ concept of hell as a place "for those who had full knowledge of God (Father, Son, and Spirit) and refused to acknowledge the Trinity, denied its truth, and defied its power."[280] Only those who are not redeemable because of their knowing and rejecting God will find themselves in hell. This is not Community of Christ doctrine. Indeed, an official Community of Christ doctrine on hell likely does not exist at this time.

Community of Christ does not put limitations on who can receive a reward in the celestial kingdom. Members do not believe it is the only church with authority and they do not teach that people must be members of Community of Christ to inherit a celestial glory. They believe that little children who die before the age of accountability will be heirs

---

277 *We Share*, 16.
278 Gunderson, "Toward Defining the Source of True Mormon Doctrine," in *Restoration Studies IX*, 244.
279 Ibid. 244–45.
280 Ibid., 244.

of the celestial kingdom. They also believe that all faithful members of the various Christian denominations, being part of the body of Christ, can enter the highest heaven.[281]

There is no official Community of Christ view on the nature of the celestial kingdom. World Church Secretary Andrew Shields wrote:

> The church focuses on a loving God who is beyond the bounds we can place on God. Community of Christ does not claim to know for certain what shape life after death takes specifically. (Members are, of course, free to study our scripture and tradition and draw their own conclusions—a healthy eschatology brings hope and energy to life, and an unhealthy one brings fear that interferes with discipleship and causes damage). Community of Christ does not believe that we are saved primarily through our efforts, but that God's love will finally overcome all that demeans and degrades creation. Our response of generosity and sacrifice and service comes as a response to generosity that God shows to us.[282]

The concept of the "end time" and a belief in the Second Coming of Jesus Christ is found in Community of Christ. As members anticipate the future, they devote themselves to seek Christ's peace and pursue it. A Basic Belief statement asserts:

> We do not know the day or hour of Christ's coming but know only that God is faithful. With faith in God, Christ, and the Holy Spirit, we face the future in hopeful longing, and with the prayer that Jesus taught us to pray: "Thy kingdom come! They will be done, on earth as it is in heaven."[283]

LATTER-DAY SAINTS

The Church of Jesus Christ of Latter-day Saints believes that humanity existed prior to mortality as spirit children of God. According to LDS theology, it was in this premortal world that the plan of salva-

281 "As for heaven and hell, and degrees of glory, the church does not express a center belief on those matters." Andrew Shields, personal response to the author's questions.
282 Personal response to the author in answer to several questions.
283 *We Share*, 16.

tion was presented to all the spirits present, and God the Father chose Jesus Christ to be the Redeemer. Latter-day Saint Apostle Richard G. Scott taught:

> We lived in the presence of God our Holy Father and His Be-loved Son, Jesus Christ, in a premortal existence. There we gained an understanding of the Father's plan of salvation and the promise of help when we would be born as mortals on earth. The primary purpose of life was explained. . . . The most fundamental purpose of your being here on earth . . . is to prove yourself obedient to the commandments of the Lord and thereby grow in understanding, capacity, and every worthy trait. It is to receive every required ordi-nance and to make and keep every needed covenant. It is to form and nourish a family. This experience includes having periods of trial and happiness, with the objective of returning triumphantly, having met well the challenges and opportunities of mortal life to receive the glorious blessings promised for such obedience.[284]

As previously stated, both churches believe that people are upon the earth to follow God's will and become what God wants them to become. The difference between the two theologies appears to be that the LDS Church believes God intends for people to become like God. It would take the injunction given by Jesus to "be ye therefore perfect, even as your Father which is in heaven is perfect" quite literally. [285] Latter-day Saints view that statement as evidence that God intends for humankind to become like Him.

Latter-day Saints believe that, under the direction of God the Fa-ther, Jesus Christ created the earth. They believe that "the elements are eternal"[286] and, therefore, Jesus used existing material to "organize" the earth rather than creating the elements. Some see this Mormon view of the creation as limiting what God can do, but Latter-day Saints do not believe in *Ex Nihilo* creation.

Mortal probation and adversity is an important part of the plan of salvation. The Latter-day Saint belief is that people could not become

---

284   Scott, "Truth Restored," 78.
285   Matthew 5:48.
286   LDS Doctrine and Covenants 93:33 (1833); Community of Christ Doctrine and Covenants 90:5e (1833).

like God without receiving physical bodies. Trials, temptations, and life's experiences are also valuable in the quest of returning to Father in Heaven becoming like Him.

In LDS doctrine, the devil is an actual personage. He was Lucifer, a premortal spirit son of God the Father. Lucifer, like all spirit children of God, was endowed with agency and allowed freedom of choice. Because "he chose the evil part from the beginning, thus placing himself in eternal opposition to the divine will," he lost his position of power and authority, was cast out of God's presence, and became Satan. The LDS Church believes that Satan and his followers are denied physical bodies, and, as evil spirits, spend their efforts tempting people to leave the path of truth and walk in darkness.[287]

In LDS doctrine there is a space between a person's mortal death and resurrection known as the Spirit World. Brigham Young taught that the transition from this life to the world of spirits is "from a state of sorrow, grief, mourning, woe, misery, pain, anguish and disappointment into a state of existence, where I can enjoy life to the fullest extent."[288] It is a condition of paradise for those who have accepted the fullness of the gospel of Jesus Christ.

The Spirit World also houses Spirit Prison, a situation or condition where the gospel is preached "to those who died in their sins, without a knowledge of the truth, or in transgression, having rejected the prophets."[289] Part of Spirit Prison could be considered as Spirit World hell—that temporary hell that exists prior to the resurrection. The LDS version of Spirit World hell is very different from the hell of mainstream Christianity.

LDS Apostle James E. Talmage described the conditions and purpose of hell within LDS doctrine:

> Hell is no place to which a vindictive Judge sends prisoners to suffer and to be punished principally for his glory; but it is a place prepared for the teaching, the disciplining of those who failed to learn here upon the earth what they should have learned. . . . that condition or state or possibility will ever exist for the sinner who

287   McConkie, *Mormon Doctrine*, 2d ed., 192–95.
288   Brigham Young, in *Journal of Discourses*, 17:142.
289   LDS Doctrine and Covenants 138:32 (1918).

deserves and really needs such condemnation; but this does not mean that the individual sufferer or sinner is to be kept in hell longer than is necessary to bring him to a fitness for something better. When he reaches that stage the prison doors will open and there will be rejoicing among the hosts who welcome him into a better state.[290]

Following the Spirit World experience, all who have lived on the earth and died will be resurrected. LDS doctrine teaches that because of the Atonement and Resurrection of Jesus Christ, all who came to earth and received bodies will be resurrected. Their spirits will be re-united with their physical bodies. However, their physical bodies will no longer be mortal. They will be immortal and perfected. After the resurrection, each person will "stand before God to be judged accord-ing to the deeds which have been done in the mortal body."[291] LDS Apostle, Joseph B. Wirthlin taught, "By virtue of the Savior's atoning sacrifice, we all will be resurrected. Each of us will stand before the judgment bar of the great Jehovah and be rewarded according to our deeds in mortality."[292]

The LDS Church teaches that there are three degrees of glory or salvation.[293] Although each kingdom is a place of joy and peace and is provided by a loving Father, the differing levels offer lesser or greater rewards. The Apostle Paul wrote to the Corinthians about the degrees of glory that can be attained after the resurrection. He used the imag-ery of brightness to describe the glory of each kingdom: the telestial was likened to stars, the terrestrial was likened to the moon, and the celestial was likened to the sun in glory.[294]

According to LDS doctrine, baptism by the proper authority is the gateway by which people gain the opportunity of entering the celestial kingdom. Another requirement is found in a revelation given to Joseph

290   Talmage, Conference Report, April 1930, 97.
291   LDS Book of Mormon, Alma 5:15. Community of Christ Book of Mormon, Alma 3:31.
292   Wirthlin, "The Time to Prepare," 16-17.
293   Joseph Smith learned of these degrees of glory in a vision he and Sidney Rigdon received on February 16, 1832. Accounts of this vision are found in section 76 of both the LDS and Community of Christ editions of the Doctrine and Covenants.
294   1 Corinthians 15:40–42.

Smith: "In the celestial glory there are three heavens or degrees; and in order to obtain the highest, a man must enter into this order of priesthood [meaning the new and everlasting covenant of marriage]."[295] Mormons believe that in order to enter the highest degree of the highest kingdom, a person must be sealed in the temple to a spouse for time and all eternity.

It is clear from the name "Latter-day Saints" that they not only believe in the "end time;" they affirm that these are the latter days. They believe that Jesus Christ will come again in power and glory, ushering in a millennial era of peace and an earth that will be raised to a paradisiacal glory.

SUMMARY

Similarities between the LDS Church and Community of Christ regarding the plan of salvation include the belief that God has a plan for all people, earth life is a time of growth and development, we are to learn to submit to the will of God in all things, and each person is of great worth. Both churches also believe that the Fall of Adam brought changes to the earth and to life upon the earth, including spiritual and physical death.

The Church of Jesus Christ of Latter-day Saints and Community of Christ both believe in the divine nature of Jesus Christ and the importance of His life, death, and resurrection. Both acknowledge that humankind is saved primarily by the grace of Jesus Christ. However, both churches also believe that our works in this life do matter and we will be judged according to our works in the flesh.

Both theologies teach of a life after this life, of judgment, and of the blessed state of those who accept Jesus Christ as their Lord and Savior. The two churches believe that God's work of salvation continues after this mortal life has ended. The grace of Jesus Christ provides opportunities beyond mortality for people to accept the word of God and be blessed accordingly. They also agree that Christ will return to the earth, ushering in an era of peace.

---

295   LDS Doctrine and Covenants 131:1–2 (1843).

Despite the many corresponding beliefs, there are a number of differences. The LDS Church teaches the absolute necessity of ordinances for salvation. Members believe that ordinances must be performed on the earth for those who have died if the deceased are to receive a fullness of salvation. Temples are built for the purpose of performing sacred ordinances for the living and the dead.

Community of Christ does have ordinances, but it views them more as blessings and support to a person's spirituality in this life than as necessities for salvation. Members do not believe in performing ordinances for those who have died. They hold as sacred the ordinance of marriage but do not believe in eternal marriage.

Other differences would simply be the way that the two churches see particular aspects of God's plan. For example, both believe that God created the heaven and the earth. Mormons believe that God could not create something from nothing, while Community of Christ adheres to the mainstream Christian belief of *Ex Nihilo* creation.

Community of Christ has no official doctrines concerning the nature or reality of Satan. It also declares that there is no specific doctrine or knowledge of what life beyond mortality will be like. While the LDS Church would admit there are many specifics about God's plan that have not been revealed, LDS doctrine appears to be somewhat more defined than that of Community of Christ in certain areas.

SCRIPTURES

When it comes to what is considered official scripture, both churches differ from much of mainstream Christianity in that they believe in extra-biblical books of scripture.[296] Community of Christ and the LDS Church believe in an open canon, meaning they both believe in modern revelation and that God can and does reveal sacred truths to humanity.

Community of Christ accepts the Bible, the Book of Mormon, and the Doctrine and Covenants as scripture. The Church of Jesus

---

296   It needs to be noted that while many Christians believe in the thirty-nine books of the Hebrew Bible and the twenty-seven books of the Greek New Testament, there are many others within mainstream Christianity, such as Catholics and the Eastern Orthodox, that hold the apocrypha as deuterocanonical. James H. Charlesworth wrote:

Mere perusal of the biblical books discloses that their authors depended upon sources that are no longer extant. . . . Moreover, the assumption that all Christians have the same canon is further shattered by the recognition that the Copts and Ethiopians have added other documents to their canon. Even in America today there are different canons among the various Christian communions: for example, Protestants exclude from the canon the Apocrypha, the additional books in the Greek Old Testament; the Roman Catholics, following the edicts of the Council of Trent in 1546, include them as deuterocanonical. The Mormons, moreover, argue that more books belong in the canon, and that it should remain open. (Charlesworth, ed., *The Old Testament Psuedepigrapha*, volume 1, xxi & xxiv.)

Various Christian religions have different books in their canonized bibles, but Community of Christ and LDS Church believe in an open canon and continue to add modern revelations to their scriptures. Thanks to Dr. Alonzo L. Gaskill for his help in understanding the diverse views of canonized scripture within Christianity and pointing out Charlesworth's comments.

Christ of Latter-day Saints considers the Bible, the Book of Mormon, the Doctrine and Covenants, and the Pearl of Great Price canonized scripture. These books are often referred to as the standard works. We will examine the views of both churches on each of these books of scripture.

COMMUNITY OF CHRIST

In 2003, a paper entitled "Scripture in the Community of Christ" was presented to the church by the First Presidency. It was "prepared by the Theological Task Force with input from the World Church Leadership Council." The following is the opening statement from that paper:

> Scripture provides divine guidance and inspired insight for life when responsibly interpreted and faithfully applied. Scripture helps us believe in Jesus Christ. Its witness guides us to eternal life and enables us to grow spiritually, to transform our lives, and to participate actively in the life and ministry of the church.[297]

BIBLE

Community of Christ affirms, with other Christian churches, the Bible as the foundational scripture for the church. The other scriptures of Community of Christ are not used "to replace the witness of the Bible or improve upon it, but because they confirm its message that Jesus Christ is the Living Word of God."[298] Community of Christ sees Joseph Smith's statement that the Bible is the "word of God as far as it is translated correctly,"[299] as being applicable to all books of scripture.

It reasons that because the Spirit "operates in and through the natural faculties of its recipients," those who experience divine manifestations or receive revelation "struggle in vain for the language to communicate the totality of the experience."[300] Written scripture is simply human attempts to convey the revelations of God; and because people are imperfect, the written word would be imperfect.

---

297   Community of Christ, *Church Administrator's Handbook*, 2005 ed., 83.
298   "Scripture in the Community of Christ," *Church Administrator's Handbook*, 2005 ed., 84.
299   *History RLDS* 2:570.
300   Howard, *Restoration Scriptures*, 2d. ed., 211.

Former counselor in the First Presidency of Community of Christ Duane E. Couey described revelation to humans as God breaking through into a person's mortal experience to "confront [one] who is biologically, psychologically, and sociologically limited." This inspiration comes to those who are "always to a greater or lesser degree estranged from God." This, he concludes, will always result in the description of what was experienced or seen being "to some degree distorted."[301]

COMMUNITY OF CHRIST CANONIZED SCRIPTURE: BIBLE, BOOK OF MORMON, DOCTRINE AND COVENANTS.
Courtesy Community of Christ Archives, Independence, Missouri

Community of Christ maintains that there is a difference between eternal truths that are revealed and the temporal expression of those revealed truths. This belief that all written scripture is incomplete or imperfect opens the way to a broader interpretation by the Spirit of the written word of God. The Committee on Basic Beliefs explained Community of Christ's view on scripture with this statement of belief:

> We believe that the scriptures witness to God's redemptive action in history and to man's response to that action. When studied through the light of the Holy Spirit they illumine men's minds and hearts and empower them to understand in greater depth the revelation in Christ. Such disclosure is experienced in the hearts of men rather than in the words by which the revelation is interpreted and communicated. The scriptures are open because God's redemptive work is eternal, and our discernment of it is never complete.[302]

---

301   Ibid., 212.
302   *Exploring the Faith*, 206.

INSPIRED VERSION OR
JOSEPH SMITH TRANSLATION OF THE BIBLE

Shortly after Joseph Smith Jr. organized the restored church in 1830, the Lord commanded him to go through the Bible and make corrections and clarifications by altering, deleting, or adding to the written text. Joseph called this process a translation although "it did not involve creating a new rendering from Hebrew or Greek manuscripts. He never claimed to have consulted any text for it other than his English Bible, but he 'translated' it in the sense of conveying it in a new form."[303]

Joseph Smith planned to complete the "translation" and publish it for the church, but he was killed before he could have it printed. The large, family-sized edition of the King James Version of the Bible that he used and the written manuscripts that resulted from the translation remained with Emma Smith after his death. After Joseph Smith III became the leader of the Reorganization, he decided to have his father's work published. In 1867, the Reorganized Church published the first edition of Joseph Smith's translation of the Bible.[304] The title *Holy Scriptures: Inspired Version* "was popularly attached to the work in the late nineteenth century." The title officially changed to *Holy Scriptures: Inspired Version* in 1936 and has been used in all editions since then.[305]

For many years, Community of Christ saw the Holy Scriptures: Inspired Version, which it published, as Joseph Smith's revelatory revision of the Old and New Testament. It believed that many precious truths that had been lost from the Bible over time had been restored through the Prophet Joseph.

---

303   Jackson, *The Restored Gospel and the Book of Genesis*, 31.
304   On the title page of the first edition it read: "THE HOLY SCRIPTURES TRANSLATED AND CORRECTED BY THE SPIRIT OF REVELATION BY JOSEPH SMITH, JR., THE SEER PUBLISHED BY THE CHURCH OF JESUS CHRIST OF LATTER-DAY SAINTS PLANO, ILLINOIS JOSEPH SMITH, I. L. ROGERS, E. ROBINSON, PUBLISHING COMMITTEE. 1867" Thanks to my friend Keith Longmore at the Orem Institute of Religion for allowing me to examine his copy of the first edition of the RLDS Holy Scriptures.
305   Foreword to the 1991 Edition of Holy Scriptures: Inspired Version, 6.

In more recent years, Community of Christ appears to be changing its view of the Inspired Version.[306] In 1970, Francis Holm Sr. stated that the Reorganized Church "accepts at face value practically all translations that have been made of the Bible." However, "they do accept the Inspired Version as the most authentic, because they feel the corrections made were done under the direction of the spirit of God."[307] That may have been Holm's personal opinion and still might be the opinion of some in Community of Christ, but it is not the generally accepted view among Community of Christ leaders and scholars today.

In a 1983 article entitled, "History and the Mormon Scriptures," William D. Russell "concluded that the New Translation might not be a restoration of the original meaning of the Biblical documents;" Joseph Smith had "watered down certain ideas in the New Testament which I considered to be the core of the Christian gospel;" and that the "New Translation is simply the King James Version with changes based on the personal hunches of Joseph Smith."[308]

Several years later, Dale Luffman commented, "the 'insights' which are to be found in the New Translation can be more responsibly viewed as Joseph Smith's commentary."[309] In his 2006 address to the John Whitmer Historical Association, W. Grant McMurray stated:

> I grew up being taught that not only did we have the original church restored, but we were also given the Bible in its perfected, pristine form resulting from Joseph Smith's call to translate it under the influence of the Holy Spirit. We have known for decades that it is not a restoration of the original text. That would be even more compelling a statement if there were such a thing as an original text of the Bible. What we do have is a theological commentary by Joseph Smith, demonstrably incomplete, that gut some of the most significant scriptural language, particularly the

---

306 William D. Russell commented that after he reviewed Robert J. Matthew's book, *Joseph Smith's Revision of the Bible*, he was struck by the irony "that Matthews, a Mormon, had a high appreciation for the New Translation while his RLDS reviewer had a limited appreciation for the book." Russell, "History and the Mormon Scriptures," 56.
307 Holm, *The Mormon Churches: A Comparison from Within*, 89.
308 Russell, "History and the Mormon Scriptures," 55–56.
309 Luffman, "The Roman Letter: An Occasion to Reflect on 'Joseph Smith's New Translation of the Bible," in *Restoration Studies III*, 199. Luffman currently serves as an apostle in Community of Christ.

theology of grace so beautifully expressed in the Pauline letters and butchered in the Inspired Version. It is time to identify it properly as a product of Joseph Smith's fertile and creative mind. I have not preached from it for decades. There are many fine versions available based on current scholarship and with poetic and literary power. The Inspired Version should have no standing as an authoritative Biblical version for the church.[310]

A more moderate approach found in Community of Christ is to not be concerned about trying to "decide which translation is 'right' but to see the Word of God using all available resources at our disposal."[311] Howard quotes former member of the First Presidency F. Henry Edwards, who said that when we use any or all of the various translations of the Bible with the Inspired Version, "we come close to having Joseph Smith at our elbow to explain the points of difference which we find there. When this happens, we find ourselves sharing the same spirit of the early Restoration."[312] Howard's conclusion is that "the Inspired Version, like all other versions, has the greatest value for those who study it intelligently, in the spirit of prayer, and in consultation with others who approach it is similar fashion."[313]

There is no single translation of the Bible prescribed by Community of Christ, and members are free to use the version or translation they choose. In the First Presidency-signed, new preface found in the 1991 edition of the Holy Scriptures: Inspired Version, it states, "Ultimately, the version we use is not as important as our openness to the guidance of the Holy Spirit."[314]

BOOK OF MORMON

One of the fundamental features of the Restoration in the latter days was the coming forth of the Book of Mormon. Both churches accept the Book of Mormon as scripture, yet there are some central

---

310   McMurray, "'Something Lost, Something Gained,': Restoration History and Culture Seen from 'Both Sides Now,'" 53.
311   Howard, *Restoration Scripture*, 2d ed., 235.
312   Ibid.
313   Ibid.
314   Ibid.

differences in the official position the two religions take on the Book of Mormon.

For the first one hundred years of the Reorganization's existence, its members would have agreed with LDS Church members "that the Book of Mormon was true in every sense of the word. It was true history, its doctrines were true, and it was a fundamental sign of the truthfulness of Joseph Smith's prophetic role. Most of us hadn't read it, but we knew it was true."[315]

The RLDS view of the Book of Mormon began to change in the second half of the twentieth century. For example, in a 1962 *Saints' Herald* article, James Lancaster suggested that the "translation" process should only be understood as conceptual and not taken literally.[316]

The 1979 First Presidency papers stated that the Book of Mormon "is one of the three standard books of scripture, but that we take no position on its historicity as a pre-Columbian document or one of any other origin."[317] The unofficial view appears to be that "most of the RLDS leaders, and many of the rank-and-file members, have come to doubt the Book of Mormon's historicity as well as some of its doctrinal affirmations." The Book of Mormon is still part of the official canon of Community of Christ scriptures, but "it is not revered as highly as it used to be. It is used less in worship services and is cited far less in church publications than previously. Most leaders and many members doubt its historicity."[318]

---

315   Russell, "The LDS Church and Community of Christ: Clearer Differences, Closer Friends," 185–86. I'm not sure of the reliability of Russell's statement that most of the RLDS Church had not read the Book of Mormon. In another article he admitted that when he was hired to teach religion at Graceland College, he had not read the Book of Mormon and neither had his two colleagues in the Religion Department. Perhaps he conducted surveys in the Restoration Scripture classes he taught that gave him a sense that few people had read the Book of Mormon, but I tend to think he is simply using hyperbole. Russell did say that he "came to appreciate why the Book of Mormon was the vehicle through which many early Mormons were converted to the Church," Russell, "History and the Mormon Scriptures," 59–60.

316   Cited in Conrad and Shupe, "An RLDS Reformation? Construing the Task of RLDS Theology," 93.

317   McMurray, "'Something Lost, Something Gained,': Restoration History and Culture Seen from 'Both Sides Now,'" 53.

318   Russell, "The LDS Church and Community of Christ: Clearer Differences, Closer Friends," 186.

Among the members of Community of Christ one might find three different camps when it comes to the Book of Mormon: 1) those who find "little value in the book and would just as soon it were not in our canon of scriptures;"[319] 2) those who regard "it as scripture because of its message and its place as the founding document of the movement;" (most likely the largest group)[320] and 3) those who cling to the original belief that Joseph Smith translated an ancient record by the gift and power of God.

Despite the differing views among Community of Christ members, scholars, and leaders, the official position of the church was made very clear at the 2007 world conference:

> Whereas. Current confusion exists as to the official position of the church concerning the Book of Mormon; therefore be it *Resolved*. That we, the Community of Christ, reaffirm the Book of Mormon as a divinely inspired record.[321]

DOCTRINE AND COVENANTS

Under the direction of the Prophet Joseph Smith, many of the revelations he received were compiled into a volume of scripture published by the restoration church. It was originally called the Book of Commandments. Later, other revelations were added, and it became known as the Doctrine and Covenants.

A comparison of the Doctrine and Covenants of the two churches will reveal substantial differences. There are some sections dating from the time of Joseph Smith that are accepted as scripture by the LDS Church that Community of Christ has rejected as uninspired.[322] Many

---

319   Ibid. W. Grant McMurray said, "I honestly don't know what to make of the Book of Mormon. There are so many reasons to question the traditional accounts of its translation 'by the gift and power of God' from golden plates. But neither have I yet encountered a sufficiently persuasive account of its nineteenth-century origins. . . . I suspect if we remain on the present course it will fall into disuse and simply go away in a couple of generations." McMurray, "'Something Lost, Something Gained': Restoration History and Culture Seen from 'Both Sides Now,'" 53–54.

320   Ibid.

321   *Herald* (February 2007): 21.

322   Included with the sections rejected by Community of Christ are revelations dealing with baptism for the dead and eternal marriage. These particular doctrines are discussed in other chapters of this book. In considering why certain doctrines were

sections have been added to the Community of Christ Doctrine and Covenants over the years. In the LDS Doctrine and Covenants, only three sections that were not received by Joseph Smith have found inclusion as canonized revelations.[323]

Community of Christ accepts the Doctrine and Covenants as scripture. It is one of the three standard books of scripture of the faith. The introduction to the 2002 printing of Community of Christ's Doctrine and Covenants states, "The Book of Doctrine and Covenants is a compilation of scriptural writings accepted by the Community of Christ as inspired."[324]

The largest portion of Community of Christ's Doctrine and Covenants was received by Joseph Smith during the early, formative years of the church, but many sections have been added by the prophet-presidents that followed Joseph Smith.

> It is the practice of the church today to consider the inspired documents from its prophet-president at biennial World Conferences, where all of the quorums, orders, and councils have an opportunity, along with the main legislative body representing the entire church, to consider them. When approved in this manner, additional sections may be added to the book.[325]

---

rejected, Community of Christ scholar William D. Russell contends that "we RLDS rejected the Nauvoo innovations and developed a theology that was fairly consistent with Mormon theology in the Kirtland period, . . . the theology we finally settled on about 1880 was essentially the theology of the church at the end of the Kirtland period in 1838." Russell, "The LDS Church and Community of Christ: Clearer Differences, Closer Friends," 184. Paul M. Edwards stated that "the most startling changes [in the doctrine of the church] appear to have occurred between 1836 and 1844, a period when the Reorganization suggests the church—and very probably Joseph Smith—was falling away from the truth." Edwards, "Persistences That Differ: Comments on the Doctrine of Man," 43.

323   These include section 135, written by John Taylor; section 136, received by Brigham Young; and section 138, a 1918 revelation received by President Joseph F. Smith. Section 137 was canonized in 1976, but it is a revelation received by Joseph Smith in 1836. There have also been two official declarations added to the LDS version of the Doctrine and Covenants.

324   Book of Doctrine and Covenants, "Introduction to the 2002 Printing of the 1990 Edition," Independence, Missouri: Community of Christ, 2004.

325   Ibid. World Church Resolution 1288 approved March 25, 2007 changed the interval of world conferences from every two years to every three years. The next world conference is scheduled for April 2010. *Herald* (June 2007): 8.

As of this writing, there are 163 sections in the version of the Doctrine and Covenants used by Community of Christ. The most recent section was added during the 2007 world conference.[326] Section 163 was received and presented to the world conference by prophet-president Stephen M. Veazey. It is consistent with the pragmatic, "what would God have us do today" approach that Community of Christ has embraced. It asks church members to "generously share the invitation, ministries, and sacraments through which people can encounter the Living Christ."[327]

Also in section 163, the Council of Twelve is "urged to enthusiastically embrace its calling as apostles of the peace of Jesus Christ in all of its dimensions," for which they will be "blessed with an increased capacity for sharing Christ's message of hope and restoration for creation."[328] It warns that "it is not pleasing to God when any passage of scripture is used to diminish or oppress races, genders, or classes of human beings."[329]

Probably the most surprising and controversial section of the Community of Christ's Doctrine and Covenants to date is section 156 . . . Although the majority of church members were pleased with the new developments, the announcement regarding women receiving the priesthood received some intense opposition.[330]

THE PEARL OF GREAT PRICE

The Pearl of Great Price is not accepted by Community of Christ as a book of scripture. That being said, some clarification and explanation is necessary. Selections from the Book of Moses found in the Pearl of Great Price are simply the first part of the Joseph Smith Translation of the book of Genesis. To the degree that Community of Christ accepts the Inspired Version of Genesis, it would also accept the chapters of Moses in the Pearl of Great Price.

---

326   World conferences have typically been held every two years. In a recent conversation with a Community of Christ leader, I was informed that there will be a three year space before the next world conference.
327   Community of Christ Doctrine and Covenants 163:2b (2007).
328   Ibid., 163:5a
329   Ibid., 163:7c
330   Women and the priesthood is discussed in another chapter of this book.

Joseph Smith—Matthew in the Pearl of Great Price is the Inspired Version of Matthew chapter twenty-four. Therefore, this part of the Pearl of Great Price would also be accepted by Community of Christ members to the extent that they accept the Inspired Version of the New Testament.

Joseph Smith—History and the Articles of Faith were taken from Joseph Smith's dictated history and personal writings, consequently this part of the Pearl of Great Price would likely be accepted by Community of Christ. The real problem with the Pearl of Great Price for Community of Christ is the Book of Abraham.

In 1835, a man named Michael Chandler arrived in Kirtland, Ohio, with four mummies and some papyrus scrolls that were said to have been acquired by Antonio Lebolo from a tomb near Thebes and Karnak in Upper Egypt sometime around 1820. After Lebolo's death in Italy in 1830, eleven mummies and the papyri ended up in the United States with Chandler. He sold seven of the mummies, likely to museums and universities, as he traveled to cities in the Eastern part of the U.S. and put the mummies on display.

After arriving in Kirtland, Chandler showed the papyri to Joseph Smith, who assured Chandler that he could read what was written on the scrolls. Joseph felt impressed to purchase the scrolls but did not want the mummies. Chandler would not sell the scrolls of papyrus without the mummies, so the Kirtland Saints purchased the scrolls and mummies in July 1835.

Although Joseph Smith worked on the translation from time to time beginning in 1835, it was not until 1842 that the first two installments of the translated Book of Abraham appeared in the *Times and Seasons* in Nauvoo.[331]

Initially, the Reorganization appears to have taken the Book of Abraham seriously. It was published in the Reorganized Church's monthly periodical, the *True Latter Day Saints' Herald*, in 1862 and again in 1864.[332] Early RLDS leaders "quoted passages from the Book

---

331   Information about Lebolo, Chandler, and the mummies was found in Peterson, *The Pearl of Great Price: A History and Commentary*, 36–46.

332   Howard, "A Tentative Approach to the Book of Abraham," 89–90.

of Abraham" and "considered it inspired and authoritative enough to reference in advancing doctrinal positions."[333]

Years later *The History of the Reorganized Church of Jesus Christ of Latter Day Saints* included this statement on the Book of Abraham:

> The church has never to our knowledge taken any action on this work, either to indorse or condemn; so it cannot be said to be a church publication; nor can the church be held to answer for the correctness of its teachings. Joseph Smith, as the translator, is committed of course to the correctness of the translation, but not necessarily to the endorsement of its historical or doctrinal contents.[334]

With the development of modern Egyptology and the discovery of eleven Egyptian papyri, once thought lost or destroyed, that were owned by Joseph Smith, Community of Christ distanced itself from the Book of Abraham and doctrines found therein.[335] In 1970, the president of the Reorganized Church, W. Wallace Smith, wrote, "I do not consider the Book of Abraham to be anything other than the speculative writings of its author, and certainly neither intended by him nor endorsed officially by the Reorganized Church at any time since its founding in 1852 to qualify as 'inspired' writing."[336]

One aspect of the Book of Abraham that is particularly troubling to the Community of Christ is the part dealing with judgment based on lineage that sounds like racism. In this particular account of Noah and the flood, Ham, one of Noah's sons, marries Egyptus. Her very name "signifies that which is forbidden." Because of her particular bloodline, the children of Egyptus and Ham are blessed "with the blessings of the earth, and with the blessings of wisdom, but cursed" because they do not have the right to hold the priesthood.[337]

---

333 Howard, *Restoration Scriptures,* 2d ed., 193.

334 *History RLDS* 2:569.

335 One of these doctrines, the plurality of gods, is discussed in another chapter.

336 Smith, "Race and Priesthood," *Saints' Herald* (March 1970): 5, as cited in Howard, *Restoration Scriptures,* 2d ed., 204.

337 Abraham 1:21–27 in the Pearl of Great Price. These verses in the Book of Abraham could very possibly have something to do with the men of black African descent being banned from holding the priesthood. The RLDS Church lifted the ban in 1865. The LDS Church lifted the ban in 1978.

Today, Community of Christ rejects the Book of Abraham both historically and doctrinally. "Whatever the early Saints felt about the Book of Abraham," wrote Richard P. Howard, "it seems not to have been either an inspired or scholarly translation."[338]

LATTER-DAY SAINTS

BIBLE

The LDS Church takes its view of the Bible from Joseph Smith, who wrote, "We believe the Bible to be the word of God as far as it is translated correctly."[339] Elder Joseph B. Wirthlin declared:

> The fragmentary nature of the biblical record and the errors in it, resulting from multiple transcriptions, translations, and interpretations, do not diminish our belief in it as the word of God "as far as it is translated correctly." We read and study the Bible, we teach and preach from it, and we strive to live according to the eternal truths it contains. We love this collection of holy writ.[340]

JOSEPH SMITH TRANSLATION OF THE BIBLE

The LDS Church uses the King James Version as its official version of the Bible. Even though Joseph Smith's translation was available for one hundred years, the LDS Church was hesitant to use the Inspired Version of the Bible published by the RLDS Church. This is likely because Mormons were suspicious of the Reorganization and assumed that it had made changes to the Prophet's work before publishing his version of the Bible.

Things changed in 1968 when Robert J. Matthews completed his doctoral dissertation comparing Joseph Smith's manuscript and the published Inspired Version. Since that time, The Church of Jesus Christ of Latter-day Saints and its members have used what they call the Joseph Smith Translation to a much greater extent. In 1979, with the permission of the Reorganized Church, many of Joseph Smith's

---

338   Howard, *Restoration Scriptures,* 2d ed., 204.
339   Article of Faith 8, in Pearl of Great Price, 60.
340   Wirthlin, "Christians in Belief and Action," 71.

changes were included in the footnotes and appendix of the official LDS edition of the King James Version of the Bible.

In recent years, the LDS Church has begun to use Joseph Smith's translation more and more. However, it continues to use the King James Version of the Bible as the official Bible of the church.

BOOK OF MORMON

For Community of Christ the foundational scripture of the church is the Bible. It would be safe to say that the foundational scripture for The Church of Jesus Christ of Latter-day Saints is the Book of Mormon. While it believes that the Bible is the word of God "as far as it is translated correctly," the second part of that article of faith states, "we also believe the Book of Mormon to be the word of God."

This does not mean that the LDS Church believes in the infallibility of the Book of Mormon, for even the title page of the Book of Mormon states, "And now, if there are faults they are the mistakes of men; wherefore, condemn not the things of God." But the church does hold to Joseph Smith's assertion that the Book of Mormon is the "most correct of any book on earth, and the keystone of our religion, and a man would get nearer to God by abiding by its precepts, than by any other book."[341]

LDS Church leaders have strongly urged its membership to read from the Book of Mormon regularly. In the 1980s, LDS Church President Ezra Taft Benson made the Book of Mormon a particular focus in his addresses. "There is a book we need to study daily, both as individuals and as families, namely the Book of Mormon," he admonished. He promised "that from this moment forward, if we will daily sup from its pages and abide by its precepts, God will pour out upon each child of Zion and the Church a blessing hitherto unknown."[342] In the First Presidency message of the August 2005 *Ensign*, President Gordon B. Hinckley challenged each member of the church to read or reread the Book of Mormon before the end of the year.[343]

---

341   Smith, *Teachings of the Prophet Joseph Smith*, 194.
342   Benson, "A Sacred Responsibility," 78.
343   Hinckley, "A Testimony Vibrant and True," 6.

The official LDS view of the Book of Mormon is that it comes from a sacred record kept by ancient prophets and that it was translated by Joseph Smith through the gift and power of God. The people in the Book of Mormon really existed, and the events actually happened. The LDS Church believes that the Book of Mormon is another testament of Jesus Christ that comes to us from the writings of those who lived anciently in the western hemisphere.

DOCTRINE AND COVENANTS

The Church of Jesus Christ of Latter-day Saints accepts the Doctrine and Covenants as scripture. President Ezra Taft Benson called it the capstone of the church to accompany the Book of Mormon, or keystone of Mormonism.[344]

The LDS Church has fewer sections in its Doctrine and Covenants—there were 136 up until 1978. Sections 137, received by Joseph Smith Jr., and 138, received by Joseph F. Smith in 1918, were canonized in 1976 and added to the Doctrine and Covenants in 1978.

PEARL OF GREAT PRICE

The Pearl of Great Price was the last book of scripture to be canonized as part of the standard works of the LDS Church. It was originally compiled and published in 1851 by Franklin D. Richards while he served as president of the British Mission. Brought to the Utah Territory by British immigrants and missionaries returning from Great Britain, the Pearl of Great Price soon became popular with Saints in America.

John Taylor called upon Orson Pratt to prepare an American version of the Pearl of Great Price, which was then published in 1878. At the 1880 October general conference of the church, it was canonized by the vote of the church.[345]

The Church of Jesus Christ of Latter-day Saints accepts the Pearl of Great Price as scripture. It is considered one of the four standard works of the church. Church scholars have done and continue to do

---

344   Benson, "The Book of Mormon and the Doctrine and Covenants," 83.
345   Information on the history of the Pearl of Great Price was taken from Peterson, *The Pearl of Great Price: A History and Commentary*, 11–23.

considerable research concerning Abraham and his writings. The LDS Church upholds the authenticity and value of the Book of Abraham, along with the rest of the Pearl of Great Price.

SUMMARY

Community of Christ and The Church of Jesus Christ of Latter-day Saints accept the Bible as scripture. In addition to the Bible, both Community of Christ and The Church of Jesus Christ of Latter-day Saints use the Book of Mormon and the Doctrine and Covenants as scripture. The LDS Church also considers the Pearl of Great Price to be scripture and includes it as part of its standard works. Community of Christ rejects the Pearl of Great Price as scripture.

The foundational scripture of Community of Christ is the Bible. The foundational scripture of The Church of Jesus Christ of Latter-day Saints is the Book of Mormon.

SACRAMENTS AND ORDINANCES

The word "sacrament" comes from a Latin term that means "an oath of allegiance." In the broadest sense when dealing with Christianity, "sacrament" stands for the affirmation of our allegiance to the Lord Jesus Christ through any sacred rite or ceremony. There are eight sacraments recognized by Community of Christ: baptism, confirmation of membership, the Lord's Supper or Communion, ordination, marriage, blessing of children, laying on of hands for the sick, and the evangelist's blessing.[346]

In The Church of Jesus Christ of Latter-day Saints the word "sacrament" has come to "refer almost exclusively to the Lord's Supper."[347] In the LDS Church, baptism, confirmation (laying on of hands for the gift of the Holy Ghost), ordination to the priesthood, blessing of children, administering to the sick, being set-apart for specific church callings, receiving patriarchal blessings, dedication of graves, temple marriage, and other sacred temple rites are usually referred to as ordinances.

BAPTISM

Both churches recognize baptism as an act of commitment to the Lord Jesus Christ and as requisite for membership in the church. Both groups consider children under the age of eight to be "without

---

346 *We Share*, 8–9. Previously, laying on of hands for the sick was known as administering to the sick, *Walking With Jesus*, 86.

347 Ludlow, ed. *Encyclopedia of Mormonism* 3:1243.

sin," therefore baptismal candidates must be at least eight years old.[348] Worthy Priests in the Aaronic Priesthood and Melchizedek Priesthood holders in both the LDS Church and Community of Christ are qualified to perform baptisms.[349] In both religions baptism by immersion is the accepted practice, and both use the same wording of the baptismal prayer found in the Doctrine and Covenants.[350] "The act of baptism," wrote John S. Wight, President of the First Quorum of Seventy in Community of Christ, "unites the individual symbolically with Jesus in his death and resurrection, but also with every other Christian disciple, and particularly within the Community of Christ when performed within that specific denomination."[351]

CONFIRMATION

The second part of the "entrance act into the Community of Christ" is confirmation. "It consists of a prayer offered by one of two officiating ministers, both of whom place their hands on the head of the candidate. Only members of the Melchisedec priesthood perform confirmation."[352] In Community of Christ, confirmation is "seen as the ritual act of intentionally celebrating, within the body of believers, the presence and work of the Holy Spirit in the life of the newly baptized person."[353] Baptism emphasizes the individual's decision to follow Christ and "the emphasis in confirmation is on God's gift of the Spirit."[354]

Like Community of Christ, confirmation in the LDS Church must be performed by those holding the Melchizedek priesthood. Also simi-

---

348   RLDS, *Church Members Manual*, 58.

349   Community of Christ, *Church Administrator's Handbook*, 2005 ed., 35.

350   Community of Christ Doctrine and Covenants 17:21 (1830); LDS Doctrine and Covenants 20:73 (1830). Community of Christ "tradition recognizes the word 'Spirit' instead of 'Ghost' but no other word substitutions." Community of Christ, *Church Administrator's Handbook*, 2005 ed., 35.

351   Wight, "The Sacraments: Baptism," 21.

352   Community of Christ, *Church Administrator's Handbook*, 2005 ed., 35. The Community of Christ uses the spelling "Melchisedec," while the LDS Church uses the spelling "Melchizedek." They both represent the same higher priesthood in each church.

353   Judd, "Confirmation: Baptism of the Spirit," 20. Peter Judd is chair of the Theological Task Force in Community of Christ.

354   Ibid.

lar, is the connection between baptism and confirmation. Joseph Smith taught, "Baptism by water is but half a baptism, and is good for nothing without the other half-that is, the baptism of the Holy Ghost."[355]

Confirmation or the laying on of hands for the gift of the Holy Ghost is the second half of baptism referred to by the Prophet. In The Church of Jesus Christ of Latter-day Saints and in Community of Christ, the two ordinances required for admission to church membership are baptism and confirmation. There is a possibility for future change of these requirements in Community of Christ.[356]

---

355   Smith. *Teachings of the Prophet Joseph Smith*, 314.
356   For Community of Christ, there has been some discussion on the conditions of membership. Approved at the world conference in March 2007 was the following:
Whereas, The First Presidency is the authority that interprets the scripture and law of the church, including the requirements for church membership; and
Whereas, The Community of Christ invites all disciples to the Communion table regardless of their baptismal circumstances; and
Whereas, There is incongruence in our theology as it embraces those Christians not yet baptized in the Community of Christ and yet does not view their baptism as acceptable for church membership; and
Whereas, Our requirement that individuals must be rebaptized is problematic and growth-inhibiting in many parts of our worldwide church; and
Whereas, For some individuals who desire to be considered members, this requirement for rebaptism diminishes the power, value, and beauty of their previous baptism and commitment to Christ; and
Whereas, The church has received instruction saying, "Be respectful of tradition and sensitive to one another, but do not be unduly bound by interpretations and procedures that no longer fit the needs of a worldwide church. In such matters direction will come from those called to lead" [Doctrine and Covenants 162:2d]; therefore, be it
Resolved, That the World Conference request the First Presidency to examine the issue of rebaptism in the context of the worldwide mission of the Community of Christ; and be it further
Resolved, The following prayer, reflection, and discernment of God's will for the Community of Christ, the First Presidency issue instructions relevant for today regarding requirements for church membership. (*Herald* [June 2007]: 40.)
Andrew Shields informed me that "the Presidency is involved in a discernment process with the church as the Presidency considers and takes very seriously its responsibility for sacraments and polity for this important issue." He also said that he does not know how this will turn out, but "we take discernment very seriously, we do not have a preconceived outcome, and we are listening for God's desire for us and call to us in this important issue."

THE LORD'S SUPPER

Community of Christ's *Church Administrator's Handbook* declares: "The Lord's Supper (often called Communion or Eucharist) is the act of partaking of bread and wine in symbolic remembrance of the life, teachings, death, and resurrection of Jesus Christ."[357] In the LDS Church the same ordinance is typically referred to as "the sacrament."

The Communion wine used in Community of Christ is "unfermented grape juice, water, or a culturally appropriate substitute where grapes are not readily available."[358] Bread and water are used in the sacrament of the LDS Church. Members of the LDS Church partake of the sacrament in a weekly sacrament meeting held on the Sabbath.[359] In Community of Christ, the Lord's Supper "is traditionally celebrated on the first Sunday of the month, but may be held more frequently as circumstances dictate."[360]

In both churches, this sacrament or ordinance consists of priesthood holders blessing bread and wine or bread and water, and then distributing the emblems of the sacrament to members of the congregation.[361] In the LDS Church, only the priesthood holder offering the sacrament prayer kneels while offering the prayer. In Community of Christ, all who are participating kneel while the prayer in being offered.[362] Both church-

---

357   Community of Christ, *Church Administrator's Handbook*, 2005 ed., 36.

358   Ibid.

359   On Sundays when general conferences or stake conferences are held, the ordinance of the sacrament is not conducted.

360   Community of Christ, *Church Administrator's Handbook,* 2005 ed., 36.

361   In the LDS Church, the bread and water are taken to members of the congregation. In the Community of Christ, "this is done either as the servers take the emblems to the congregation or as the congregation comes forward to receive." Community of Christ, *Church Administrator's Handbook*, 2005 ed., 82.

362   Ibid., 36. The practice of the congregation kneeling during the ordinance of the sacrament was not required, but it was not uncommon in the LDS Church during the nineteenth century.

In 1902, an *Improvement Era* reply in the "Questions and Answers" section observed that it had been the custom 'when the congregations were not so large as they are now' for the whole congregation to kneel, and that it was still not improper. This was in response to a question about whether more than one of the brethren administering the sacrament should kneel during the prayer. 'This matter, however,' the editorial concluded, 'may be regulated by the presiding authority, according to local surroundings, circumstances and conditions.' *Improvement Era* (April 1902), 473–74. The custom of all kneeling together was clearly disappearing at that time, though we do not know when the practice finally ended. (James B. Allen, "I Have a Question," 23.)

es have set prayers that are to be offered.[363] Both Community of Christ and the LDS Church do not prohibit those who are not church members from partaking of this sacrament.

The ordinance of the Lord's Supper is seen by both churches as closely connected with the ordinance of baptism. A Community of Christ manual reminds members that whenever they share the Communion meal, it is appropriate "to remember the commitment each of

---

363 LDS sacrament prayers are found in the LDS Doctrine and Covenants 20:77, 79 (1830). There has been one word altered from these verses; the word "water" has been substituted for "wine" found in verse 79. This change is based on Doctrine and Covenants 27:2, which states: "For, behold, I say unto you, that it mattereth not what ye shall eat or what ye shall drink when ye partake of the sacrament, if it so be that ye do it with an eye single to my glory—remembering unto the Father my body which was laid down for you, and my blood which was shed for the remission of your sins." The Community of Christ prayer uses the word "wine," but it also has the verse in its Doctrine and Covenants that states that it does not matter "what ye shall eat or drink when ye partake of the sacrament." Community of Christ Doctrine and Covenants 26:1b; 1830. Community of Christ uses grape juice, water, or whatever is culturally appropriate. The prayers of the Lord's Supper in Community of Christ are found in the Community of Christ Doctrine and Covenants 17:22d and 23b (1830). In addition to the Communion prayers found in the Doctrine and Covenants, the First Presidency of Community of Christ has also approved the following alternate prayers: **Combined Prayer on the Bread and Wine** "O God, the eternal Father, we ask thee in the name of thy Son Jesus Christ, to bless and sanctify this bread and wine to the souls of all those who partake of them, that they may eat and drink in remembrance of the body and blood of thy Son, and witness unto thee, O God, the eternal Father, that they are willing to take upon them the name of thy Son, and always remember him and keep his commandments which he has given them, that they may always have his Spirit to be with them. Amen." **Combined Prayer on the Bread and Wine (Contemporary Language)** "Eternal God, we ask you in the name of your Son Jesus Christ, to bless and sanctify this bread and wine to the souls of all those who receive them, that they may eat and drink in remembrance of the body and blood of your Son, and witness to you, O God, that they are willing to take upon them the name of your Son, and always remember him and keep the commandments which he has given them, that they may always have his Spirit to be with them. Amen." In the contemporary language Communion prayer, "the attempt has been to replace archaic language with wording that is in current use; this includes gender-specific references to God." Community of Christ, *Church Administrator's Handbook*, 2005 ed., 82–83.

us has made to God through our baptism into the covenant."[364] Mormon doctrine considers partaking of the sacrament as a renewal of the covenant made at baptism. LDS Apostle, Dallin H. Oaks wrote:

> The sacrament of the Lord's Supper is a renewal of the covenants and blessings of baptism. We are commanded to repent of our sins and come to the Lord with a broken heart and a contrite spirit and partake of the sacrament. In the partaking of the bread, we witness that we are willing to take upon us the name of Jesus Christ and always remember Him and keep His commandments. When we comply with this covenant, the Lord renews the cleansing effect of our baptism. We are made clean and can always have His Spirit to be with us.[365]

BLESSING OF CHILDREN

The Doctrine and Covenants states: "Every member of the church of Christ having children is to bring them unto the elders before the church, who are to lay their hands upon them in the name of Jesus Christ, and bless them in his name."[366] Giving children a name and a blessing is a traditional ordinance or sacrament in both churches.[367]

In both the LDS Church and Community of Christ, this particular sacrament or ordinance can be performed only by Melchizedek priesthood holders. There are some slight differences in the way the ordinances are performed in the two churches. Traditionally in Community of Christ, the parents bring the child forward for the blessing. One elder holds the small child, "while another elder places his or her hands on the child and offers the prayer of blessing."[368] It is common for the parents to stand next to the elders who are officiating during the prayer.

---

364 RLDS, *Church Members Manual*, 46.
365 Oaks, "Special Witnesses of Christ," 13.
366 Community of Christ Doctrine and Covenants 17:19 (1830); LDS Doctrine and Covenants 20:70 (1830).
367 It should be noted that the blessing of children is not an ordinance necessary for salvation. It would be considered a blessing ordinance rather than a saving ordinance.
368 Community of Christ, *Church Administrator's Handbook*, 2005 ed., 35.

The blessing of a child is typically performed within the first few weeks of the child's birth. However, it can take place up until the child's eighth birthday. In the case of the blessing of an older child, a parent may sit in a chair and hold the child, or an older child may sit alone in the chair.[369]

In the LDS Church, the blessing of babies normally takes place during fast and testimony meetings, held once each month. Melchizedek Priesthood holders gather in a circle and hold the infant in their hands, while one, often the child's father, pronounces the blessing. In the case of blessing an older child, the priesthood holders lay their hands lightly on the child's head.[370]

LAYING ON OF HANDS FOR THE SICK

As does the blessing of children, laying on of hands for the sick has scriptural basis: "Is any sick among you? Let him call for the elders of the church; and let them pray over him, anointing him with oil in the name of the Lord" (James 5:14). Also like the blessing of children, laying on of hands for the sick is a blessing and not a saving ordinance.[371]

Only those who are worthy and hold the Melchizedek, or higher, Priesthood in both churches may perform this administering or laying on of hands ordinance. Usually, two priesthood holders perform the laying on of hands in Community of Christ. In the LDS Church, two or more priesthood holders generally perform this ordinance.

In both churches, an elder anoints with consecrated oil the head of the person who is ill or injured. After this brief anointing with oil, the other priesthood holder(s) place their hands upon the person receiving

---

369   Ibid.

370   LDS *Church Handbook of Instructions*, 2006 ed., Book 1, 32.

371   This statement may be confusing to some considering James 5:15 which states: "And the prayer of faith shall save the sick, and the Lord shall raise him up; and if he have committed sins, they shall be forgiven him." While a person may receive great blessings from receiving an administration for the sick, it must be remembered that a person who never receives such a blessing can still be saved in the kingdom of God. It is not a necessary saving ordinance.

the blessing, as does the elder who just performed the anointing, and the anointing is sealed and a blessing is pronounced.

Community of Christ Theologian in Residence Tony Chavala-Smith noted that laying on of hands for the sick "is possibly the most frequently celebrated sacrament of the church." He wrote:

> For us, no sacrament is more closely bound to the human condition and God's yearning to meet us in the tangle of life. Administration is the sacrament of emergency rooms, hospital rooms, and living rooms; of camps, reunions, and retreats; of pastors' studies, inner-city streets, and even prisons; of bad news from the doctor, of phone calls at 2 a.m., and of life's final moments.[372]

Administering to the sick is very similar in both churches.[373] The method of consecrating the oil used in administering to the sick is also similar. The cap is removed from a container of oil and a Melchizedek Priesthood holder offers a prayer to consecrate the oil. An official statement from Community of Christ's *Church Administrator's Handbook* says, "Oil should not be consecrated in large quantities then divided into smaller portions and distributed."[374]

In 1958, the Standing High Council of the Reorganized Church prepared this statement:

> There is no law known to us directing what kind of oil shall be used in administering to the sick, or indicating how, when, or why the oil should be set apart or consecrated for such use. It has become the custom of the church to use olive oil, which was presumably the oil used by the Savior and the early saints. In view of this tradition, we believe that the oil should be olive oil, except in case of an emergency when we feel that other oil is equally acceptable. The oil used should be of good quality and . . . once it has

---

372   Chvala-Smith, "Administration: Sacrament of Healing Grace," 18.

373   In Community of Christ, it is not uncommon for a few family members and friends to join the elders surrounding the chair or bed of the person who is ill. "The practice of many people holding onto the person is discouraged." Community of Christ, *Church Administrator's Handbook*, 2005 ed., 34.

374   Community of Christ, *Church Administrator's Handbook*, 2005 ed., 34–35. I am not sure what "large quantities" means in this statement. It is not uncommon in the LDS Church to consecrate a 10-16 ounce bottle of oil and then put some in smaller containers for the use of Melchizedek Priesthood holders.

been blessed, or consecrated, this oil should not be used for any purpose other than that for which it has been set apart.[375]

In The Church of Jesus Christ of Latter-day Saints, no oil other than olive oil may be consecrated.[376]

Both Community of Christ and The Church of Jesus Christ of Latter-day Saints recognize that administering to the sick or the laying on of hands for the sick is a form of prayer. As such, priesthood holders seek the will of God in the administration. Just as Jesus "fully submitted to God," the laying on of hands for the sick "calls us to this attitude of yielding."[377]

EVANGELIST'S OR PATRIARCHAL BLESSING

"An Evangelist is a Patriarch," taught the Prophet Joseph Smith, and like Jacob of old who gave patriarchal blessings to his sons, "wherever the Church of Christ is established in the earth, there should be a Patriarch for the benefit of the posterity of the Saints."[378] Community of Christ and the LDS Church have had patriarchs since their earliest years.

Joseph Smith Jr. gave the first patriarchal blessings of this dispensation on December 18, 1833. On that day, Joseph blessed his parents, three of his brothers, and Oliver Cowdery. Also on that same day, Joseph Smith Sr. was ordained as the first Patriarch to the Church.[379]

Both churches have people who hold the priesthood office of patriarch or evangelist. In Community of Christ today, these people are referred to as evangelists and blessings formerly called patriarchal blessings are now known as evangelist's blessings.[380] In the LDS Church,

---

375   Quoted in *Question Time* 3:184.
376   LDS *Church Handbook of Instructions*, 2006 ed., Book 1, 38.
377   Chvala-Smith, "Administration: Sacrament of Healing Grace," 19.
378   Smith, *Teachings of the Prophet Joseph Smith*, 151.
379   Smith, *Essentials in Church* History, 141–42.
380   Thanks to William Russell for pointing out to me that Community of Christ likely began referring exclusively to "evangelists" and not "patriarchs" because women began being ordained as evangelists about 1986 and, of course, the word patriarch refers to the male gender.

they are still known as patriarchs, and the blessings they give are called patriarchal blessings.

Evangelists in Community of Christ belong to the Order of the Evangelists. The evangelist's blessing is a prayer given to an individual by an evangelist. The blessing is usually recorded and a transcript is given to the person who received the blessing. The same procedure is practiced in the LDS Church.

The evangelist's blessing is a very personal thing, "perhaps the most personal of all sacraments," wrote David R. Brock, Presiding Evangelist of Community of Christ. "As a recipient of a blessing, the focus is on *my* life, *my* relationship with God, *my* needs, *my* potential, *my* calling as a disciple of the Lord Jesus."[381]

Any person eight years old or older can receive an evangelist's blessing in Community of Christ. While no set age is required in the LDS Church, the bishop issuing the recommend is to make sure that the person is of sufficient age to understand the importance of the patriarchal blessing, but, ideally, still young enough that many of life's important decisions still lie ahead. Every worthy Mormon is entitled and encouraged to receive a patriarchal blessing.[382]

A Community of Christ evangelist "places his or her hands on the head of the candidate and delivers words of thanksgiving, affirmation, counsel, life direction, and blessing."[383] The blessing usually takes place in a home or other appropriate site.[384] Because of the sacred and personal nature of patriarchal blessings, the LDS Church instructs its members that it should be "given in private except that a limited number of family members may be present."[385]

A declaration of lineage has long been a part of the patriarchal blessing. In the LDS Church, it remains one of the most important aspects of the blessing. If a patriarch does not include a declaration of

381 Brock, "The Evangelist's Blessing," 20.
382 Information about evangelist's and patriarchal blessings were found in Community of Christ's *Church Administrator's Handbook,* 2005 edition and in the LDS *Church Handbook of Instructions,* 2006 edition.
383 Community of Christ, *Church Administrator's Handbook,* 2005 ed., 35.
384 Ibid.
385 LDS *Church Handbook of Instructions,* 2006 ed., Book 1, 43.

lineage in the blessing, typically he will later give an addendum to the blessing to pronounce the recipient's lineage.

The evangelist's blessing in Community of Christ can still include the declaring of lineage, but it is not seen as important as it once was.[386] Former Presiding Patriarch Elbert A. Smith wrote: "Naming of lineage is *not* the primary function of the blessing. It is more important to be counseled concerning a Christian way of life and to be blessed and dedicated and inspired for such a life than it is to learn about one's far-off ancestry."[387] Since Elbert Smith's statement was published in 1955, there has been even less importance given to lineage in today's Community of Christ.

Former Reorganized Church Presiding Patriarch Roy Cheville pointed out that "in the earlier days of our church the Saints were quite interested in lineage since this meant to them security and assignment in God's program." However, today's Community of Christ members are much less concerned about lineage than before. "Now, they are concerned that they qualify as saints to be in the working company of God's reliable people."[388]

Evangelists in Community of Christ also offer blessings to congregations. In addition, Community of Christ members can now get more than one evangelist's blessing over the course of a lifetime.[389]

---

386   Presiding Evangelist David R. Brock said:
      Though on occasions the tribal lineage is shared in blessings offered by evangelists, we find that it is included less and less in blessings given today. As evangelists have continued to explore the meaning and purpose of the blessing for these times, it has seemed increasingly important to emphasize the greater lineage that we share with all of humankind, that of being creatures named and called 'beloved' by God. It has seemed more important to lift up the principle that all are of equal worth. And it has seemed important to emphasize that we all belong to the 'tribe' or 'family' called the body of Christ. That is the heritage which defines us most deeply. Our identity lies more deeply there, in Christ, than in tribal heritage. (Personal communication with David R. Brock.)
387   Quoted in *Question Time* 1:242.
388   *Question Time* 3:339.
389   Thanks to Community of Christ World Church Secretary Andrew Shields for the more up-to-date information about evangelists.

**OLD STONE CHURCH,
INDEPENDENCE, MISSOURI**
Courtesy Community of Christ Archives,
Independence, Missouri—photograph by John Hamer

ORDINATION

In the LDS Church, to confer the priesthood and ordain someone to a specific office, one must have permission from ecclesiastical leadership and hold a priesthood office either equal to or higher than that which is being given.[390] An elder cannot ordain a person to be a high priest. It is the same in Community of Christ in that "Aaronic priests and members of the Melchisedec priesthood may officiate at the ordinations of members of the Aaronic priesthood, and high priests and elders at the ordination of elders. High priests may be ordained by other high priests."[391]

MARRIAGE

The importance of marriage and the family unit are stressed by both religions. Both would agree that marriage is "a sacred covenant between husband and wife in which God participates with sanction, blessing, and guidance."[392] The LDS Church and Community of Christ would

---

390   LDS *Church Handbook of Instructions* 1:39. The question of a stake president ordaining a man to the office of patriarch might arise. In most cases, the stake president will not have been ordained a patriarch. Can a man who does not hold that office ordain someone to an office he does not hold? Both are high priests in the Melchizedek Priesthood. In a case such as this, the stake president is authorized by the Quorum of the Twelve to ordain a patriarch. With keys delegated to him by the Twelve, a stake president can ordain a patriarch. But, the stake president cannot assign one of his counselors to perform the ordination. He is to ordain the patriarch himself, and no others are to stand with him during the ordination. Ibid., 6.

391   Community of Christ, *Church Administrator's Handbook*, 2005 ed., 36. Information on who can be ordained to the various offices of the priesthood is found in a previous chapter.

392   RLDS, *Church Members Manual*, 66. In recent years, there has been much discussion about homosexuality and the church. It has been a topic for world conferences and "Listening Circles," groups established for listening and dialogue. A committee was created after the world conference in 2002 and charged by the First Presidency of

agree that "marriage is a vital part of all world cultures. It helps provide opportunity for healthy, constructive development of persons. This includes the marriage partners and the children who may result from their union."[393] They would also agree that "marriage is ordained of God."[394]

The following are traditional views of marriage within Community of Christ:

1. It is a sacred covenant between a man and a woman with God as the unseen partner in the relationship.
2. It is a life-long commitment of mutual support, companionship, and trust involving physical, emotional, spiritual, and economic factors.
3. Marriage is a *monogamous* relationship. The phrase "keeping yourselves wholly for each other from all others…" (Doctrine and Covenants 111:2b) stressed the importance of marital fidelity.
4. Marriage should not be entered into lightly. Prayer and spiritual preparation and premarital counseling should be the norms for marriage covenants in the Community of Christ. Some countries legally require a specified number of counseling sessions for the couple before a marriage may be performed.
5. According to church law, any member of the Melchisedec priesthood or any Aaronic priest may officiate at the wedding ceremony. This is subject to the legal restrictions of the country.[395]

The LDS Church teaches that marriage and family is an essential part of God's plan for humanity. "Mormons place particularly strong

Community of Christ to oversee and provide guidance to the church-wide dialogue process concerning homosexuality in the church. "This will be an issue that will grow in magnitude in the foreseeable future and one that is crucial for the church to be able to address in a way that does not foster divisiveness and polarization." *Herald* (April 2007): 20-21.

393   RLDS, *Church Members Manual*, 65.
394   Community of Christ Doctrine and Covenants 49:3a (1831); LDS Doctrine and Covenants 49:15 (1831).
395   Fielding, "The Sacrament of Marriage," 20–21.

emphasis on family as the basic unit of the Church and of society. We have a deep commitment to marriage."[396] Through the years, LDS leaders have reminded the Latter-day Saints that no amount of success a man or woman might attain in the various aspects of life can ever compensate for failure within one's home.[397]

Community of Christ "reaffirms marriage as an institution, a covenant, a sacrament ordained of God, and a legal contract."[398] There is an expectation in the church that "husband and wife will remain married to each other as long as they both live."[399]

Despite the similarities in the two church's views on the importance of marriage, the marriage ordinance or sacrament differs greatly between the two restoration theologies. The LDS Church believes that a marriage or "sealing" of a worthy man and woman that is performed in the temple by the proper authority lasts beyond this life. "The Family: A Proclamation to the World" states that "sacred ordinances and covenants available *in* holy temples make it possible for individuals to return to the presence of God and for families to be united eternally."[400]

Community of Christ does not believe that marriage or family exists beyond this earthly life. Speaking of the "sealing" of marriage partners, RLDS scholar Fred L. Young wrote that it was "a practice which was instituted during the dark and troublesome days of Nauvoo. It has no foundation in scripture and certainly is not accepted by the Reorganization." He declared that the very idea that people are married in life after death was contrary to scriptures.[401]

Marriage in Community of Christ is considered a lifelong commitment. Section 111 of the Community of Christ Doctrine and Covenants is not considered a revelation, but it is regarded as the law of marriage for the church. It states:

> Marriage should be celebrated with prayer and thanksgiving; and at the solemnization, the persons to be married, standing together, the man on the right, and the woman on the left, shall be

396   Ballard, "Faith, Family, Facts, and Fruits," 26.
397   McKay,
398   Community of Christ, *Church Administrator's Handbook,* 2005 ed., 57.
399   Ibid.
400   "The Family: A Proclamation to the World," 102; emphasis added.
401   *Question Time* 3:217.

addressed, by the person officiating, as he shall be directed by the
Holy Spirit; and if there be no legal objections, he shall say, calling
each by their names: "You both mutually agree to be each other's
companion, husband and wife, observing the legal rights belonging to this condition; that is keeping yourselves wholly for each
other, and from all other during your lives?" And when they have
answered "Yes," he shall pronounce them "husband and wife" in
the name of the Lord Jesus Christ, and by virtue of the laws of the
country and authority vested in him.[402]

Any member of Community of Christ's Melchisedec priesthood
or a priest holding the Aaronic priesthood has authority to perform
wedding ceremonies for the church. They also uphold "the validity of a
legal marriage authorized by civil and other religious authorities."[403]

The LDS Church recognizes any legal civil or religious marriage as
binding for time, meaning for the duration of the mortal lives of the
couple. An ecclesiastical leader such as a bishop or stake president can
perform LDS marriages of this type. However, for a couple not sealed
in the temple, "their covenant and marriage are not of force when they
are dead."[404]

The Reorganized Church never accepted Joseph Smith's revelation
on eternal marriage. Most Community of Christ members would consider Joseph's doctrine of eternal marriage, along with plural marriage,
baptism for the dead, and other ordinances of the temple to be radical
and even heretical. Paul Edwards gave his opinion that during the latter years of the Prophet Joseph's life, when the most startling doctrinal
changes occurred, was "a period when the Reorganization suggests the
church—and very probably Joseph Smith—was falling away from the
truth."[405]

---

402   Community of Christ Doctrine and Covenants 111:2a–c (1835). This article on mar-
      riage appeared in the LDS Doctrine and Covenants as section 101 in the 1835 edition.
      It remained in the LDS Doctrine and Covenants until its removal in 1876.
403   Community of Christ, *Church Administrator's Handbook*, 2005 ed., 57.
404   LDS Doctrine and Covenants 132:15 (1843). Temples and temple ordinances are
      discussed in another chapter.
405   Edwards, "Persistences That Differ: Comments on the Doctrine of Man," 43.

TEMPLES

Six years after the church was founded by Joseph Smith, the first temple was dedicated in Kirtland, Ohio. The Saints sacrificed much to complete this building during a time of great poverty. It was not a typical church building or chapel. It was a temple to God—the house of the Lord. Brigham Young said that Joseph received the pattern for the temple through revelation "as did Moses for the Tabernacle, and Solomon for his Temple; for without a pattern, he could not know what was wanting, having never seen one, and not having experienced its use."[406]

The early Saints also dedicated sites for temples in Independence, Far West, and Adam-ondi-Ahman, Missouri, and in Nauvoo, Illinois. Because of persecution, the temples in Missouri were never completed.[407] The building of the temple in Nauvoo started in 1841 and was completed following the death of Joseph Smith Jr.

---

406   Brigham Young, in *Journal of Discourses*, 2:31.
407   Joseph Smith dedicated the temple site and cornerstones were placed for the temple
       to be built in Independence, Missouri. A site was dedicated, ground was broken, and
       cornerstones laid for the Far West Temple. As far as a temple at Adam-ondi-Ahman is
       concerned, the following comes from Heber C. Kimball: "While there we laid out a
       city on a high elevated piece of land, and set the stakes for the four corners of a temple
       block, which was dedicated, Brother Brigham Young being the mouth; there were
       from three to five hundred men present on the occasion, under arms. This elevated
       spot was probably from two hundred and fifty to five hundred feet above the level of
       the Grand River, so that one could look east, west, north, or south as far as the eye
       could reach: it was one of the most beautiful places ever beheld." Cited in Whitney,
       Life of Heber C. Kimball, 209.

The two restoration churches believe that the Prophet Joseph was inspired to build temples. Community of Christ owns the original temple in Kirtland, Ohio; and it has built a large temple in Independence, Missouri. Well over one hundred LDS temples are in operation and the LDS Church continues to build temples around the world. One of the most obvious differences between the two churches is their position on the importance and purpose of temples. Ordinances such as the endowment and eternal marriage are performed for the living in LDS temples. In addition, these ordinances and others, such as baptism, are performed in behalf of those who have died.

Joseph Smith Jr. publicly introduced the concept of baptism by proxy for those who are dead in a sermon he gave at the funeral of Seymour Brunson in August 1840. In January 1841, the Prophet Joseph received a revelation informing the Saints that baptism for the dead was an ordinance to be performed in the temple. However, during that time of poverty when there was no temple, the members were given a period of time in which they were allowed to perform baptisms for the dead in the Mississippi River.

> But I command you, all ye my saints, to build a house unto me; and I grant unto you a sufficient time to build a house unto me; and during this time your baptisms shall be acceptable unto me. But behold, at the end of this appointment your baptisms for your dead shall not be acceptable unto me; and if you do not these things at the end of the appointment ye shall be rejected as a church, with your dead, saith the Lord your God.[408]

Joseph Smith received several other revelations concerning baptism for the dead and continued to preach that principle until the end of his life. In a March 27, 1842, journal entry, Wilford Woodruff recorded that Joseph Smith taught that the Bible supported the doctrine of baptism for the dead (1 Corinthians 15:29). Joseph taught:

---

408 LDS Doctrine and Covenants 124:31–32 (1841); formerly found in the Community of Christ Doctrine and Covenants 107:10f–11a. This section was placed in the appendix of the Community of Christ Doctrine and Covenants in 1970 and removed by the 1990 world conference. It is not found in the current Community of Christ Doctrine and Covenants.

> If we can baptize a man in the name of the Father and of the Son and of the Holy Ghost for the remission of sins it is just as much our privilege to act as an agent and be baptized for the remission of sins for and in behalf of our kindred dead who have not heard the gospel or the fulness of it.[409]

In a general conference of the church held just a few months before his death, Joseph Smith taught that not only baptism, but other ordinances for the dead should be performed in the temple when it was completed. He said to the congregation, "as soon as the Temple and baptismal font are prepared, we calculate to give the Elders of Israel their washings and anointings, and attend to those last and more impressive ordinances, without which we cannot obtain celestial thrones."[410]

COMMUNITY OF CHRIST

Not yet twelve years old when his father was killed, Joseph Smith III knew very little of his father's teachings of ordinances performed in temples.[411] He did become, to some extent, aware of the Utah Mormons' belief in temple rites. As president of the Reorganized Church, Joseph III "always asserted that they (Mormon temple rituals) were largely doctrinal baggage added to the church without a useful purpose."[412]

The Reorganized Church did not believe in the temple ceremonies of washing and anointing, endowments, and sealing marriages for eternity. Joseph Smith III led the opposition to Mormon temple ordinances, once writing in a

THE MULTI-WOOD CROSS IN THE FOYER OF THE TEMPLE IN INDEPENDENCE, MISSOURI
Courtesy Community of Christ Archives, Independence, Missouri

---

409   Kenney, *Wilford Woodruff's Journal*, 2:165.
410   *HC* 6:319.
411   Joseph III's mother, Emma, did participate in the ordinances of the temple with her husband, Joseph Smith Jr. I am unaware of Emma teaching Joseph III anything about the temple ceremonies.
412   Launius, "Joseph Smith III and the Quest for a Centralized Organization, 1860–1873," in *Restoration Studies II*, 113.

**KIRTLAND TEMPLE,
DEDICATED IN 1836.**
Courtesy Community of Christ Archives,
Independence, Missouri—photograph by
Val Brinkerhoff

letter: "I cannot see anything sacred or divine in it."[413]

One RLDS writer suggested that part of the criticism of LDS temple ordinances by the Reorganized Church may have been due to the secrecy involved with LDS temple rites. He wrote, "We could cite the denunciation of secret societies in the Book of Mormon, then build upon the general antipathy in American society toward other secret societies such as the Masons."[414]

There are no temple ordinances performed for the living or the dead in Community of Christ. When the Reorganized Church was contemplating the building of the temple in Independence, Missouri, there was concern among a few RLDS members that ordinances similar to those performed in LDS temples might be part of the new temple.[415]

This anxiety was unjustified. In a letter addressed to Reorganized Church President W. Wallace Smith, his two counselors in the First Presidency wrote:

> We have probably reached the point at which attention can
> be given to temple worship in terms other than those rooted in
> the Nauvoo setting . . . If the "magic" were purged from temple
> functions in the Mormon sense, the construction of a temple for
> the Center Place . . . as places for seeking "learning by study and
> by faith" would be a great challenge to our priesthood to quali-

---

413   Quoted in Launius, "Joseph Smith III and the Quest for a Centralized Organization,
      1860–1873," in *Restoration Studies II*, 113.
414   Russell, "The LDS Church and the Community of Christ: Clearer Differences, Closer
      Friends," 182.
415   Ibid., 181.

fy for high level ministry and should quicken the morale of the Saints.[416]

Community of Christ has never accepted temple ordinances for the living or the dead, except in the case of baptism for the dead. That is the one vicarious ordinance that was not initially rejected by the Reorganization.

The 1844 edition of the Doctrine and Covenants was already canonized scripture in the RLDS Church when Joseph Smith III became its prophet-president in 1860. This edition of the Doctrine and Covenants contained three sections concerning baptism for the dead.

COMMUNITY OF CHRIST TEMPLE IN INDEPENDENCE, MISSOURI, DEDICATED 1994
Courtesy Community of Christ Archives, Independence, Missouri

Some who had belonged to the church led by Joseph Smith Jr. believed baptism for the dead to be a valid ordinance. They came into the Reorganization with that belief. Others did not accept it as a true doctrine.

In 1865, Joseph III discussed the topic of baptism for the dead with the Council of the Twelve. The first official position taken by the Reorganized Church was established at that time. They decided that baptism for the dead was not commanded, and permitted only under special circumstances. The situation in Nauvoo had been such that the Saints were granted this blessing for a limited time.[417] When the temple was not completed in the allotted time, the special permission was revoked.[418]

---

416   Cramm, "The 150-Year Journey of Rejection of Baptism for the Dead," in *Restoration Studies IX*, 90.

417   Emma Smith, Joseph III's mother, actually acted as proxy for the baptisms of at least six deceased family members, including her mother and father. These baptisms took place in 1841 and 1843. Black and Black, *Annotated Record of Baptisms for the Dead 1840–1845 Nauvoo Hancock County Illinois* 6:3354–56.

418   Cramm, "The 150-Year Journey of Rejection of Baptism for the Dead," in Restoration Studies IX, 88–89, "Joseph Smith III and the Quest for a Centralized Organization,

The Reorganized Church considered baptism for the dead to be "a question concerning which the Reorganization has received no commandment, and that it is not binding under these circumstances." The common belief for many years was that "baptism for the dead could not be practiced without further divine guidance."[419]

Many early RLDS leaders and members pondered the possibility that baptism for the dead might be practiced once the Reorganized Church had an appropriate temple. "As late as 1960," Community of Christ scholar William D. Russell noted, "one of our Presidents of Seventy, Russell F. Ralston (later an apostle) suggested we didn't baptize for the dead because we didn't yet have a temple built for that purpose."[420]

Doctrine and Covenants section 149A, a revelation given through prophet-president W. Wallace Smith, helped settle the issue on whether baptisms for the dead or "temple" ordinances would be performed in the Reorganized Church's temple. "It is also to be noted that the full and complete use of the temple is yet to be revealed but that there is no provision for secret ordinances now or ever."[421]

In 1970, the world conference voted to take the sections of the Doctrine and Covenants that referred to baptism for the dead from the main part of the text and place them in the appendix. Former counselor in the RLDS First Presidency Maurice Draper said, "It was not until 1970 [that] we were willing to say, 'Baptism for the dead is an aberration. If it's not a heresy then at least it's a worthless speculation and at its worst, it may actually be un-Christian and damaging to the spirit of the gospel.'"[422]

In 1990, construction began on the Independence Temple. In that same year at the world conference, the appendix, with the assorted former Doctrine and Covenants sections, was removed from the book

---

1860–1873," in *Restoration Studies II*, 113. See also Launius, "Joseph Smith III and the Quest for a Centralized Organization, 1860–1873," in Restoration Studies II, 113.

419   Ibid.

420   Russell, "The LDS Church and the Community of Christ: Clearer Differences, Closer Friends," 181.

421   Community of Christ Doctrine and Covenants 149A:6 (1968).

422   Quoted in Cramm, "The 150-Year Journey of Rejection of Baptism for the Dead," in *Restoration Studies IX*, 91.

entirely. "For all practical purposes, the church of the twentieth century was no longer interested in magical rituals for the dead."[423]

The question might be asked, "With no specific temple ceremonies, for what purpose did Community of Christ build a temple?" One compelling reason is that in July 1831, Joseph Smith received a revelation that Independence, Missouri, was to be the "center place" of Zion, "and a spot for the temple is lying westward, upon a lot which is not far from the courthouse."[424] In early August 1831, Joseph and a few men traveled to the site where the Prophet indicated the temple was to be built. They placed a stone to mark the northeast corner of the future temple and dedicated the site.

Persecution forced the Mormons from the area, but the dream of building a temple in Independence did not fade. Through the years, leaders and members of the Reorganization discussed the building of the temple. A 1968 revelation received through President W. Wallace Smith announced: "The time has come for a start to be made toward building my temple in the Center Place. It shall stand on a portion of the plot of ground set apart for this purpose many years ago by my servant Joseph Smith, Jr."[425]

After years of preparation and waiting, President Wallace B. Smith submitted what would become Doctrine and Covenants section 156 at the April 1984 world conference. It included the following about the temple:

> The temple shall be dedicated to the pursuit of peace. It shall be for reconciliation and for healing of the spirit. It shall also be for the strengthening of faith and preparation for witness. By its ministries an attitude of wholeness of body, mind, and spirit as a desirable end toward which to strive will be fostered. It shall be the means for providing leadership preparation for priesthood and member. And it shall be a place in which the essential meaning of the Restoration as healing and redeeming agent is given new life and understanding, inspired by the life and witness of the Redeemer of the world.[426]

---

423   Ibid.
424   Community of Christ Doctrine and Covenants 57:1d (1831); LDS Doctrine and Covenants 57:3 (1831).
425   Community of Christ Doctrine and Covenants 149:6a (1968).
426   Community of Christ Doctrine and Covenants 156:5a–e (1984).

The building of Community of Christ's temple in Independence, Missouri, was begun in 1990. It was completed and dedicated at the world conference in 1994. This temple "is a house of public worship, and entrance into the Temple or participation in its ministries is open to all."[427] As far as ordinances or sacraments are concerned, "communion (the Lord's Supper) is often served during special services in the Temple sanctuary. Other sacraments are provided in local congregations."[428]

The Independence Temple of Community of Christ has become a landmark in that area. Each year, thousands of people are welcomed as they tour the temple. The purpose of building the Independence Temple was to fulfill the revelation of Joseph Smith Jr. and to create a place of peace and worship—"an ensign to the world of the breadth and depth and devotion of the Saints."[429]

Because the ministries of Community of Christ "can be shared anywhere the church is gathered, there is need for only one temple."[430] There are no plans to build any other Community of Christ temples.

THE LATTER-DAY SAINTS

Since the days of the Prophet Joseph Smith, temple building and the ordinances performed in the temples have been essential components of The Church of Jesus Christ of Latter-day Saints. LDS teachings proclaim that Jesus Christ is the center of the gospel, and the temple is necessary to bring people to Jesus Christ.

The LDS Church proclaims its three-fold mission is to proclaim the gospel, perfect the Saints, and redeem the dead. Former LDS Church President Howard W. Hunter, taught that at the center of the mission of the LDS Church is the temple. To LDS Church members, he taught that "all of our efforts in proclaiming the gospel, perfecting the Saints, and redeeming the dead lead to the holy temple. This is because the

---

427 Official website of Community of Christ, "Frequently Asked Questions." Several months ago, my wife and I attended one of the Daily Prayer for Peace services that are held in the Community of Christ Temple.

428 Ibid. It is my understanding that no marriages, baptisms, confirmations, or any ordinance other than communion is performed in the Community of Christ Temple.

429 Community of Christ Doctrine and Covenants 156:6 (1984).

430 Official website of Community of Christ, "Frequently Asked Questions."

temple ordinances are absolutely crucial; we cannot return to God's presence without them."[431]

Individuals perform LDS temple ordinances for themselves and by proxy for the dead. Baptism, confirmation, and priesthood ordination are performed for the dead. The endowment and its ordinances, plus the sealing of couples (marriages), and the sealing of families are done for the living and for those who have died. James E. Faust, former counselor in the First Presidency, said this of the ordinances done in the temples: "It is an important part of the work of salvation for both the living and the dead."[432]

Former LDS President Ezra Taft Benson taught that temple ordinances were more important than academic degrees,[433] and Elder Russell M. Nelson, an LDS Apostle, said, "No accountable individual can receive exaltation in the celestial kingdom without the ordinances of the temple."[434] Howard W. Hunter also said, "It is in the temple where things of heaven and earth are joined. Temples are sacred for the closest communion between the Lord and those receiving the highest and most sacred ordinances of the holy priesthood."[435]

People who are not members of The Church of Jesus Christ of Latter-day Saints are not permitted into dedicated temples. Not even all LDS Church members are allowed to enter the temples. A person must receive a recommend from ecclesiastical leaders, who determine worthiness based on an evaluation of faithfulness, honesty, morality, and obedience to commandments. The recommend is renewed every two years.

Because only worthy Latter-day Saints are allowed to enter the temple and participate in temple ordinances, there have been feelings of anxiety and suspicion expressed by outsiders over the perceived secret nature of the ordinances. Latter-day Saints would concede that there is much symbolism in the temple, and "many aspects of the temple

431 Williams, ed., *Teachings of Howard W. Hunter*, 237-8.
432 Faust, "Spiritual Healing," 7.
433 Kimball, *Teachings of Spencer W. Kimball*, 390.
434 Nelson, "Perfection Pending," 87. Exaltation in the celestial kingdom is the highest heaven in LDS theology.
435 Williams, ed., *Teachings of Howard W. Hunter*, 237.

experience are significantly different than regular worship services."[436] However, Mormons insist that there is absolutely nothing sinister that takes place in the temple. The ordinances are viewed as sacred and are not to be shared with the spiritually unprepared. All Latter-day Saint temple ordinances, covenants, and activities are focused on worship of God the Father and His Son, Jesus Christ.

SUMMARY

Both Community of Christ and The Church of Jesus Christ of Latter-day Saints have functioning temples. Temple building and temple worship was important to the early Saints of the Restoration. Joseph Smith Jr. instructed the early members about the necessity of temples for salvation.

The two churches see the purpose of temples very differently. It might be said that the differences between the two churchs' views on temples could be exemplified by comparing the temples in Kirtland, Ohio, and Nauvoo, Illinois. The Kirtland Temple was the center of Church administration, a place for congregational meetings, revelation, and learning. There were no ordinances for the dead and very limited ordinances of any kind performed in the Kirtland Temple. Community of Christ temple theology and use is patterned after the Kirtland Temple.

In the Nauvoo Temple, ordinances for the living and the dead were performed. Access to the temple was much more limited in Nauvoo than it was in Kirtland. The Church of Jesus Christ of Latter-day Saints aligns its temple worship with what took place in the Kirtland Temple, coupled with what took place in the Nauvoo Temple.

The LDS Church builds temples to provide its members with holy places to receive sacred ordinances members believe are required to enter the highest degree of heaven. Community of Christ does not believe in the temple ordinances of Mormonism. Community of Christ built its temple in Independence because of the prophecy that a temple would be built in Independence, Missouri, and as a sacred house of worship and learning.

---

436   Scott, "Receive the Temple Blessings," 26.

There are no temple rites for the living or the dead in Community of Christ. The Kirtland Temple is an historic site and visitor's center to help guests gain an appreciation for the sacrifice of the early Saints and the rich history of the Restoration. In addition to the historical role it plays, the Kirtland Temple is still used as a place of worship.

The purposes of the Community of Christ temple in Independence, Missouri, are the pursuit of peace, reconciliation, healing of the spirit, strengthening of faith, and preparation for witness.[437] It is to "stand as a towering symbol of a people who knew injustice and strife on the frontier and who now seek the peace of Jesus Christ throughout the world."[438]

The Church of Jesus Christ of Latter-day Saints continues performing saving ordinances for the living in each of its temples. In addition, the ordinance of baptism, confirmation, priesthood ordination, and endowment are done for deceased persons. The sealing of couples and families are also performed for those who died without receiving those ordinances.

Entrance into Mormon temples is restricted to members of the LDS Church who are living a standard of worthiness established by the Church. The Community of Christ temple is open to all in the hope that all who enter will find peace in Jesus Christ.

---

437   Community of Christ Doctrine and Covenants 156:5a–5b (1984).
438   Community of Christ Doctrine and Covenants 161:2b (2000).

COMMANDMENTS

A man asked Jesus what he needed to do to have eternal life, and the Savior responded, "if thou wilt enter into life, keep the commandments."[439] On another occasion, Jesus said to His disciples, "If ye love me, keep my commandments."[440] Keeping God's commandments, or following His will, has always been an essential aspect of the gospel of Jesus Christ. However, a comparison of the philosophies of the LDS Church and Community of Christ concerning obedience to the commandments reveals a substantial difference.

Beginning with the organization of the church by Joseph Smith Jr. in 1830, an increasing number of commandments became part of the restoration church. Initially, the revelations received by the Prophet Joseph were viewed as commandments. They were specific assignments or instructions from the Lord. "Wherefore, I the Lord, knowing the calamity which should come upon the inhabitants of the earth, called upon my servant Joseph Smith, Jun., and spake unto him from heaven, and gave him commandments; and also gave commandments to others."[441]

Just prior to the organization of the church, the believers who would become members of the church were instructed to "keep the

---

439   Matthew 19:17
440   John 14:15
441   Community of Christ Doctrine and Covenants 1:4a (1831); LDS Doctrine and Covenants 1:17–18 (1831).

commandments which you have received by the hand of my servant Joseph Smith, Jun." They were then commanded to repent and to learn of Christ and listen to His words.[442]

As the restoration church developed, Joseph Smith Jr. would instruct the Saints to be obedient to more general, institutional commandments. These would include the Ten Commandments as received by Moses—injunctions against murder, adultery, lying, theft, and coveting.[443] The payment of tithing for the building of the kingdom of God upon the earth was instituted through Joseph Smith. A health code known as the Word of Wisdom was introduced to the early Saints through a revelation received by Joseph Smith "to be sent greeting, not by commandment or constraint."[444]

COMMUNITY OF CHRIST

Commandments in Community of Christ have evolved since its beginning. The church, of course, encourages the basic standards of honesty, morality, kindness, and avoiding actions that would be harmful to oneself and to others.

Tithing is practiced in Community of Christ, but in a somewhat different variation than that found in the LDS Church. The concept of stewardship is vitally important in Community of Christ. The philosophy of the church is that all that we receive and all that we have comes to us from God. Church members have a sacred responsibility to use resources wisely.

The financial and other gains received each year would be the annual increase. For most people, a substantial portion of their income goes toward the necessities of life. The amount left over after necessities have been met is called surplus. It is from this surplus that one cre-

---

442   Community of Christ Doctrine and Covenants 18:2f–g, 2n (1830); LDS Doctrine and Covenants 19:13–15, 23 1830).

443   Although keeping the Sabbath Day holy is part of the Ten Commandments, we have no instructions from Joseph Smith concerning the Sabbath. "The Prophet Joseph Smith apparently taught little or nothing about certain subjects. An excellent example would be the Sabbath day. We do not have a single statement on that subject." Dahl and Cannon, eds., *Teachings of Joseph Smith*, ix.

444   Community of Christ Doctrine and Covenants 86: section heading (1833); LDS Doctrine and Covenants 89:2 (1833).

ates an inheritance. The term "inheritance" does not simply mean the acquisition of wealth. "It includes all the resources and opportunities required to exercise responsible stewardship for one's self and family, consecrating all beyond this for the benefit of others."[445]

Tithing in Community of Christ used to be one tenth of one's surplus after deducting the basic living needs. Now, instead of using a percentage or formula, Community of Christ members are "called out of the relative security of a clear guideline, and called to respond to the generosity God has shown us through Jesus."[446] Community of Christ members "honor what we have received from God by reaching toward sharing 10 percent or more through Mission and Community Tithes." It is not so much a question of "How much should I give?" as it is "How much tithing can I hope to share?"[447] Paying tithing is not a requirement for church membership, but it is encouraged.[448] In addition to tithing, there are also opportunities to help build the kingdom in the form of oblations[449] and consecrations.

Many members of Community of Christ "contribute 10 percent or more of total income to tithing, offerings, and other good causes."[450] Unlike the LDS Church, Community of Christ members can determine where a portion of their tithing goes by donating directly to institutions such as SaintsCare, Graceland University, Outreach International, World Accord, or other nonprofit charitable organizations.[451]

Joseph Smith Jr. received a revelation known as the Word of Wisdom in February 1833. Community of Christ accepts the Word of

---

445 RLDS, *Church Members Manual*, 75–76.
446 Personal communication with Community of Christ World Church Secretary Andrew Shields.
447 "A Disciple's Generous Response," found on the official website: cofchrist.org/generosity.
448 Tithing is not required for membership in the LDS Church, but it is necessary for those who desire to attend the temple and participate in temple ordinances to live the law of tithing.
449 An oblation is a gift used to help the poor and others with special needs. "It has become a tradition in the RLDS Church to include an oblation offering as part of the regular monthly Communion Service." RLDS, *Church Members Manual*, 77. This is similar to the fast offerings donated by members of the LDS Church, typically given on the first Sunday of each month.
450 RLDS, *Church Members Manual*, 76.
451 *Walking with Jesus*, 73.

Wisdom as it was originally given to the Prophet Joseph: "not by commandment or constraint."[452] Over the years RLDS Church leaders have made official statements at general conferences against the use of alcoholic beverages and tobacco. For example, at the April general conference in 1868, it was "resolved that this conference deprecates the use of intoxicating drinks, (as beverages,) and the use of tobacco, and recommends to all officers of the church, total abstinence."[453]

In today's Community of Christ, one of the questions concerning standards and qualifications for a potential priesthood holder reads: "Does this candidate exhibit good stewardship of health and hold high standards of behavior, avoiding the abuse of chemical substances and refraining from the use of alcohol and tobacco?"[454]

There is no restriction of coffee and tea as there is in the LDS version of the Word of Wisdom. Community of Christ leaders and priesthood holders are encouraged to abstain from intoxicating beverages, tobacco, and the abuse of chemical substances. Because the Word of Wisdom never became an official commandment of the Reorganization, it is left a personal matter between each Community of Christ member and God as to whether to live the Word of Wisdom.

The Word of Wisdom is still a matter of concern for Community of Christ members and leaders. It was discussed at a recent world conference. A resolution was presented stating that since the Word of Wisdom was given in 1833 when almost all members were from the United States, and because it was "to be sent by greeting, not by commandment, or constraint,"[455] that it must be reconsidered for an international church. The resolution did not pass but is slated for further discussion and discernment efforts on the part of church leaders and members.[456]

---

452   Community of Christ Doctrine and Covenants 86: section heading (1833); LDS Doctrine and Covenants 89:2 (1833).
453   *History RLDS* 3:494.
454   Community of Christ, *Church Administrator's Handbook,* 2005 ed., 89.
455   Preface to section 86 of Community of Christ Doctrine and Covenants; LDS Doctrine and Covenants 89:2 (1833).
456   In part, the resolution stated:
Resolved, That the application of the church's standards of personal conduct in all parts of the world be based on the central principles of the worth of all persons and personal agency and responsibility grounded in the principles of sound health and positive interpersonal relationships; and be it further

In recent years, Community of Christ has moved away from the institutional idea of specific commandments and is advocating a more holistic approach to following the word of God. It sees spiritual growth as a very personal thing; the journey of each disciple being unique and developing in stages. A Community of Christ member's guide states:

> A belief that we cling to today may be reconsidered tomorrow, next month, or next year in the light of our new experience. . . . Salvation is not based on getting everything right or making no mistakes: it is the gift of God offered to us in grace and mercy. Remember, your need for God looks and feels different at various stages of your life. Ask for help and give help to those who ask. Remember that discipleship is a process.[457]

Members of Community of Christ are encouraged to worship, be involved and active disciples of Christ, learn, share their witness and resources with others, and be peacemakers. Community of Christ's mission statement is: "We proclaim Jesus Christ and promote communities of joy, hope, love, and peace."[458] Community of Christ members are commanded to learn what Jesus Christ revealed and reveals about God. They use Jesus as their model for faithful discipleship, and share with others what that means to them personally.[459] This is where the "community" aspect of Community of Christ comes in. Its goal is to promote communities

---

Resolved, That the World Conference acknowledge the need for flexibility and cultural respect when dealing with the application of the church's standards of personal conduct in the varying cultures and nations of the world; and . . . that the church's standards of personal conduct be applied around the world in culturally appropriate ways under the guidance of administrative officers and with the support and approval of the members of the Twelve involved." (*Herald* [June 2007]: 21.)

This resolution is about more than just the Word of Wisdom. Andrew Shields wrote: "the central issue at stake in the resolution is the request to decentralize expectations of conduct for church members in different parts of the world. . . . What is a sin and what is a cultural difference?" The Expanded World Church Leadership Council will continue to discuss this and other issues dealing with cultural differences and the Enduring Principles.

457 *Walking with Jesus* 27.
458 Ibid., 56–57.
459 Community of Christ efforts to promote communities of joy, hope, love, and peace is in keeping with the establishing Zion theme of their heritage.

that live out the Zionic ideal by following Christ.[460] Discipleship is about obedience to Jesus in every aspect of one's life. "Discipleship is both an inward and outward journey. Jesus calls us to follow him and to invite others to experience the transforming power of his grace."[461] God provides each person the ability to make choices. Choosing wisely contributes to the good in our lives and in the world. Unwise actions can diminish a person's ability to make choices. "We are called to make responsible choices within the circumstances of our lives."[462] Because circumstances vary with each individual, to some degree choices will also vary.

God wants all of His creations to obtain what Community of Christ refers to as "shalom" or justice, reconciliation, well-being, peace, and wholeness. Because "Jesus Christ, the embodiment of God's shalom (peace), reveals the meaning of God's peace in all aspects of life,"[463] those who are led by the Spirit to follow Christ are keeping the ultimate commandment of "come, follow me."[464] With this approach to the commandments, "faithful disciples interweave mind, body, spirit and relationships into a holistic cycle of ministry."[465]

Based on their continuing experience with God, Christ, and the Holy Spirit, Community of Christ members strive to uphold what they call the Enduring Principles or core values. These Enduring Principles include grace and generosity, sacredness of creation, continuing revelation, worth of all persons, all are called, responsible choices, pursuit of peace (Shalom), unity in diversity, and blessings of community.[466]

---

460 Personal communication with Andrew Shields, Community of Christ World Church Secretary.
461 *We Share*, 15.
462 Ibid., 11.
463 Ibid.
464 Luke 18:22.
465 Shields, *Claimed by Christ's Vision*, 34.
466 *We Share*, 10.

LATTER-DAY SAINTS

The LDS Church would agree with Community of Christ that the restored gospel is designed for its members to be more responsible and spirit-directed. The Doctrine and Covenants teaches:

> Behold, it is not meet that I should command in all things; for he that is compelled in all things, the same is a slothful and not a wise servant; wherefore he receiveth no reward. Verily I say, men should be anxiously engaged in a good cause, and do many things of their own free will, and bring to pass much righteousness; for the power is in them, wherein they are agents unto themselves.[467]

In addition to following the direction of the Spirit in individual spiritual guidance, Mormons are also to adhere to the fundamental laws found in the Ten Commandments that have been reiterated in our dispensation. They also live other commandments as instructed by Joseph Smith Jr. To be a Latter-day Saint in good standing, one must live the laws of chastity, honesty, tithing, and the Word of Wisdom.

The LDS Church views these specific commandments and any others received by revelation through living prophets as "divine directives for righteous living."

> Latter-day Saints believe that commandments . . . bring happiness and spiritual and temporal blessings; and are part of God's way to redeem his children and endow them with eternal life. Therefore, commandments provide not only a test of faith, obedience, and love for God and Jesus Christ but also an opportunity to experience love from God and joy both in this life and in the life to come.[468]

SUMMARY

Both religious groups believe that by doing the will of God and following Christ, people will find greater peace and happiness in this life. Both churches believe that God's will is communicated through the

---

467   Community of Christ Doctrine and Covenants 58:6c–d (1831); LDS Doctrine and Covenants 58:26–28 (1831).
468   Ludlow, ed. *Encyclopedia of Mormonism* 1:296.

Spirit to those who desire to follow Christ. Joseph Smith Jr. introduced specific commandments to early church members, in addition to those found in the Bible. The LDS Church continues to focus on the institutional commandments revealed through the Prophet Joseph. Community of Christ has a more open interpretation of commandments. Disciples open themselves to the Holy Spirit and discern how best to live out God's commandments in their context and in their calling. The two great commandments of loving God with all of one's heart, soul, mind, and strength, and loving one's neighbor would encompass all other commandments.[469]

---

469   Mark 12:30–31.

DISSIDENTS

Like many other religions, The Church of Jesus Christ of Latter-day Saints and Community of Christ have had individuals and groups of former members who were once believers but are now at odds with their former churches. These are not people who have simply lost interest in being involved in church; they have become irritated and sometimes even hostile toward the religion to which they once belonged.

Some of these dissidents from the two restoration churches have come to believe that the religions are a complete hoax and that church members are being deceived by false doctrines and fraudulent leaders. Others support earlier versions of the religions, but they feel that the current churches have strayed from the fundamentals they once upheld.

The term "fundamentalist" comes from their desire to return to the way the churches used to be—to the old traditions. "Fundamentalists of all persuasions are reactionists. They react to changes in the mother church, changes they believe are harmful or unauthorized."[470] There are dissidents who are antagonistic and fundamentalist organizations that have broken off from the LDS Church and from Community of Christ.

---

470   Hales, *Mormon Fundamentalists*, 40.

COMMUNITY OF CHRIST

There has been dissent in the Reorganized Church for nearly as long as there has been a Reorganized Church. The Reorganization "originated as a dissenting sect of Mormonism," which rejected the claims and denounced the doctrines of all other factional leaders.[471] In the past fifty years, much of the dissent found in the Reorganization has been in the form of fundamentalism. RLDS fundamentalism is not related to polygamy, but it is based on holding to the traditional views of scripture, doctrine, and church history.

The beginning of modern RLDS fundamentalism likely began in the latter part of the 1950s, when W. Wallace Smith became president of the Reorganized Church of Jesus Christ of Latter Day Saints.[472] During the early years of his presidency, a few individuals from the church's religious education department and some RLDS staff members began taking graduate courses and receiving post-graduate degrees from Protestant theological seminaries. William D. Russell noted that "formal theological training of church staff members had a liberalizing effect on the materials published for Sunday School use, on the materials published in the *Saints' Herald,* and on other church publications."[473]

In 1969, a series of theological articles called the "Position Papers" were written by the curriculum committee—a committee that included some of the members of the Council of Twelve and even members of the First Presidency. "When these papers were leaked to the church public," wrote Russell, "fundamentalist saints were shocked at their extremely liberal contents."[474] In his 1970 book, *The Mormon Churches: a Comparison from Within,* RLDS author Francis W. Holm Sr. penned this concern about his church, "The trend towards 'protestant' thinking seems to be emerging and is of deep concern to the author."[475]

RLDS historian Roger Launius wrote that in the 1960s, "Reorganization liberals emerged to engage in the steady dismantling of what

---

471   Howard, *The Church Through the Years,* 2:413–14.
472   This is not to say that there was not dissent from the RLDS Church prior to this time. The current fundamentalist movement simply appears to have begun in the second half of the twentieth century.
473   Russell, "Defenders of the Faith: Varieties of RLDS Dissent," 15.
474   Ibid.
475   Holm, *The Mormon Churches: a Comparison from Within,* 209.

had been a traditional Reorganized Church theological consensus." Launius pointed to the tensions between the liberals and conservatives. The liberals thought it was time to re-think many of the church's traditions in light of the best scholarship available, while the conservatives desired "to remain faithful to the stories, symbols, and events of early Mormonism."[476]

In 1970, after a ten-year process of preparation, a committee of RLDS scholars published a very important theological work entitled *Exploring the Faith*. Its foreword states that "a more adequate statement of beliefs of the church," beyond Joseph Smith's Epitome of Faith was necessary.[477] The foreword also included this statement: "Historical and traditional points of view needed to be expanded in view of contemporary religious experience and scholarship."[478]

Exploring the Faith "deemphasized the Reorganization's most unique aspects and stressed those more characteristic of 'orthodox' Christian denominations."[479] RLDS traditionalists saw their church changing in ways that they disagreed with and found difficult to accept.

In the first part of 1979, the RLDS First Presidency "invited all of the church's fulltime appointee ministers and their wives to Independence where the new president and his counselors read theological papers which clearly showed the presidency to be in a liberal camp."[480] The lectures became known as the Presidential Papers. These papers "brought the fundamentalists' search for heresy right to the door of the prophet and his counselors."[481]

One of the changes from the traditional to the new theology was seeing scripture as "the inspired human witness to God's revelation," rather than the inerrant "words, revelations, and commandments of

476 Launius, "Coming of Age? The Reorganized Church of Jesus Christ of Latter Day Saints in the 1960s," 39. It should be noted that liberals also appeared to desire respectability and openness to Protestantism.
477 *Exploring the Faith*, 5. The Epitome of Faith is known in the LDS Church as the Articles of Faith.
478 Ibid.
479 Launius, "Coming of Age? The Reorganized Church of Jesus Christ of Latter Day Saints in the 1960s," 44.
480 Russell, "Ordaining Women and the Transformation from Sect to Denomination," 61.
481 Russell, "Defenders of the Faith: Varieties of RLDS Dissent," 15.

God to the church."[482] Another progressive change was to no longer view church history as "selected records of the past which prove the rightness of the church."[483] The concept of doctrine changed from being "divinely, inerrantly communicated, meant for all times and places" to "theologically grounded inferences drawn from scriptural interpretation and responsive to unique times, places, and cultures."[484] Authority was no longer seen as exclusive to the RLDS Church. It emanated from God to each faith community. RLDS Church leaders no longer saw their church as the "one true church." Modern RLDS leaders began getting involved with ecumenical movements, something which traditionalists opposed.[485]

William Russell cited five changes during Wallace B. Smith's administration that "created a gulf so wide between the RLDS Church and its Old School schismatics that it appears impossible to close."[486] The five changes were as follows: 1) the ordination of women to the priesthood; 2) the building and dedication of the Independence Temple to the pursuit of peace; 3) changing the policy on the Lord's Supper from a closed to an open communion; 4) the announcement of W. Grant McMurray as the first prophet-president who was not a descendant of Joseph Smith Jr.; and 5) changing the name of the church to Community of Christ.[487]

When what would become Community of Christ Doctrine and Covenants section 156 was presented at the April 1984 world conference, it came as a stunning announcement to many because it opened the way for women to be ordained to the priesthood. The ordination of women to the priesthood "was merely the last straw for many Old School Saints who had been concerned about the Church's de-emphasis

---

482   Howard, *The Church Through the Years* 2:416.

483   Ibid., 417.

484   Ibid.

485   Ibid., 411, 417.

486   Russell, "The Remnant Church: An RLDS Schismatic Group Finds a Prophet of Joseph's Seed," 87–88.

487   Ibid., 87. Russell has since named two additional changes during the administration of Wallace B. Smith that led to a rift between traditionalists and revisionists in the RLDS Church. One was the way the revisionists were dealing with the old issue of Joseph Smith and polygamy. The other is doctrinal revisionism. "The Last Smith Presidents and the Transformation of the RLDS Church," 61–66.

of many beliefs that had been central tenets of the RLDS faith for more than a century."[488] By 1990, "about one-fourth of the active RLDS members ceased their involvement in the church."[489]

In his book *The Saints at the Crossroads*, RLDS fundamentalist Richard Price identified nine fundamental distinctions that set the Reorganized Church apart from other Christian churches. According to an article on RLDS reformation, these nine characteristics can be summarized into three basic declarations:

> First, Jesus Christ founded a specific church organization which later departed from the truths of the gospel and thereby lost the authority to represent God and administer the sacraments. After centuries of dark apostasy, light again burst forth as God intervened to restore the true church through Joseph Smith, Jr. This restoration is preserved in the Reorganization.
>
> Second, the church enjoys and possesses a sacred deposit of modern, infallible revelations given through the founder and his successors in the prophetic office. The Inspired Version of the Holy Bible, Book of Mormon, and Doctrine and Covenants contain the words of God as dictated to the prophets.
>
> Third, the church's chief mission is to participate in God's redeeming activity by building Zion, a literal city of God, at Independence, Missouri.[490]

The dissenters from the today's Community of Christ have responded in essentially three ways. First are those who could be referred to as non-separatists. These are church members who have formed separate groups for worship—independent restoration branches—who do not ask for their names to be withdrawn from the Community of Christ rolls. They believe that someday the church leaders will see their errors and return to the traditional beliefs. Non-separatists have traditionally been the largest group of RLDS fundamentalists.[491]

488   Russell, "The Remnant Church: An RLDS Schismatic Group Finds a Prophet of Joseph's Seed," 79.
489   Russell, "Ordaining Women and the Transformation from Sect to Denomination," 63.
490   As quoted in Conrad and Shupe, "An RLDS Reformation? Construing the Task of RLDS Theology," 94.
491   This may no longer be true. William Russell said that as time goes on, more and more give up and resign their membership. Personal communication with William Russell.

The second group of fundamentalists would be the separatists. These people have withdrawn from the Reorganization because they don't believe that Community of Christ will ever change back to the way it was originally. Separatists have created their own churches, and some groups do acknowledge a prophet as their guide.

Finally, there are the typically very small groups that follow self-proclaimed prophets. These groups are what Russell refers to as schismatics. Their numbers are very small, and they can appear suddenly and then disappear almost as quickly. Not considered as one of the three basic groups of fundamentalists are those Community of Christ members who simply quit attending any of the restoration churches.[492]

At present, there are numerous break-off groups from Community of Christ and several hundred independent branches whose members maintain their RLDS membership, hoping that someday they might return to the church they once knew and still love.

Another type of dissenter is the church member who becomes antagonistic toward the church, having lost all belief in every aspect of the Restoration. Most of what little anti-RLDS sentiment exists comes from the early roots of the Restoration and Community of Christ's ties with the LDS Church. Websites that demonstrate antagonism toward Community of Christ typically connect it to Mormonism. Ignoring the current beliefs of Community of Christ, vitriolic writers link the two "Mormon" churches by their common origin. They see Mormonism as fraudulent at best and possibly satanic. Community of Christ is guilty by association.

LATTER-DAY SAINTS

There are a myriad of books, pamphlets, Internet sites, television programs, and films dedicated to undermine and ultimately destroy Mormonism. Ministers will devote entire sermons to the evils of the LDS Church. Points of attack have included the historicity of the Book of Mormon, the Book of Abraham, Joseph Smith, plural marriage, perceived sexism and racism, and the LDS doctrine of God and the plural-

---

492   The three types of fundamentalists were labeled by Russell, "The Fundamentalist Schism, 1958–Present," in Launius and Spillman, eds., *Let Contention Cease*, 125–51.

ity of gods. Many of the dissidents from the LDS Church have become involved with the Anti-Mormon movement. Some of the most embittered anti-Mormons are former LDS Church members. As Elder Neal A. Maxwell said, "Then there are the dissenters who leave the Church, either formally or informally, but who cannot leave it alone."[493]

There are "fundamentalists" who claim a historical connection to The Church of Jesus Christ of Latter-day Saints. Most of these have either never belonged to the LDS Church or have been excommunicated from The Church of Jesus Christ of Latter-day Saints. In some ways, the original Reorganized Church of Jesus Christ of Latter Day Saints could be considered a fundamentalist-type of movement. These were Saints who rejected what they considered to be the more radical teachings of Joseph Smith during the Nauvoo era. They desired to return to the traditions and doctrines of Kirtland Mormonism.

The major reason for Mormon fundamentalism today is polygamy. Modern Mormon fundamentalism has its roots in the reaction to the 1890 Manifesto and the second manifesto of 1904. They believe in the restoration of the gospel through the Prophet Joseph Smith. They believe in the divine calling of both Brigham Young and John Taylor as prophets of God. Opinions among fundamentalist Mormons about later prophets, such as Wilford Woodruff and Joseph F. Smith, range from believing they were called of God to lead the main body of Saints who were not worthy to live the higher law to calling them "sell-outs" who gave in to pressure from the United States government rather than follow the commandments of God.

Most of today's Mormon fundamentalists claim authority to perform plural marriages and live the law of plural marriage based on a secret ordination that purportedly took place in 1886 under the hands of President John Taylor. According to the story, certain men were ordained at this time to "a previously unheard of priesthood office called 'High Priest Apostle' and thereby became a member of a previously unheard of priesthood council called 'The Council of Seven Friends.'"[494]

This Council of Seven Friends was supposedly "outside of the Church as part of a 'priesthood' organization that existed independent

---

493   Maxwell, *Men and Women of Christ*, 4.
494   Hales, *Mormon Fundamentalism*, 71.

of all other religious entities . . . more powerful than any priesthood quorum within the Church including the First Presidency."[495] Although "most Mormon fundamentalists have discarded the teachings of High Priest Apostles and the Council of Seven Friends," most still trace their "authority" to the event that purportedly took place in 1886.[496]

According to one report, there is an "estimated 37,000 men, women, and children who refer to themselves as fundamentalist Mormons."[497] Most of these Mormon fundamentalists live in the western part of the United States and Canada. There are also some in northern Mexico. In addition to plural marriage, many fundamentalist Mormons believe in the "one mighty and strong" that will "set in order the house of God."[498] The building up of Zion, restriction of priesthood to certain races, and belief in what is known as the Adam-God theory are also common in Mormon fundamentalism.

SUMMARY

Through the years there have been dissidents from both The Church of Jesus Christ of Latter-day Saints and Community of Christ. Some of these dissenters have left the LDS Church or Community of Christ entirely, finding other religions that suited them better or remaining without religious affiliation.

Some have left the churches because they felt that they had been deceived by false teachings. Often, these people will get involved with anti-Mormonism, speaking out and writing against Joseph Smith and any church that claims him as a prophet.

There have also been dissidents who continue to believe in various aspects of the Restoration but are in disagreement with the two largest existing churches that began with Joseph Smith. There have been numerous divisions and break-offs from both The Church of Jesus Christ of Latter-day Saints and Community of Christ. Community of Christ

---

495   Ibid.

496   Ibid., 77.

497   Wilde, "Fundamentalist Mormonism," in Bringhurst and Hamer, eds., *Scattering of the Saints: Schism within Mormonism*, 263.

498   LDS Doctrine and Covenants 85:7 (1832); not found in the Community of Christ Doctrine and Covenants.

scholar Steven Shields estimates that there have been over four hundred different churches or religious groups that based their doctrine, at least in part, on the Restoration through the Prophet Joseph Smith.[499] Most of these divisions resulted from differing views on doctrine or changes that have occurred in the LDS and RLDS churches.

Some of these schisms refer to themselves as fundamentalists. Most Mormon fundamentalists have separated themselves from the LDS Church because of the doctrine of plural marriage. When the Mormon Church discontinued the practice of plural marriage around the turn of the twentieth century, fundamentalist individuals and organizations outside of the church kept the practice going. They see themselves as loyal followers of the Prophet Joseph Smith. The LDS Church views them as apostates who are not willing to follow the living prophet.

The fundamentalist movement that came from the Reorganized Church is composed of a group of conservatives who seek for doctrines and beliefs that were originally in the Reorganization. They disagree with current Community of Christ leadership and what they see as the "de-emphasis of certain RLDS fundamentals—such as the idea that the primitive church fell into apostasy and was later restored,"[500] and the inerrancy of the Bible, Book of Mormon, and the early Doctrine and Covenants. RLDS fundamentalists also disagree with the ecumenical movement that Community of Christ has embraced. They "believe that the leaders of the church have been moving away from many of the unique and distinctive features of RLDS thought and, in the process, are becoming more like mainstream Protestantism."[501]

Both the LDS Church and Community of Christ have lost some of their membership to dissidents. They are both concerned with dissidents and make efforts to help these people return to church fellow-

---

499   Shields, "Foreword," in *Scattering of the Saints: Schism within Mormonism*, ix.
500   Russell, "Defenders of the Faith: Varieties of RLDS Dissent," 14.
501   Ibid.

ship. However, each church maintains the course it is on, believing that it is being guided in its growth and development by the Lord.[502]

---

502   One note of interest concerning Community of Christ: I was surprised to see how willing the church was to publish varying views concerning doctrines and other issues in their magazine, the *Herald*. Controversial topics and disagreements with Community of Christ leaders and decisions are openly addressed. I believe this comes from Community of Christ's desire to get everyone involved in the discernment process. It appears that the opinions of members concerning doctrine and policy are listened to and considered.

CONCEPT OF ZION

According to Joseph Smith Jr., "The building up of Zion is a cause that has interested the people of God in every age; it is a theme upon which prophets, priests and kings have dwelt with peculiar delight."[503] He once remarked, "The people of the Lord, those who have complied with the requirements of the new covenant, have already commenced gathering together to Zion, which is in the state of Missouri."[504]

A revelation given through the Prophet Joseph pronounced the center place of Zion to be Independence, Missouri.[505] He stated that Zion was to be a New Jerusalem.[506] On another occasion, Joseph said, "the whole of America is Zion itself from north to south."[507] He spoke often of building or establishing Zion. How do the two restoration churches see the concept of Zion today?

COMMUNITY OF CHRIST

In the earliest days of the Reorganization, the concept of establishing Zion was similar to what was taught by Joseph Smith Jr.: "We believe in the literal gathering of Israel and in the restoration of the

---

503   Smith, *Teachings of the Prophet Joseph Smith*, 231.
504   Ibid., 17.
505   Community of Christ Doctrine and Covenants 57:1d (1831); LDS Doctrine and Covenants 57:3 (1831).
506   Smith, *Teachings of the Prophet Joseph Smith*, 84.
507   Ibid., 362.

Ten Tribes. That Zion will be built upon this continent."[508] As a young boy, Joseph Smith III experienced hardships as a result of his father's attempts to gather the Saints into communities united in the cause of Zion and separated from worldly society.

Whether it was his experiences with his father's gathering experiments, societal changes caused by the Civil War and the Industrial Revolution, his personal philosophy, or a combination of these things, Joseph Smith III discouraged the gathering of RLDS members into a particular geographical location or central gathering place. He saw the role of the Reorganized Church "more in Christian terms of 'leaven' rather than that of being the chosen elect of a wrathful God." The RLDS Church "made the decision to adapt to its environment and to live in peace with its neighbors."[509]

Nearly one hundred fifty years later, Community of Christ continues to move in the direction initiated by Joseph Smith III and beyond. It seeks more than simply adapting to its environment and getting along with others. Its goal is to influence and improve the world in which we live. No longer do members see Zion in the apocalyptic sense as they did in earlier times.

Richard P. Howard wrote, "zionic objectives, concepts, and procedures have changed with the transition from the nineteenth-century to the present." He continued:

> Changing social, economic, and political conditions and structures have vastly complicated Zion building processes. The church's theological horizons have widened, heightening the felt need to grasp essential historical and theological principles and to apply them as foundational to any physical, geographic Zion. We seek the universals of Zionic endeavor in order to capture the imagination and commitment of the Saints everywhere. Universals are elusive, because no culture or people is identical with any other; no one culture can speak for all.[510]

---

508   *Times and Seasons* 3 (March 1, 1842): 710. It was later clarified that "Zion will be built on this [the American] continent.

509   Bouissou, "Evolution of Institutional Purpose in The Restoration Movement," in *Restoration Studies VI*, 118.

510   Howard, "The Emerging RLDS Identity," in *Restoration Studies III*, 52.

Today's Community of Christ is driven by modern revelation and social conscience to help heal an ailing world. William D. Russell wrote, "there seems to be very little concern about life after death in the Community of Christ." Rather, there is more of an interest in this world than in the next.[511] This worldview has become an expanded concept of Zion. Consider the following verses from the most recently added section to Community of Christ Doctrine and Covenants:

> You are called to create pathways in the world for peace in Christ to be relationally and culturally incarnate. The hope of Zion is realized when the vision of Christ is embodied in communities of generosity, justice, and peacefulness. Above all else, strive to be faithful to Christ's vision of the peaceable Kingdom of God on earth. Courageously challenge cultural, political, and religious trends that are contrary to the reconciling and restoring purposes of God. Pursue peace.[512]
>
> God, the Eternal Creator, weeps for the poor, displaced, mistreated, and diseased of the world because of their unnecessary suffering. Such conditions are not God's will. Open your ears to hear the pleading of mothers and fathers in all nations who desperately seek a future of hope for their children. Do not turn away from them. For in their welfare resides your welfare.[513]
>
> The earth, lovingly created as an environment for life to flourish, shudders in distress because of creation's natural and living systems are becoming exhausted from carrying the burden of human greed and conflict. Humankind must awaken from its illusion of independence and unrestrained consumption without lasting consequences.[514]

Community of Christ has also developed a worldwide scope of interest. It is taking Christ's vision for peace, or its Zion view, to many countries in the world. Community of Christ World Church Historian Mark Scherer wrote: "Today's Community of Christ is in fact a world church. On any given Sunday, more people—members, and

---

511   Russell, "The LDS Church and Community of Christ: Clearer Differences, Closer Friends," 189.

512   Community of Christ Doctrine and Covenants 163:3a–b (2007).

513   Ibid., 163:4a.

514   Ibid., 163:4b.

non-members alike—worship with us in French than in English."[515] Community of Christ Apostle Susan Skoor spoke of the changes that have come to the church as it has taken the message of Christ to various parts of the world:

> Variety of belief and differences in culture increased as our church spread throughout the world. Today, we can truly say that we are a church of great diversity, unified by our affirmation of Jesus Christ and our desire to transform our communities into an expression of the reign of God, the cause of Zion that is so vital to our movement.[516]

Community of Christ is seeking to establish Zion; not the Zion perceived by Joseph Smith Jr., but the Zion that it believes Jesus came to proclaim: a kingdom of Zion communities, all living Zion principles. This Zion is "a holistic approach to every sector—health care, welfare, counseling, architecture, education, legislation, administration, family, sexuality, *ad infinitum.*"[517]

In 1986, one RLDS author stated it this way: "My understanding of Christian history with regard to apostasy is that the people who believed in Christ labored for so long under a heavy load of tradition, form, and ritual, that they could not experience abundant life." The Restoration, then, was not "to reinstate some ancient church organizational pattern, but God's movement to create a people who would seek new depths in realizing human potential."[518]

Community of Christ's view of Zion would be in harmony with a verse found in the Joseph Smith Translation of Genesis: "And the Lord called his people, Zion; because they were of one heart and one mind, and dwelt in righteousness; and there was no poor among them."[519]

---

515   Scherer, "Answering Questions No Longer Asked," 32.
516   Skoor, "Called by Your Name," in *Claimed by Christ's Vision*, ed. Andrew Shields, 16.
517   Jones, "Demythologizing and Symbolizing the RLDS Tradition," in *Restoration Studies V*, 111–12.
518   Worthington, "Crises in the RLDS Tradition: New Grasps of Essential/Instrumental Faith," in *Restoration Studies III*, 39.
519   Holy Scriptures: Inspired Version, Genesis 7:23.

LATTER-DAY SAINTS

According to LDS theology, Zion can be used to describe a place or land, a people, or the condition of a society. In the Doctrine and Covenants Zion is described as "the pure in heart."[520] For members of The Church of Jesus Christ of Latter-day Saints, "the Church and its stakes are called Zion because they are for gathering and purifying a people of God."[521]

Although the Mormons failed in their first attempt in the 1830s to establish the center place of Zion in Jackson County, Missouri, they still believe that this will eventually be the center stake of Zion. Through Joseph Smith the Lord revealed, "Zion shall be redeemed, although she is chastened for a little season."[522] In 1847 Brigham Young received the word of the Lord stating, "Zion shall be redeemed in my own due time."[523]

In the early years of the LDS Church, converts were encouraged to gather from all over the world to the environs near the seat of church government: Kirtland, Independence, Far West, Nauvoo, Salt Lake City. This type of gathering in a central location had much to do with temple building. Concerning the gathering of the people of God in any age of the world, Joseph Smith taught that "the main object was to build unto the Lord a house whereby He could reveal unto His people the ordinances of His house and the glories of His kingdom, and teach the people the way of salvation."[524]

Since the turn of the twentieth century, Church leaders have counseled members in countries outside of the United States "to remain and build up the Church in their own countries."[525] Initially, "the gathering was necessary to build a temple, and a temple was a prerequisite for the establishment of Zion."[526] With LDS temples being built all over the

---

[520]   LDS Doctrine and Covenants 97:21 (1833); Community of Christ Doctrine and Covenants 94:5c (1833).
[521]   Ludlow, ed. *Encyclopedia of Mormonism* 4:1624.
[522]   LDS Doctrine and Covenants 100:13 (1833); Community of Christ Doctrine and Covenants 97:4a (1833).
[523]   LDS Doctrine and Covenants 136:18 (1847).
[524]   Smith, *Teachings of the Prophet Joseph Smith*, 308.
[525]   Clark, ed. *Messages of the First Presidency*, 5:268.
[526]   Ludlow, ed. *Encyclopedia of Mormonism* 2:536–37.

world, the need to gather to a particular place at present is not necessary or desired.

For Latter-day Saints today, the building of Zion includes missionary work, raising righteous families, serving in the organizations of the church, and any other effort that will build and strengthen the kingdom of God anywhere in the world. Brigham Young's statements about Zion illustrate the broader LDS view of Zion: "Zion will extend, eventually, all over this earth."[527] "Where is Zion? Where the organization of the Church of God is."[528] "When we conclude to make a Zion we will make it, and this work commences in the heart of each person."[529]

SUMMARY

Community of Christ and The Church of Jesus Christ of Latter-day Saints believe in the concept of establishing and building Zion. Although Independence, Missouri, is the world headquarters of Community of Christ, it is far removed from the concept of that location being a gathering point. Instead, it views the temple in Independence as a place from which ministry flows instead of a place to gather.

The LDS Church still sees Independence, Missouri, as the center place of Zion. The LDS Church has a presence in Independence, Missouri, but not to the degree that Community of Christ does. In addition to Independence being its world headquarters, Community of Christ has built a temple in Independence, Missouri, as prophesied by Joseph Smith.

Both restoration churches are striving to expand their membership around the world, which is considered a method of building up Zion. Both view Zion as eventually covering the earth. For LDS Church members, there remains a more literal aspect of the fulfillment of prophecy concerning Zion. Despite the broader LDS view of Zion being anywhere the Saints of God dwell, the original concept expressed by Joseph Smith Jr. remains. LDS Church members "still look for an

---

527   *Discourses of Brigham Young*, 120.
528   Ibid., 118.
529   Ibid.

eventual temple and permanent headquarters to be built in Zion, a New Jerusalem in Missouri."[530]

---

530   Ludlow, ed. *Encyclopedia of Mormonism* 2:536.

FUTURE CHALLENGES OF COMMUNITY OF CHRIST

There are challenges that Community of Christ is facing at present and will likely have to deal with in the future. Following the revelation that permitted women to receive the priesthood, about one fourth of the active RLDS members ceased their involvement with the Reorganized Church. With decreased membership came a decrease in tithing funds, which has brought a financial challenge to Community of Christ.

Another current issue challenging Community of Christ is homosexuality. The RLDS Church began to address the issue of homosexuality in the 1990s. It was during those debates that "the church leadership began to recognize an organization of church members called GALA (Gay and Lesbian Acceptance), allowing the organization to have a booth and to sponsor special worship services at conference."[531] At present, the official policy of Community of Christ allows a homosexual to be a priesthood holder only if he or she is celibate. This will certainly be a topic of discussion at future conferences.

Another possible challenge could be how the rank-and–file membership of Community of Christ will relate to a leadership that is increasingly being trained in theological schools and Protestant seminaries. In recent years, the church has established its own seminary, but even with its own seminary, these questions likely remain: Will church

---

531   Russell, "The LDS Church and Community of Christ: Clearer Differences, Closer Friends," 188.

leaders become more progressive, more theologically mainstream, and less likely to believe in traditional Reorganized teachings? In the years to come, will the Book of Mormon and the Doctrine and Covenants lose their status as canonized scripture in Community of Christ?

Another challenge facing Community of Christ is its shifting focus to the international membership as it becomes a global church. Can the church maintain growth in areas outside of the United States? Can it provide central leadership from its world headquarters in Independence, Missouri, and still allow branch leadership to make decisions according to their unique circumstances? Can Community of Christ retain its global membership without developing schisms?

A concern at present is how Community of Christ as a church will handle the need for some kind of standards of conduct that are rigid enough for unity but flexible enough for a worldwide church. What is considered negotiable and what is central to the doctrine of the church? How will it be able to articulate and enforce standards that increase unity and not cause division? Speaking of these concerns, Andrew Shields wrote, "It is a question as old as the New Testament, and one we engage for our time."[532]

Community of Christ has become very involved with the ecumenical movement. Its acceptance by other Christians is challenged by its unusual origin and beliefs: Joseph Smith, the Book of Mormon, the early doctrine of restoration from the Great Apostasy, and other distinctive "Mormon" doctrines. A challenge for Community of Christ is to gain acceptance from other Christians.

The development of ecumenical relationships has been a concern for some of the more conservative Community of Christ members. However, church leaders see Community of Christ theology and experience bringing something unique and important to ecumenical and interfaith conversation. Community of Christ World Secretary Andrew Shields said "that we do not serve the ecumenical community well by simply conforming to them." He went on to say that "We do not frame the question as a decision between shedding distinctives to belong or walking our own path, but instead [it is] a question of how we can use

---

532   Personal communication with Andrew Shields, Community of Christ World Church Secretary.

our call and our testimony as we join with other faiths in making the world more just and more peaceful."[533]

The ecumenical movement will likely continue, with Community of Christ theology perhaps becoming more mainline Christian, with the hope that Protestantism will be more accepting of a church that began with Joseph Smith. Regarding the challenges faced in their ecumenical efforts, Stacy A. Evans wrote:

> The opportunity for the contribution of the church to the greater ecumenical enterprise of world Christianity has been limited. Much of the reason has been the prejudice that existed over many generations in response to the origins of the Restoration movement through the mind and ministry of Joseph Smith, Jr.[534]

If the church is successful ecumenically and becomes more accepted by other Christian religions, how will the more conservative or traditional members of the church cope with the possibility of losing the aspects of their faith that once made them unique: latter day prophets, modern scripture, and the traditional views of the Apostasy and Restoration? Will the progressive changes taking place in Community of Christ bring more dissention and schisms?

A particular challenge Community of Christ faces is one that it has taken upon itself. That is, to make a significant difference in the world through sharing as Christ would share—a noble and lofty goal. A recent Community of Christ publication contained this outlook on sharing:

> What we share with one another, as members and participants in Community of Christ shapes identity, mission, message, and beliefs as a worldwide faith community. Just as important, the phrase "we share" emphasizes our call and commitment to share our witness, ministries, sacraments, resources, and message with the world. So, the phrase "we share" defines both what we generally hold in common and what we generously offer to the world.[535]

---

533   Ibid.
534   Evans, "The Past Can Be Prologue: A Proposal for a Zionic Bridge to the Ecumenical Church," in *Restoration Studies IX*, 1.
535   *We Share*, 2.

What does the future hold for Community of Christ? It is safe to say that it will continue its efforts in countries around the world, involving international members, bringing together different cultures, languages, and perspectives in discerning the proper path for a global church.

In the years to come, it is probable that the leadership and members of Community of Christ will distance themselves even further from The Church of Jesus Christ of Latter-day Saints. For over a century they have spent a considerable amount of energy convincing people that they are not Utah Mormons. Now, there is more of an effort to define what they are, rather than what they are not.

"What of the future?" wrote Galen Worthington, "I believe that God is working through the RLDS community to lay the foundation for the creation of a whole new humanity—a people that will be free to have more abundant lives."[536]

---

536 Worthington, "Crises in the RLDS Tradition: New Grasps of Essential/Instrumental Faith," in Restoration Studies III, 39.

CONCLUSION

Joseph Smith Jr. organized the Church of Christ in April 1830. At the time of his death in 1844, it had become known as The Church of Jesus Christ of Latter-day Saints. Joseph's death caused confusion among church members who believed him to be a prophet of God but were unclear as to whom his replacement should be. Men vied for leadership and control of the church Joseph had begun. Many schisms resulted from the rifts caused by the struggle for power.

The two largest groups that came from the division among early church members were The Church of Jesus Christ of Latter-day Saints led by Brigham Young and the Quorum of the Twelve Apostles, and the Reorganized Church of Jesus Christ of Latter Day Saints, which was eventually directed by Joseph Smith III. These two churches shared a common origin, but in doctrinal matters the Community of Christ has moved purposefully away from The Church of Jesus Christ of Latter-day Saints within a very short time frame.

Each of the two churches saw itself as the continuation of the church begun by Joseph Smith. Each believed it held the legitimate authority of priesthood and that the other was an apostate organization. From the very beginning, there were unkind feelings and distrust between the two organizations.

The development of the RLDS Church was patterned after the earlier Mormon doctrines and organization Joseph Smith established during the time he led the Church in Kirtland, Ohio. The personality of the Reorganized Church was greatly influenced by Joseph Smith III, who was pragmatic, "open minded, slow to form opinions, logical with a sense of humor, able to see various sides of a question, but capable of coming to his own conclusions and holding to them."[537]

The LDS Church followed the teachings of Joseph Smith from the Kirtland era as well as from the Nauvoo era, including temple ordinances, plurality of gods, and plural marriage. The Mormons who went west were led by the strong-willed, determined, and capable leadership of Brigham Young. The LDS Church established a stronghold in the American West. The greater number of early Saints followed Brigham Young and the Twelve.

As the Mormon Church became infamous in the nation for polygamy, the Reorganized Church attempted to distance itself from the Utah church by informing the public that even though it traced its roots to Joseph Smith, it was in no way like the religion led by Brigham Young. Joseph Smith III was a strong advocate for the eradication of polygamy. His anti-polygamy position and his plan of sending missionaries to Utah to bring back the lost souls who had followed Brigham Young added further fuel to the fire of antagonism between the LDS and RLDS churches.

The LDS Church ended its practice of polygamy around the beginning of the twentieth century. Over the years that have followed, the LDS Church, although not considered a mainstream Christian church, has become more readily accepted as a people with strong values and moral ethics. It has experienced a high rate of growth in many countries of the world.

The RLDS Church, for the most part, has never been considered as unusual as the LDS Church to outsiders. From the mid-twentieth century, the RLDS Church adopted a much more mainstream Christian view of theology. Leaders and staff have received graduate degrees from Protestant theological seminaries. Some aspects of the church's early doctrine and history have been questioned and reevaluated by leaders and members alike.

---

537   Blair, A. R., "Reorganized Church of Jesus Christ of Latter Day Saints: Moderate Mormonism," in *The Restoration Movement: Essays in Mormon History*, 218.

The changes that have taken place in the Reorganized Church have caused some friction among the membership. Although there is a faction of RLDS and former RLDS members that clings to the traditional doctrines of the early church, they have found themselves out of step with Community of Christ leaders and the majority of the church's membership.[538] The number of Community of Christ members has decreased and break-off churches have emerged.

Still, Community of Christ moves ahead in its development toward the Christian mainstream. It no longer sees itself as the only true church, but as part of Christ's true church. It no longer believes that it is the only church with authority from God. Its focus is on Jesus Christ and His vision for humanity. It is not defined by its history, former beliefs, or the teachings of its founder. It continues to maintain that the canon is not closed, and that God communicates His will through the Spirit to those who are listening.

Community of Christ is very much aware that its theology is not "fixed." President Stephen M. Veazey said he is often asked, even by church members, "What does the church really believe anyway?" President Veazey has responded:

> While the temptation is to try to answer definitively once and for all, our faith story teaches us the importance of striking a balance between certainty regarding basic beliefs and humility in the realization that human words can never fully communicate the eternal purposes of God. To migrate to one extreme (rigid dogmatism) or the other (whatever feels right) poses serious problems and pitfalls. . . . The Community of Christ is a church that provides light for the way as well as space for the personal faith journey. This is in contrast to other expressions of Christianity that assert strict answers that bring comfort to some, but that are woefully inadequate for others.[539]

---

538   It has been fascinating to me to see what those on the fringe of each of the two restoration churches believe and why they are troubled by the current state of their church. It seems to me that some of those who are bothered by the conservative nature of the LDS Church and the lack of democracy in the church's decisions would find themselves very comfortable as members of Community of Christ. On the other hand, some of the traditionalists in Community of Christ who are irritated by the direction their church has taken might find far more shared beliefs in the LDS Church.

539   Veazey, "Up Front," *Herald* (August 2006): 5

The LDS Church holds to the traditional restoration concepts introduced by Joseph Smith. It continues to see itself as the one true church, believing it is the only church with God's authority. It views scripture as inspired writings recorded by prophets. It believes in eternal progression and the potential of God's children to become like God, and it continues to build temples where worthy members may perform sacred ordinances for the living and the dead.

Perhaps not in spite of their differences, but rather because the two churches have become so dissimilar in the last half century, there is a closer tie between the LDS Church and Community of Christ today than has ever existed in the past. There is really no competition in comparison any more. Their common origin and early history binds them together. Historians from the two churches share insights and discoveries, and there is a united desire to preserve historical sites and documents.

The general membership of Community of Christ and of The Church of Jesus Christ of Latter-day Saints needs to gain a greater understanding and appreciation for each other. Regardless of differing doctrines, both churches believe in God and that Jesus Christ is our Lord and Savior. Both religions seek to serve others, improve society, and make the world a better place. Given this common ground, working together for the common good of the world is always better than working alone.

APPENDIX A:
A STATEMENT OF BELIEF

[Taken from *Exploring the Faith: A Series of Studies in the Faith of the Church*, 10–15]

For many years the most widely circulated statement of the beliefs of the church was the Epitome of Faith.[540] The Epitome was originally written by Joseph Smith, Jr. in answer to a request by a Chicago newspaper editor. . . . In more recent times it has been recognized that a more adequate statement of the beliefs of the church should be developed. Historical and traditional points of view needed to be expanded in view of contemporary religious experience and scholarship. Recognizing that the understanding of religious experience is always qualified by the human nature of those involved, the church has traditionally avoided creedal statements and has sought to preserve the openness and humility of the admonition "by study and by faith." Over a period of nearly a decade a dedicated group of ministers has worked carefully and consistently to bring insights to this task. . . . Such a work is never finished because each generation brings its own unique insights and experience to the task.

—*First Presidency of Community of Christ, Foreword to* Exploring the Faith

PARAGRAPH ONE

We believe in God the eternal Father, source and center of all love and life and truth, who is almighty, infinite, and unchanging, in whom and through whom all things exist and have their being.

---

540   Known in the LDS Church as the Articles of Faith.

PARAGRAPH TWO

We believe in Jesus Christ, the Only Begotten Son of God, who is from everlasting to everlasting; through whom all things were made; who is God in the flesh, being incarnate by the Holy Spirit for man's salvation; who was crucified, died, and rose again; who is mediator between God and man, and the judge of both the living and the dead; whose dominion has no end.

PARAGRAPH THREE

We believe in the Holy Spirit, the living presence of the Father and the Son, who in power, intelligence, and love works in the minds and hearts of men to free them from sin, uniting them with God as his sons, and with each other as brethren. The Spirit bears record of the Father and of the Son, which Father, Son, and Holy Ghost, are one God.

PARAGRAPH FOUR

We believe that the Holy Spirit empowers men committed to Christ with gifts of worship and ministry. Such gifts, in their richness and diversity, are divided severally as God wills, edifying the body of Christ, empowering men to encounter victoriously the circumstances of their discipleship, and confirming the new creation into which men are called as sons of God.

PARAGRAPH FIVE

We believe that the Holy Spirit creates, quickens, and renews in men such graces as love, joy, peace, mercy, gentleness, meekness, forbearance, temperance, purity of heart, brotherly kindness, patience in tribulation, and faithfulness before God in seeking to build up his kingdom.

PARAGRAPH SIX

We believe that man is endowed with freedom and created to know God, to love and serve him, and to enjoy his fellowship. In following the dictates of pride and in declaring his independence from God, man loses the power to fulfill the purpose of his creation and becomes the servant of sin, whereby he is divided within himself and estranged from

God and his fellows. This condition, experienced by our ancestors who first came to a knowledge of good and evil, is shared by all who are granted the gift of accountability.

PARAGRAPH SEVEN

We believe that men cannot be saved in the Kingdom of God except by the grace of the Lord Jesus Christ, who loves us while we are yet in our sins, and who gave his life to reconcile us unto God. Through this atonement of the Lord Jesus Christ and by the gift of the Holy Spirit, men receive power to choose God and to commit their lives to him; thus are they turned from rebellion, healed from sin, renewed in spirit, and transformed after the image of God in righteousness and holiness.

PARAGRAPH EIGHT

We believe that all men are called to have faith in God and to follow Jesus Christ as Lord, worshiping the Father in his name. In this life those who hear the gospel and repent should commit their lives to Christ in baptism by immersion in water and by the laying on of hands. Through living by these principles they participate in God's promise of forgiveness, reconciliation, and eternal life.

PARAGRAPH NINE

We believe that the church was established by Jesus Christ. In its larger sense it encompasses those both living and dead, who, moved by the Spirit of God, acknowledge Jesus as Lord. In its corporate sense, it is the community of those who have covenanted with Christ. As the body of Christ through which the Word of God is tangibly expressed among men, the church seeks to discern the will of God and to surrender itself to him in worship and service. It is enlightened, sustained, and renewed by the Holy Spirit. It is to bring the good news of God's love to all people, reconciling them to God through faith in Jesus Christ. The church administers the ordinances through which the covenant is established, cares for all within its fellowship, ministers to the needy, wages war on evil, and strives for the kingdom of God.

PARAGRAPH TEN

We believe that all men are called to be stewards under God. They are accountable to him, in the measure of their perception of the divine purpose in creation and redemption, for managing all gifts and resources given into their care. In the exercise of stewardship, men embody the divine will and grow in spiritual maturity through developing native powers and skills achieving dominion over the physical order and perfecting human relationships in the Spirit of Christ.

PARAGRAPH ELEVEN

We believe that the kingdom of God sustains men as the stable and enduring reality of history, signifying the total Lordship of God over all human life and endeavor. The kingdom is always at hand in judgment and promise, confronting men with the joyful proclamation of God's rule and laying claim upon them as they acknowledge the new Creation in Christ. The full revelation of the kingdom awaits the final victory over evil, when the will of God shall prevail and his rule shall extend over all human relations to establish the dominion of peace, justice, and truth. To this end the church proclaims the gospel of the kingdom both as present reality and future hope in the midst of a faithless world.

PARAGRAPH TWELVE

We believe that Zion is the means by which the prophetic church participates in the world to embody the divine intent for all personal and social relations. Zion is the implementation of those principles, processes, and relationships which give concrete expression to the power of the kingdom of God in the world. It affirms the concern of the gospel with the structures of our common life together and promotes the expression of God's reconciling love in the world, thus is bringing forth the divine life in human society. The church is called to gather her covenant people into signal communities where they live out the will of God in the total life of society. While this concrete expression of the kingdom of God must have a central point of beginning it reaches out to every part of the world where the prophetic church is in mission.

PARAGRAPH THIRTEEN

We believe that all are called according to the gifts of God unto them to accept the commission and cost of discipleship. Some are chosen through the spirit of wisdom and revelation and ordained by those who are in authority in the church to serve in specialized ministries. These include ministry to persons, families, and community, as well as preaching, teaching, administering the ordinances, and directing the affairs of the church. The authority of every member of the body in his respective calling emerges out of divine endowment to him and his faithfulness in servanthood with Christ.

PARAGRAPH FOURTEEN

We believe that the ordinances witness the continuing life of Christ in the church, providing the experiences in which God and man meet in the sealing of covenant. In the ordinances God uses common things, even the nature of man, to express the transcendent and sacramental meaning of creation. God thereby provides the continuing means of investing his grace in human life for its renewal and redemption.

PARAGRAPH FIFTEEN

We believe that God reveals himself to man. He enters into the minds of men through the Holy Spirit to disclose himself to them and to open their understanding to the inner meaning of his revelation in history and in the physical order. Revelation centers in Jesus Christ, the incarnate word, who is the ultimate disclosure of truth and the standard by which all other claims to truth are measured.

PARAGRAPH SIXTEEN

We believe that the scriptures witness to God's redemptive action in history and to man's response to that action. When studied through the light of the Holy Spirit they illumine men's minds and hearts and empower them to understand in greater depth the revelation in Christ. Such disclosure is experienced in the hearts of men rather than in the words by which the revelation is interpreted and communicated. The scriptures are open because God's redemptive work is eternal, and our discernment of it is never complete.

PARAGRAPH SEVENTEEN

We believe in the resurrection. This principle encompasses the divine purpose to conserve and renew life. It guarantees that righteousness will prevail and that, by the power of God, men move from death into life. In resurrection God quickens and transforms the soul, i.e. the body and spirit, bringing man into fellowship with his Son.

PARAGRAPH EIGHTEEN

We believe in eternal judgment. It is the wisdom of God bringing the whole creation under divine judgment for good. This judgment is exercised through men as they are quickened by the Holy Spirit to comprehend the eternal implications of divine truth. Through the judgment of God the eternal destiny of men is determined according to divine wisdom and love and according to their response to God's call to them. The principle of eternal judgment acknowledges that Christ is the judge of all human aspiration and achievement and that he summons men to express the truth in decision until all things are reconciled under God.

PARAGRAPH NINETEEN

We believe that the inner meaning and end toward which all history moves is revealed in Christ. He is at work in the midst of history, reconciling all things unto God in order, beauty, and peace. This reconciliation brings to fulfillment the kingdom of God upon earth. Christ's presence guarantees the victory of righteousness and peace over the injustice, suffering, and sin of our world. The tension between our assurance that the victory has been won in Christ and our continuing experience in this world where God's sovereignty is largely hidden is resolved in the conviction that Christ will come again. The affirmation of his coming redeems us from futility and declares the seriousness of all life under the unfailing and ultimate sovereignty of God.

Appendix B:
Scripture in the
Community of Christ

[Taken from Community of Christ's *Church Administrator's Handbook,* 2005 ed., 83–84.]

We are pleased to present to the church the following paper titled "Scripture in the Community of Christ." This has been prepared by the Theology Task Force with input from the World Church Leadership Council. The statement is presented for reflection and study by the church, a process that could lead to further refinements as the result of our experience with it. This foundational set of affirmations provides the context for the church's continuing quest to become more knowledgeable about our three books of scripture. The focus is on how we understand scripture and its role in the life of the church. Study of and reflection on these affirmations will assist us all in our prayerful consideration and use of the scriptural witness. With this in mind, we have added some questions to aid in an exploration of these affirmations.

—The First Presidency (June 2003)

Scripture provides divine guidance and inspired insight for life when responsibly interpreted and faithfully applied. Scripture helps us believe in Jesus Christ. Its witness guides us to eternal life and enables us to grow spiritually, to transform our lives, and to participate actively in the life and ministry of the church.

    1. We declare that Jesus Christ—who lived, was crucified, was raised from the dead, and comes again—is the Living Word of God. It is to Christ that scripture points. It

is through Christ that we have life (John 5:39–40). It is Christ whom we must hear (Mark 9:7).

2. We find the Living Word in and through scripture. Scripture is the indispensable witness of the saving, transforming message that God has entrusted to the church. The church formed the canon of scripture so that it might always have a way to hear the good news, nurture its faith, measure its life, test its experience, and remember its identity.

3. Scripture is a library of books that speaks in many voices. These books were written in diverse times and places, and reflect the languages, cultures, and conditions under which they were written. God's revelation through scripture does not come to us apart from the humanity of the writers, but in and through that humanity. In the earthen vessels of scripture we have been given the treasure of divine love and grace (2 Corinthians 4:7).

4. Scripture's authority is derived from the model of Christ, who came to be a servant (Mark 10:45). Therefore, the authority of scripture is not the authority to oppress, control, or dominate. If Jesus came to serve, how much more should the books that point to him be treated as a servant of the saving purposes of God.

5. Scripture is vital and essential to the church, but not because it is inerrant (in the sense that every detail is historically or scientifically correct). Scripture makes no such claim for itself. Rather, generations of Christians have found scripture simply to be trustworthy in keeping them anchored in revelation, in promoting faith in Christ, and in nurturing the life of discipleship. For these purposes, scripture is unfailingly reliable (2 Timothy 3:16–17).

6. Faith, experience, tradition, and scholarship each have something to contribute to our understanding of scripture. In wrestling to hear and respond to the witness of scripture, the church must value the light that each of these sources may offer.

7. As the church tries to interpret scripture responsibly, it seeks the help of the Holy Spirit. Jesus promised that the Spirit would guide his disciples into new truth (John 16:12–15). By the Spirit, the ancient words of scripture can become revelatory; allowing us to grasp what may not have been seen or heard before.

8. Disciples are called to grow in their knowledge and understanding of the scriptures so that they may ever increase in love for God, neighbor, and self (Matthew 22:37–40; Mosiah 1:49), uphold the dignity and worth of all persons (Doctrine and Covenants 16:3c–d), and faithfully follow the Way of Jesus Christ.

9. With other Christians, we affirm the Bible as the foundational scripture for the church. In addition, the Community of Christ uses the Book of Mormon and the Doctrine and Covenants as scripture. We do not use these sacred writings to replace the witness of the Bible or improve upon it, but because they confirm its message that Jesus Christ is the Living Word of God (Preface of the Book of Mormon; Doctrine and Covenants 76:3g). We have heard Christ speak in all three books of scripture, and bear witness that he is "alive forever and ever" (Revelation 1:18).

10. For our time we shall seek to live and interpret the witness of scripture *by* the Spirit, *with* the community, *for the sake of* mission, *in the name of* the Prince of Peace.

—Theology Task Force (May 3, 2003)
With the concurrence of the World Church Leadership Council (May 12, 2003)

APPENDIX C:
CHURCH HISTORY PRINCIPLES

[Taken from President Stephen M. Veazey, "Perspectives on Church History," *Herald* (October 2008): 10–12.]

As the First Presidency has joined with others in exploring issues emerging from the ongoing study of Restoration history, we decided it would be timely to provide a set of "Church History Principles" to help guide the church's reflections and discussions. These principles have been distilled from the insights of past and present World Church leaders, church historians, theologians, and others. We hope the statements will prove useful as the church continues to explore the personalities, events, and meanings of our church's colorful, inspiring story.

1. **Continuing exploration of our history is part of identity formation.**

    As a church we seek always to clarify our identity, message, and mission. In our faith story, we see clearly God's Spirit giving this faith community tools, insights, and experiences for divine purposes. A people with a shared memory of their past, and an informed understanding of its meaning, are better prepared to chart their way into the future.

2. **History informs but does not dictate our faith and beliefs.**

   The foundation and continuing source of our faith is God's revelation is Jesus Christ. Studying history is not about proving or disproving mystical, spiritual, or revelatory experiences that birth or transform religious movements. Sound history informs faith, and healthy faith leads to insights about history. Theology and faith, guided by the Holy Spirit, must play an important role in discovering the enduring meaning of such events as well as the deeper truths found in them. Our understanding of our history affects our faith and beliefs. However, our past does not limit our faith and beliefs to what they were historically.

3. **The church encourages honest, responsible historical scholarship.**

   Studying history involves related fields. Historians use academic research to get as many facts as they can; then, they interpret those facts to construct as clear a picture as possible of what was going on in the past. This includes analyzing human culture to see how it affected events. Historians try to understand patterns of meaning to interpret what the past means for our future. This process should avoid "presentism," or interpreting the past based on a current worldview and culture instead of the culture of the time.

4. **The study of church history is a continuing journey.**

   If we say that a book on history is the only true telling of the story, we risk "canonizing" one version, a tendency we have shown in the past. This blocks further insights from continuing research. Good historical inquiry understands that conclusions are open to correction as new understanding and information comes from ongoing study.

5. **Seeing both the faithfulness and human flaws in our history makes it more believable and realistic, not less.**

    Our history has stories of great faith and courage that inspire us. Our history also includes human leaders who said and did things that can be shocking to us from our current perspective and culture. Historians try not to judge—instead, they try to understand by learning as much as possible about the context and the meaning of those words and actions at the time. The result is empathy instead of judgment. Our scriptures are consistent in pointing out that God, through grace, uses imperfect people for needed ministry and leadership.

6. **The responsible study of church history involves learning, repentance, and transformation.**

    A church with a mission focused on promoting communities of reconciliation, justice, and peace should be self-critical and honest about its history. It is important for us to confess when we have been less than what the gospel of Jesus Christ calls us to be. This honesty prompts us to repent, and it strengthens our integrity. Admitting past mistakes helps us avoid repeating them and frees us from the influences of past injustices and violence in our history. We must be humble and willing to repent, individually and as a community, to contribute as fully as possible to restoring God's shalom on earth.

7. **The church has a long-standing tradition that it does not legislate or mandate positions on matters of church history.**

    Historians should be free to draw their own conclusions after thorough consideration of evidence. Through careful study and the Holy Spirit's guidance, the church is learning how to accept and responsibly interpret all of its history. This includes putting new information and changing understandings into proper perspective, while emphasizing the parts of our history that continue to play a role in guiding the church's identity and mission today.

8. **We need to create a respectful culture of dialogue about matters of history.**

   We should not limit our faith story to one perspective. Diverse viewpoints bring richness to our understanding of God's movement in our sacred story. Of course, historians will come to different conclusions as they study. Therefore, it is important for us to create and maintain a respectful culture that allows different points of view on history. Our conversation about history should be polite and focused on trying to understand others' views. Most important, we should remain focused on what matters most for the message and mission of the church in this time.

9. **Our faith is grounded in God's revelation in Jesus Christ and the continuing guidance of the Holy Spirit.**

   We must keep our hearts and minds centered on God's revelation in Jesus Christ. As God's Word alive in human history, Jesus Christ was and is the foundation of our faith and the focus of the church's mission and message.

APPENDIX D:
EXCERPTS FROM WE SHARE: IDENTITY, MISSION, MESSAGE, AND BELIEFS

[Excerpts from *We Share: Identity, Mission, Message, and Beliefs* published by Community of Christ in 2008]

This document provides important information about the identity, mission, message, and beliefs of Community of Christ. The Expanded World Church Leadership Council, cultural interpreters, various World Church teams, the 2008 World Church Leaders Gathering, and other individuals contributed to its contents.

The phrase "we share" is used in headings throughout this document. This phrase has two important meanings:

1. What we share with one another, as members and participants in Community of Christ shapes identity, mission, message, and beliefs as a worldwide faith community.
2. Just as important, the phrase "we share" emphasizes our call and commitment to share our witness, ministries, sacraments, resources, and message with the world.

So, the phrase "we share" defines both what we generally hold in common and what we generously offer to the world.

WE SHARE A VISION OF CREATION

The vision we share is God's vision of reconciliation, salvation, wholeness, justice, and peace expressed in the scriptural definition of shalom. Shalom means a fullness or completeness of peace. God yearns to establish a lasting covenant of peace with humankind and with all of creation.

God's vision of peace for creation clearly was revealed in the life, death, and resurrection of Jesus Christ, who proclaimed the coming kingdom or peaceful reign of God on earth. The gospel or "good news" was then entrusted to the church—the community of disciples called to be the body of Christ. The purpose of the church is to form disciples who faithfully share the gospel of peace in Christ through the power of the Holy Spirit.

COMMUNITY OF CHRIST PEACE SEAL
Courtesy Community of Christ Archives,
Independence, Missouri

The Christian cross and the church seal symbolize and emphasize our commitment to God's vision of justice and peace for the entire creation. This vision was proclaimed consistently by the prophets and decisively revealed in Jesus Christ, who calls disciples in every age to share his peace throughout the world.

WE SHARE A NAME

We are Community of Christ! We share a common name throughout the world that is translated into many languages. Our name is faithful to our heritage and true to our identity and calling today.

"Community of Christ," your name, given as a divine blessing, is your identity and calling.

—Doctrine and Covenants 163:1

WE SHARE A FUTURE

We also are continuing to become "Community of Christ!" Our future is full of possibility, necessary challenges, and hope as we continue to respond to the guidance of God, who has led the church from its beginning.

"Community of Christ," your name, given as a divine blessing, is your identity and calling. If you will discern and embrace its full meaning, you will not only discover your future, you will become a blessing to the whole creation. Do not be afraid to go where it beckons you to go.

—Doctrine and Covenants 163:1

WE SHARE THE PEACE OF JESUS CHRIST

Early in its history, the church, often referred to as the restoration movement, perceived the call to share the fullness of the gospel throughout the world (Doctrine and Covenants 1:4) and to "seek to bring forth and establish the cause of Zion" (Doctrine and Covenants 6:3). Today, we understand this as the call to share the peace of Jesus Christ in all of its personal, interpersonal, community, and worldwide dimensions.

Sharing the peace of Jesus Christ involves generously and compassionately offering witness, ministry, sacraments, and community life that reconciles and restores people to right or righteous relationships with God, themselves, others, and creation. This wholistic approach to proclaiming and demonstrating the gospel is faithful to our best understanding of God's will. This approach is the fullest meaning of "restoration."

WE SHARE A MISSION

How do we share the peace of Jesus Christ in all of its personal, interpersonal, and worldwide dimensions? The church's mission statement points the way.

We Proclaim Jesus Christ and Promote Communities of Joy, Hope, Love, and Peace.

—World Church Mission Statement

WE PROCLAIM JESUS CHRIST!

We proclaim Jesus Christ through local and worldwide evangelism, including ministries of invitation, witness, inclusive fellowship, worship, caring, and lifelong disciple formation.

WE PROMOTE COMMUNITIES!

We promote local and worldwide communities that signal (exemplify, reveal) the peaceful reign of God on earth. In some areas of the world this is known as the cause or hope of Zion.

When we effectively proclaim Jesus Christ by sharing our witness, ministries, and sacraments, and promote Christ-centered communities of justice and peacefulness, we are sharing the peace of Jesus Christ.

And blessed are they who shall seek to bring forth my Zion at that day, for they shall have the gift and the power of the Holy Ghost;

—1 Nephi 3:187

WE SHARE A SACRED STORY

Do not fail to listen attentively to the telling of the sacred story, for the story of scripture and faith empowers and illuminates.

—Doctrine and Covenants 161:5

The story of Community of Christ is part of a much larger sacred story that is rooted in Christian history, including the Hebrew tradition from which Christianity emerged. Within this larger history, Community of Christ has a particular story that is inspiring, colorful, and increasingly international. The church began in the early 1800s in upper New York, USA, during a time of Christian revival. So far, the church has established a presence in close to fifty nations.

The story of the church is one of unusual faith, vision, and creativity in response to God's call. We can clearly see God's Spirit active in every chapter of our faith story. What began with a teenager seeking God in prayer in the early 1800s continues today. God gives each generation insights, experiences, and challenges for divine purposes.

WE SHARE SACRAMENTS

Look especially to the sacraments to enrich the spiritual life of the body.

— Doctrine and Covenants 158:11c

Generously share the invitation, ministries, and sacraments through which people can encounter the Living Christ who heals and reconciles through redemptive relationships in sacred community.

—Doctrine and Covenants 163:2b

The church throughout the world celebrates sacraments. These special ministries use common symbols and familiar procedures to draw us into relationship with God, who seeks to establish covenant with us. The sacraments embody God's grace and peace and lead to transformation of our lives and communities. The sacraments shape our identity and community life as followers of Jesus Christ. As we experience the blessings available through sacraments, we are empowered to share the peace of Jesus Christ and to fulfill our mission in the world.

WE SHARE ENDURING PRINCIPLES

The Foundation: God, Christ, Holy Spirit

God's revelation in Jesus Christ and continuing presence through the Holy Spirit, as proclaimed by scripture, is the foundation of our faith, identity, mission, message, and beliefs.

In faithful response to our heritage and continuing experience with God, Christ, and the Holy Spirit, we endeavor to uphold the following enduring principles (values, concepts, themes) as essential components of church identity and mission.

Enduring principles define the essence, heart, or soul of church identity, mission, and message. They describe the personality of the church as expressed through its participants, congregations, and affiliate organizations throughout the world.

Some call enduring principles "core values." Others call them "foundational concepts." Use whatever terms make the most sense in the setting where you are writing, sharing, teaching, or preaching. For general official purposes, the World Church will use the term "Enduring Principles."

ENDURING PRINCIPLES

- Grace and Generosity
- Sacredness of Creation
- Continuing Revelation
- Worth of All Persons
- All Are Called
- Responsible Choices
- Pursuit of Peace (Shalom)
- Unity in Diversity
- Blessings of Community

Each principle follows with statements that help explain its meaning. Each set of statements ends with "we" statements that emphasize calling and desired response. The statements following each principle are not meant to be limiting or comprehensive. They are provided as helps. Use phrases, illustrations, stories, testimonies, scripture passages, and additional points to provide clarity and understanding for those with whom you are sharing.

GRACE AND GENEROSITY

- God's grace, especially as revealed in Jesus Christ, is generous and unconditional.
- Having received God's generous grace, we respond generously and graciously receive the generosity of others.
- We offer all we are and have to God's purposes as revealed in Jesus Christ.
- We generously share our witness, resources, ministries, and sacraments according to our true capacity.

SACREDNESS OF CREATION

- In the beginning, God created and called it all good.
- Spirit and material, seen and unseen, are related.

- Creation's power to create or destroy reminds us of our vulnerability in this life.
- God is still creating to fulfill divine purpose.
- We join with God as stewards of care and hope for all creation.

CONTINUING REVELATION

- Scripture is an inspired and indispensable witness of human response to God's revelation of divine nature.
- God graciously reveals divine will today as in the past.
- The Holy Spirit inspires and provides witness to divine truth.
- In humility, individually and in community, we prayerfully listen to understand God's will for our lives, the church, and creation more completely.

WORTH OF ALL PERSONS

- God views all people as having inestimable and equal worth.
- God wants all people to experience wholeness of body, mind, spirit, and relationships.
- We seek to uphold and restore the worth of all people individually and in community, challenging unjust systems that diminish human worth.
- We join with Jesus Christ in bringing good news to the poor, sick, captive, and oppressed.

ALL ARE CALLED

- God graciously gives people gifts and opportunities to do good and to share in God's purposes.
- Jesus Christ invites people to follow him by becoming disciples who share his life and ministry.
- Some disciples are called and ordained to particular priesthood responsibilities and ministries for the sake of the community, the congregation, and the world.

- We respond faithfully, with the help of the Holy Spirit, to our best understanding of God's call.

RESPONSIBLE CHOICES

- God gives humans the ability to make choices about whom or what they will serve. Some people experience conditions that diminish their ability to make choices.
- Human choices contribute to good or evil in our lives and in the world.
- Many aspects of creation need redemption because of irresponsible and sinful human choices.
- We are called to make responsible choices within the circumstances of our lives that contribute to the purposes of God.

PURSUIT OF PEACE (SHALOM)

- God wants shalom (justice, reconciliation, well-being, wholeness, and peace) for all of creation.
- Jesus Christ, the embodiment of God's shalom (peace), reveals the meaning of God's peace in all aspects of life.
- The vision of Zion is to promote God's reign on earth, as proclaimed by Jesus Christ, through the leavening influence of just and peaceful communities.
- We courageously and generously share the peace of Jesus Christ with others.
- Led by the Holy Spirit, we work with God and others to restore peace (shalom) to creation.
- We celebrate God's peace wherever it appears or is being pursued by people of good will.

UNITY IN DIVERSITY

- The Community of Christ is a diverse, international family of disciples, seekers, and congregations.
- Local and worldwide ministries are interdependent and important to the church's mission.
- The church embraces diversity and unity through the power of the Holy Spirit.

- We seek agreement or common consent in important matters. If we cannot achieve agreement, we commit to ongoing dialogue and lovingly uphold our common faith in Jesus Christ and the mission of the church.
- We confess that our lack of agreement on certain matters is hurtful to some of God's beloved children and creation.

BLESSINGS OF COMMUNITY

- The gospel of Jesus Christ is expressed best in community life where people become vulnerable to God's grace and each other.
- True community includes compassion for and solidarity with the poor, marginalized, and oppressed.
- True community upholds the worth of persons while providing a healthy alternative to self-centeredness, isolation, and conformity.
- Sacred community provides nurture and growth opportunities for all people, especially those who cannot fully care for themselves.
- We value our connections and share a strong sense of trust in and belonging with one another—even if we never have met.
- Some disciples are called and ordained to particular priesthood responsibilities and ministries for the sake of the community, the congregation, and the world.
- We are called to create communities of Christ's peace in our families and congregations and across villages, tribes, nations, and throughout creation.

WE SHARE THE TEMPLE AS LIFE-GIVING SYMBOL

And, it (the Temple) shall be a place in which the essential meaning of the Restoration as healing and redeeming agent is given new life and understanding, inspired by the life and witness of the Redeemer of the world.

—Doctrine and Covenants 156:5e

Let it (the Temple) stand as a towering symbol of a people who knew injustice and strife on the frontier and who now seek the peace of Jesus Christ throughout the world.

—Doctrine and Covenants 161:2b

Become a people of the Temple—those who see violence but proclaim peace, who feel conflict yet extend the hand of reconciliation, who encounter broken spirits and find pathways for healing.

—Doctrine and Covenants 161:2a

. . . the Temple calls the entire church to become a sanctuary of Christ's peace, where people from all nations, ethnicities, and life circumstances can be gathered into a spiritual home without dividing walls, as a fulfillment of the vision for which Jesus Christ sacrificed his life.

—Doctrine and Covenants 163:8c.

The spiraling, Christ-centered symbolism of the Temple and its defined purposes reveal the essence of God's presence with us. These images and concepts serve to focus the church on its true identity, message, and mission. As we become a people of the Temple, we will be led to embrace what "matters most" in the life of the church. In fact, without the ongoing influence of the Temple, we would not be as focused as we are on:

- The need to approach the Divine in awe and wonder in an increasingly skeptical age.
- God's vision of peace for creation.
- The interconnectedness of the physical and spiritual dimensions of the universe.
- Peace, reconciliation, and healing of the spirit as the essence of Jesus Christ's ministry.
- Wholeness of body, mind, and spirit as a desirable condition for all.
- The essential meaning of the restoration as healing and redeeming agent.
- The disciple's lifelong inner and outer journey as depicted by the Temple's symbolism.

- The church's call to "pursue peace" and be "a sanctuary of Christ's peace" throughout the world.
- The call to engage in ecumenical and interfaith relationships because the Temple is a house of prayer for all faiths.

The Temple Strategy Team has defined the focus of the Temple as:

RESTORING GOD'S SHALOM: INDIVIDUAL AND COMMUNITY JOURNEY OF TRANSFORMATION.

The idea and language of "shalom" best capture a holistic and scripturally sound basis for ministries consistent with the symbol and stated purposes of the Temple.

We uphold the purpose of restoring God's shalom by integrating the disciplines of worship, formation, and praxis to bring about transformation.

WORSHIP

Loving and adoring the God of Peace

— Isaiah 55:12

Let the Temple continue to come to life as a sacred center of worship, education, community building, and discipleship preparation for all ages.

—Doctrine and Covenants 163:8b

FORMATION

Guiding our feet into the way of Peace

— Luke 1:79

God is calling for a prophetic community to emerge, drawn from the nations of the world, that is characterized by uncommon devotion to the compassion and peace of God revealed in Jesus Christ.

— Doctrine and Covenants 163:11a

PRAXIS

(A recurring process of transformative action and reflection.)
Seeking and pursuing Peace

—Psalm 34:14

Transformative encounters with the Eternal Creator and Reconciler await those who follow its (Temple) spiritual pathways of healing, reconciliation, peace, strengthening of faith, and knowledge.

—Doctrine and Covenants 163:8a

WE SHARE BASIC BELIEFS

BASIC BELIEFS OF COMMUNITY OF CHRIST

PREFACE

The Good News of Jesus Christ is at the center of the faith and beliefs of Community of Christ. We are a worldwide community and are committed to follow Jesus, bring forth the kingdom of God, and seek together the revealing, renewing presence of the Holy Spirit. We offer here our basic beliefs, not as the last word, but as an open invitation to all to embark on the adventure of discipleship. As we seek God's continuing guidance, we encourage all people to study the scriptures and think about their experiences as they engage in the life of the church.

GOD

We believe in one living God who meets us in the testimony of Israel, is revealed in Jesus Christ, and moves through all creation as the Holy Spirit. We affirm the Trinity—God who is a community of three persons. All things that exist owe their being to God: mystery beyond understanding and love beyond imagination. This God alone is worthy of our worship.

JESUS CHRIST

We believe in Jesus Christ, the Son of the living God, the Word made flesh, the Savior of the world, fully human and fully divine. Through Jesus' life and ministry, death and resurrection, God reconciles the world and breaks down the walls that divide. Christ is our peace.

THE HOLY SPIRIT

We believe in the Holy Spirit, Giver of Life, holy Wisdom, true God. The Spirit moves through and sustains creation; endows the church for mission; frees the world from sin, injustice, and death; and transforms disciples. Wherever we find love, joy, peace, patience, kindness, generosity, faithfulness, gentleness, or self-control, there the Holy Spirit is working.

CREATION

As an expression of Divine love, God created the heavens and the earth and all that is in them, and called them "good." Everything belongs to God and should be cherished and used justly according to divine purposes. God sees creation as a whole without separation of spirit and element. God calls people of every generation to join with God as stewards in the loving care of creation.

HUMANITY

Every human being is created in the image of God. In Jesus Christ, God took on the limits of human flesh and culture, and is known through them. We therefore affirm without exception the worth of every human being. We also affirm that God has blessed humankind with the gift of agency: the ability to choose whom or what we will serve within the circumstances of our lives.

SIN

God created us to be agents of love and goodness. Yet we misuse our agency individually and collectively. We take the gifts of creation and of self and turn them against God's purposes with tragic results. Sin is the universal condition of separation and alienation from God and one another. We are in need of divine grace that alone reconciles us with God and one another.

SALVATION

The gospel is the good news of salvation through Jesus Christ: forgiveness of sin, and healing from separation, brokenness, and the power of violence and death. This healing is for individuals, human societies, and all of creation. This new life is the loving gift of God's grace that becomes ours through faith and repentance. Baptism is how we initially express our commitment to lifelong discipleship. As we yield our lives to Christ in baptism we enter Christian community (the body of Christ) and have the promise of salvation. We experience salvation through Jesus Christ, but affirm that God's grace has no bounds, and God's love is greater than we can know.

THE CHURCH

God intends Christian faith to be lived in companionship with Jesus Christ and with other disciples in service to the world. The church of Jesus Christ is made of all those who respond to Jesus' call. Community of Christ is part of the whole body of Christ. We are called to be a prophetic people, proclaiming the peace of Jesus Christ and creating communities where all will be welcomed and brought into renewed relationship with God, and where there will be no poor.

REVELATION

We affirm the Living God is ever self-revealing. God is revealed to the world in the testimony of Israel, and above all in Jesus Christ. By the Holy Spirit we continue to hear God speaking today. The church is called to listen together for what the Spirit is saying and then faithfully respond.

SCRIPTURE

Scripture is writing inspired by God's Spirit and accepted by the church as the normative expression of its identity, message, and mission. We affirm the Bible as the foundational scripture for the church. In addition, Community of Christ uses the Book of Mormon and the Doctrine and Covenants—not to replace the witness of the Bible or improve on it, but because they confirm its message that Jesus Christ is the Living Word of God. When responsibly interpreted and faithfully applied, scripture provides divine guidance and inspired insight for our discipleship.

SACRAMENTS

Sacraments are special ministries given to the church to convey the grace of Jesus Christ to his followers and all those he yearns to touch with his compassion. Sacraments are baptism, confirmation, the Lord's Supper, marriage, blessing of children, laying on of hands for the sick, ordination to the priesthood, and the evangelist's blessing. In these ministries, God sanctifies common elements of creation to bless human life and to renew and form the church to seek the peaceful kingdom of God.

DISCIPLESHIP

Being a Christian is more than holding a list of right ideas; it is about radical obedience to Jesus in every part of life. God's boundless love sets us free for lives of responsible stewardship in which we generously offer our lives in service to God's reign. Discipleship is both an inward and outward journey. Jesus calls us to follow him and to invite others to experience the transforming power of his grace.

MINISTRY

Ministry is humble service offered according to the model of Jesus, who calls every disciple to share in ministry for the world. Some disciples are called by God and ordained to priesthood offices to serve the mission of the church in specialized ways. The Holy Spirit gives complementary gifts and abilities to all disciples to equip the body of Christ for its witness in the world.

THE REIGN OF GOD

The Reign of God is the coming triumph of love, justice, mercy and peace that one day will embrace all of creation. Jesus' life and ministry were the living expression of this promise. He taught his disciples to pray for the kingdom's full coming and sent them out into the world to be living emblems of that new creation. "Zion" expresses our commitment to herald God's peaceable kingdom on earth by forming Christ-centered communities in families, congregations, neighborhoods, cities, and throughout the world.

PEACE

Peace is God's shalom: justice, righteousness, wholeness, and the well-being of the entire creation. Jesus, the Prince of Peace, came to preach the kingdom and to be our peace through the cross. The Holy Spirit empowers us for the costly pursuit of peace and justice for all people.

RESURRECTION AND ETERNAL LIFE

Christ is risen! Thus we believe that God is God of life, not of death. By faith we share in eternal life even now. In Christ, God's love finally will overcome all that demeans and degrades the creation, even death itself. Easter also gives us hope that the tragic suffering and death of victims, throughout history, is not the last word. We believe the Holy Spirit will transform all creation to share in the glory of God.

JUDGMENT

The living God whom we serve is a God of justice and mercy. God cares about how we treat our neighbors and enemies and how we make use of creation's gifts. It matters supremely to God how we welcome the poor, the stranger, the sick, the imprisoned, and the rejected. We affirm in Scripture's light that Jesus Christ is advocate and judge of the living and the dead.

END TIME

We press forward together in service to God, knowing that our labor is not in vain. The future of the creation belongs to the Prince of Peace, not to those who oppress, dominate, or destroy. As we anticipate that future, we devote ourselves to seek Christ's peace and pursue it. We do not know the day or hour of Christ's coming but know only that God is faithful. With faith in God, Christ, and the Holy Spirit, we face the future in hopeful longing, and with the prayer that Jesus taught us to pray: "Thy kingdom come! Thy will be done, on earth as it is in heaven."

ENDURING PRINCIPLES AND BASIC BELIEFS

What is the relationship between enduring principles and basic beliefs?

When people try to understand the church's identity, mission, and message, they bring different ways of perceiving reality, which leads to different questions.

What is the church like? Enduring principles are the underlying truths and affirmations that shape the personality of the church. Enduring principles guide how we live in our communities, families, workplaces, congregations, and cultures. They describe how we experience and share the gospel and the church with others.

What does the church believe? Basic beliefs are the more comprehensive, rational explanations of what the church holds to be true, arranged in categories that are part of the broader Christian tradition. Basic beliefs represent a deepening level of inquiry about the gospel and the church.

We need both ways of expressing the identity, mission, and message of the church, along with the others described in this document, to ensure that people can explore and experience the gospel in ways that are the most informing and transforming for them.

BIBLIOGRAPHY

Alder, Douglas D. and Paul M. Edwards. "Common Beginnings, Divergent Beliefs." *Dialogue* (Spring 1978): 1829.

Alexander, Thomas G. and Jessie L. Embry, eds. *After 150 Years: The Latter-Day Saints in Sesquicentennial Perspective.* Provo, Utah: Charles Redd Center for Western Studies, 1983.

Allen, James B. "I Have a Question." *Ensign* (March 1978): 23.

"An Extract of Revelation." *Elders' Journal* 1 (August 1838): 52–53.

Anderson, Mary Audentia Smith, ed. *Joseph Smith III and the Restoration.* Independence, Missouri: Herald Publishing House, 1952.

Ballard, M. Russell. "Faith, Family, Facts, and Fruits." *Ensign* (November 2007): 25–27.

Barrett, Ivan J. *Joseph Smith and the Restoration.* Provo, Utah: Brigham Young University Press, 1973.

Benson, Ezra Taft. "A Sacred Responsibility." *Ensign* (May 1986): 77–78.

_____. "Godly Characteristics of the Master." *Ensign* (November 1986): 45–48.

_____. "The Book of Mormon and the Doctrine and Covenants." *Ensign* (May 1987): 83–85.

Black, Susan Easton. "Joseph Smith III and the 'Lost Sheep.'" In *Regional Studies in Latter-day Saint Church History: Illinois*, edited by H. Dean Garrett. Provo, Utah: Department of Church History and Doctrine, Brigham Young University, 1995: 55–75.

Black, Susan Easton and Harvey Bischoff Black. *Annotated Record of Baptisms for the Dead 1840–1845, Nauvoo, Hancock County, Illinois.* 7 vols. Provo, Utah: Brigham Young University Press, 2002.

Boegle, Jimmy. "Mormons Divided: The Emergence of Two Mormon Churches Following the Death of Joseph Smith." Unpublished senior honors thesis. Stanford University, May 1997.

Book of Mormon. Community of Christ revised authorized edition. Independence, Missouri: Herald Publishing House, 2002; LDS edition. Salt Lake City: The Church of Jesus Christ of Latter-day Saints, 1981.

Booth, Howard J. "Changing Concepts of Priesthood Authority." In *Restoration Studies VI*, edited by Paul M. Edwards, Wayne Ham, and Joni Wilson. Independence, Missouri: Herald Publishing House, 1995: 101–5.

_____. "Recent Shifts in Restoration Thought." In *Restoration Studies I,* edited by Maurice L. Draper and Clare D. Vlahos. Independence, Missouri: Herald Publishing House, 1980: 162–75.

_____. "Shifts in Restoration Thought." *Dialogue* (Fall 1980): 79–92.

Bouissou, Jean-Christophe. "Evolution of Institutional Purpose in The Restoration Movement." In *Restoration Studies VI*, edited by Paul M. Edwards, Wayne Ham, and Joni Wilson. Independence, Missouri: Herald Publishing House, 1995: 115–25.

Breckon, Donald J. "The Issue of Homosexuality and the Priesthood Reexamined." In *Restoration Studies V*, edited by Paul M. Edwards and Darlene Caswell. Independence, Missouri: Herald Publishing House, 1993: 139–44.

Bringhurst, Newell G. and John C. Hamer, eds. *Scattering of the Saints: Schism within Mormonism.* Independence, Missouri: John Whitmer Books, 2007.

Brock, David R. "The Evangelist's Blessing." *Herald* (July 2007): 20–21.

Charlesworth, James H., ed. *The Old Testament Psuedepigrapha.* 2 vols. New York: Doubleday and Company, 1983.

Church Educational System Administrators' Council. "Succession in the Presidency." Revised version. January 29, 2008.

Church Handbook of Instructions. Book 1. Salt Lake City: The Church of Jesus Christ of Latter-day Saints, 2006: 32.

Chvala-Smith, Anthony. "A Trinitarian Approach to World Religions." In *Restoration Studies VIII,* edited by Joni Wilson. Independence, Missouri: Herald Publishing House, 2000: 128–32.

_____. "Administration: Sacrament of Healing Grace." *Herald* (February 2007): 18–19.

Clark, James R., comp. *Messages of the First Presidency.* 6 vols. Salt Lake City: Deseret Book, 1965–1975.

Community of Christ. *Church Administrator's Handbook,* 2005 ed. Independence, Missouri: Herald Publishing House, 2005.

Community of Christ. *The Priesthood Manual,* 2004 ed. Independence, Missouri: Herald Publishing House, 2004.

Compier, Don H. "Canonization in the Reorganized Church of Jesus Christ of Latter Day Saints." In *Restoration Studies III,* edited by Maurice L. Draper and Debra Combs. Independence, Missouri: Herald Publishing House, 1986: 178–83.

Conrad, Larry. "Scripture in the Reorganization: Exegesis, Authority, and the 'Prophetic Mantle.'" *Dialogue* (Summer 1991): 65–80.

Conrad, Larry and Paul Shupe. "An RLDS Reformation? Construing the Task of RLDS Theology." *Dialogue* (Summer 1985): 92–103.

Cramm, Stassi. "Call of Bishop: An Expression of High Priest Ministry." *PA 231, Bishops: Ministers of Generosity,* compiled by the Presiding Bishopric. Community of Christ, 2006: 21–23.

_____. "The 150-Year Journey of Rejection of Baptism for the Dead." In *Restoration Studies IX,* edited by Joni Wilson. Independence, Missouri: Herald Publishing House, 2005: 87–93.

Dahl, Larry E. and Donald Q. Cannon. *Teachings of Joseph Smith.* Salt Lake City: Bookcraft, 1977. (Now published as *Encyclopedia of Joseph Smith's Teachings*).

Davis, Inez Smith. *The Story of the Church.* Independence, Missouri: Herald Publishing House, 1977.

Davis, Paul, Ken Robinson, David Schaal, Jim Slauter, and Stephen M. Veazey. *Share Christ's Peace: Going Deeper.* Independence, Missouri: Herald Publishing House, 2006.

Doctrine and Covenants. Community of Christ edition. Independence, Missouri: Herald Publishing House, 2004; LDS edition. Salt Lake City: The Church of Jesus Christ of Latter-day Saints, 1981.

Edwards, Paul M. "Being Mormon: An RLDS Response." *Dialogue* (Spring 1984): 106–11.

_____. *Our Legacy of Faith: A Brief History of the Reorganized Church of Jesus Christ of Latter Day Saints.* Independence, Missouri: Herald Publishing House, 1991.

_____. "Persistences That Differ: Comments on the Doctrine of Man." *Sunstone* (September–October 1980): 43–50.

_____. *Preface to Faith: A Philosophical Inquiry Into RLDS Beliefs.* Midvale, Utah: Signature Books, 1984.

Ehat, Andrew F. "Joseph Smith's Introduction of Temple Ordinances and the 1844 Mormon Succession Question." Unpublished thesis. Provo, Utah: Brigham Young University, 1982.

Evans, Stacy A. "The Past Can Be Prologue: A Proposal for a Zionic Bridge to the Ecumenical Church." In *Restoration Studies IX*, edited by Joni Wilson. Independence, Missouri: Herald Publishing House, 2005: 1.

Exploring the Faith: A Series of Studies in the Faith of the Church. Basic Beliefs Committee. Independence, Missouri: Herald Publishing House, 1970.

Eyring, Henry B. "Finding Safety in Council." *Ensign* (May 1997): 24–26.

Faust, James E. "Spiritual Healing." *Ensign* (May 1992): 6–8.

Fielding, Harry J. "The Church and the Sacraments—Toward a Functional Interpretation." In *Restoration Studies III*, edited by Maurice L. Draper and Debra Combs. Independence, Missouri: Herald Publishing House, 1986: 21–31.

_____. "The Sacrament of Marriage." *Herald* (April 2007): 20–21.

Flanders, Robert Bruce. "Dream and Nightmare: Nauvoo Revisited." In *The Restoration Movement: Essays in Mormon History*, F. Mark McKiernan, Alma R. Blair, and Paul M. Edwards, eds. Independence, Missouri: Herald Publishing House, 1979: 141–66.

_____. "Some Reflections on the Kingdom and Gathering in Early Mormon History." *Dialogue* (Summer 1968): 156–60.

Garr, Arnold K., Donald Q. Cannon, and Richard O., Cowan, eds. *Encyclopedia of Latter-day Saint History*. Salt Lake City: Deseret Book, 2000.

Gaskill, Alonzo L. *Know Your Religions, Volume One: A Comparative Look at Mormonism and Catholicism*. Orem, Utah: Millennial Press, 2008.

Gunderson, Robert A. "Toward Defining the Source of True Mormon Doctrine." In *Restoration Studies IX*, edited by Joni Wilson. Independence, Missouri: Herald Publishing House, 2005: 239–60.

Hales, Brian C. *Mormon Fundamentalism*. Orem, Utah: Millennial Press, 2008.

Ham, Wayne. "Comment on the Book of Abraham: A Personal Reflection." In *Restoration Studies V*, edited by Paul M. Edwards and Darlene Caswell. Independence, Missouri: Herald Publishing House, 1993: 189–94.

Hatch, Stephen V. "History of the Godhead in the Community of Christ." In *Restoration Studies IX*, edited by Joni Wilson. Independence, Missouri: Herald Publishing House, 2005: 117–22.

Higdon, Barbara. "The Reorganization in the Twentieth Century." *Dialogue* (Spring 1972): 94–100.

Higdon, Miriam Elizabeth. "Eyes Single to the Glory: The History of the Heavenly City of Zion." In *Restoration Studies I,* edited by Maurice L. Draper and Clare D. Vlahos. Independence, Missouri: Herald Publishing House, 1980: 269–77.

Hinckley, Gordon B. "A Testimony Vibrant and True." *Ensign* (August 2005): 3–6.

Holm, Francis W., Sr. *The Mormon Churches: A Comparison from Within*. Kansas City, Missouri: Midwest Press, 1970.

Holy Scriptures: Inspired Version. Independence, Missouri: Price Publishing Company, 1997.

Howard, Richard P. *Restoration Scriptures: A Study of Their Textual Development*, 2d ed. Independence, Missouri: Herald Publishing House, 1995.

_____. "A Tentative Approach to the Book of Abraham." *Dialogue* (Summer 1968): 88–92.

_____. "Joseph Smith's First Vision: The RLDS Tradition." *Journal of Mormon History* (1980): 23–29.

_____. "The Changing RLDS Response to Mormon Polygamy: A Preliminary Analysis." In *Restoration Studies III*, edited by Maurice L. Draper and Debra Combs. Independence, Missouri: Herald Publishing House, 1986: 145–62.

_____. *The Church Through the Years*. 2 vols. Independence, Missouri: Herald Publishing House, 1992–1993.

_____. "The Emerging RLDS Identity." In *Restoration Studies III*, edited by Maurice L. Draper and Debra Combs. Independence, Missouri: Herald Publishing House, 1986: 44–53.

_____. "The Reorganized Church in Illinois, 1852–82: Search for Identity." *Dialogue* (Spring 1970): 63–75.

Inouye, Henry K. "Re-Enchantment of Propositional Revelation." In *Restoration Studies VI*, edited by Paul M. Edwards, Wayne Ham, and Joni Wilson. Independence, Missouri: Herald Publishing House, 1995: 107–14.

Jackson, Kent P. *The Restored Gospel and the Book of Genesis*. Salt Lake City: Deseret Book, 2001.

Jones, W. Paul. "Demythologizing and Symbolizing the RLDS Tradition." In *Restoration Studies V*, edited by Paul M. Edwards and Darlene Caswell. Independence, Missouri: Herald Publishing House, 1993: 109–15.

Jorgensen, Danny L. "Beyond Modernity: The Future of the RLDS Church." In *Restoration Studies VIII*, edited by Joni Wilson. Independence, Missouri: Herald Publishing House, 2000: 52–60.

Journal of Discourses. 26 vols. London: Latter-day Saints' Book Depot, 1854–86.

Judd, Peter. "Confirmation: Baptism of the Spirit." *Herald* (December 2006): 20–21.

Kenney, Scott G. *Wilford Woodruff's Journal*. 9 vols. Midvale, Utah: Signature Books, 1983.

Kimball, Spencer W. *Teachings of Spencer W. Kimball.* Edited by Edward L. Kimball. Salt Lake City: Bookcraft, 1982.

Koury, Aleah G. *The Truth and the Evidence.* Independence, Missouri: Herald Publishing House, 1965.

Larson, Stan. "The King Follett Discourse: a Newly Amalgamated Text." *BYU Studies* 18 (Winter 1978): 193–208.

Launius, Roger D. "An Ambivalent Rejection: Baptism for the Dead and the Reorganized Church Experience." *Dialogue* (Summer 1990): 61–84.

_____. "Coming of Age? The Reorganized Church of Jesus Christ of Latter Day Saints in the 1960s." *Dialogue* (Summer 1995): 31–57.

_____. "Is Joseph Smith Relevant to the Community of Christ?" *Dialogue* (Winter 2006): 58–67.

_____. "Joseph Smith III and the Quest for Centralized Administration (1860–73)." In *Restoration Studies II*, edited by Maurice L. Draper and A. Bruce Lindgren. Independence, Missouri: Herald Publishing House, 1983: 104–20.

_____. *Joseph Smith III: Pragmatic Prophet.* Chicago: University of Illinois Press, 1988.

_____. "Methods and Motives: Joseph Smith III's Opposition to Polygamy, 1860–1890." *Dialogue* (Winter 1987): 105–20.

_____. "The Reorganized Church, the Decade of Decision, and the Abilene Paradox." In *Restoration Studies VIII*, edited by Joni Wilson. Independence, Missouri: Herald Publishing House, 2000: 39–51.

_____. "The RLDS Church and the Decade of Decision." *Sunstone* (September 1996): 45–55.

Launius, Roger D. and W. B. Spillman, eds. *Let Contention Cease.* Independence, Missouri: Graceland/Park Press, 1991.

Launius, Roger D. and Linda Thatcher, eds. *Differing Vision: Dissenters in Mormonism.* Chicago: University of Illinois Press, 1994.

Levi and Mosiah Hancock Journal Excerpts. Genola, Utah: Pioneer Publishing, 2006.

Ludlow, Daniel H., ed. *Encyclopedia of Mormonism*, 4 vols. New York: Macmillan Publishing Company, 1992.

_____. *Latter-day Prophets Speak*. First collector's edition. Salt Lake City: Bookcraft, 1988.

Luffman, Dale E. "The Roman Letter: An Occasion to Reflect on 'Joseph Smith's New Translation of the Bible.'" In *Restoration Studies III*, edited by Maurice L. Draper and Debra Combs. Independence, Missouri: Herald Publishing House, 1986: 197–203.

Maxwell, Neal A. *Men and Women of Christ*. Salt Lake City: Bookcraft, 1991.

May, Dean. "Dissent and Authority in Two Latter-Day Saint Traditions." *Sunstone* (June 1994): 16–20.

McConkie, Bruce R. *Mormon Doctrine*. 2d ed. Salt Lake City: Bookcraft, 1966.

McConkie, Joseph Fielding. "A Historical Examination of the Views of the Church of Jesus Christ of Latter-day Saints and the Reorganized Church of Jesus Christ of Latter-Day Saints on Four Distinctive Aspects of the Doctrine of Deity Taught by the Prophet Joseph Smith." Unpublished thesis. Provo, Utah: Brigham Young University, 1968.

McKay, David O. *Improvement Era* (June 1964): 445.

McKiernan, Mark F., Alma R. Blair, Paul M. Edwards, eds. *The Restoration Movement: Essays in Mormon History*. Independence, Missouri: Herald Publishing House, 1979.

McMurray, W. Grant. "A 'Goodly Heritage' in a Time of Transformation: History and Identity in the Community of Christ." *Journal of Mormon History* (Spring 2004): 59–74.

_____. "History and Mission in Tension: A View from Both Sides." In *Restoration Studies VIII*, edited by Joni Wilson. Independence, Missouri: Herald Publishing House, 2000: 17–25.

_____. "'Something Lost, Something Gained': Restoration History and Culture Seen from 'Both Sides Now.'" *John Whitmer Historical Association Journal* (2007): 49–56.

_____. "'True Son of a True Father': Joseph Smith III and the Succession Question." In *Restoration Studies I,* edited by Maurice L. Draper and Clare D. Vlahos. Independence, Missouri: Herald Publishing House, 1980: 131–45.

Mesle, C. Robert. "'Counted as Loss': Struggling with Troublesome Traditions." In *Restoration Studies VII*, edited by Joni Wilson and Ruth Ann Wood. Independence, Missouri: Herald Publishing House, 1998: 149–56.

_____. "Zion and the Future of the RLDS Church." In *Restoration Studies IV,* edited by Marjorie B. Troeh and Eileen M. Terrill. Independence, Missouri: Herald Publishing House, 1988: 31–39.

Nelson, Russell M. "Perfection Pending." *Ensign* (November 1995): 86–88.

Newell, Linda King and Valeen Tippetts Avery. *Mormon Enigma: Emma Hale Smith.* New York: Doubleday, 1984.

Niebuhr, Gustav. "New Leader for Church That Share Mormon Roots," *New York Times,* May 12, 1996, 16.

Nii, Dave. "Orthodoxy in RLDS Thought: The Questionable Quest for Legitimacy and Reasonableness." In *Restoration Studies VIII*, edited by Joni Wilson. Independence, Missouri: Herald Publishing House, 2000: 133–40.

Oaks, Dallin H. "Special Witnesses of Christ." *Ensign* (April 2001): 13.

Packer, Boyd K. "The Mantle is Far, Far Greater Than the Intellect." *BYU Studies* 21 (Summer 1981): 259–78.

Pearl of Great Price. Salt Lake City: The Church of Jesus Christ of Latter-day Saints, 1981.

Peffers, Diane D. "The Diffusion and Dispersion of the Reorganized Church of Jesus Christ of Latter Day Saints: An Overview." Unpublished thesis. Provo, Utah: Brigham Young University, 1980.

Peterson, H. Donl. *The Pearl of Great Price: A History and Commentary.* Salt Lake City: Deseret Book, 1987.

Porter, Larry C. "The Priesthood Restored." In *Studies in Scripture, Volume Two: The Pearl of Great Price*, edited by Robert L. Millet and Kent P. Jackson. Salt Lake City: Randall Book Company, 1985.

Position Papers by the Department of Religious Education of the Reorganized Church of Jesus Christ of Latter Day Saints. Independence, Missouri: Cumorah Books, 1970.

Pratt, Parley P. *Key to the Science of Theology.* Salt Lake City: Deseret Book, 1978.

Presidential Papers, 3rd ed. Presented by the First Presidency of the RLDS Church at the Auditorium to a seminar of appointees and executives on January 9–12, 1979. Independence, Missouri: Cumorah Books, 1984.

"On Administering the Sacrament." *Improvement Era* (April 1902): 473–74.

Quinn, D. Michael. "The Mormon Succession Crisis of 1844." *BYU Studies* 16 (Winter 1976): 187–233.

Ralston, Russell F. *Fundamental Differences between the LDS and RLDS Churches.* Independence, Missouri: Price Publishing Company, 1998.

Reorganized Church of Jesus Christ of Latter Day Saints. *Church Members Manual.* Independence, Missouri: Herald Publishing House, 1991.

Reorganized Church of Jesus Christ of Latter Day Saints. *Question Time,* vol. 1. Independence, Missouri: Herald Publishing House, 1955.

Reorganized Church of Jesus Christ of Latter Day Saints. *Question Time,* vol. 3. Independence, Missouri: Herald Publishing House, 1976.

Richards, Stephen L. *Where is Wisdom?* Salt Lake City: Deseret Book, 1955.

Roberts, Allen Dale. "Profile of Apostasy: Who Are the Bad Guys, Really?" *Dialogue* (Winter 1998): 143–62.

Ruch, Velma. "To Magnify Our Calling: A Response to Section 156." In *Restoration Studies III,* edited by Maurice L. Draper and Debra Combs. Independence, Missouri: Herald Publishing House, 1986: 97–107.

Russell, William Dean. "Beyond Literalism." In *Restoration Studies IV,* edited by Marjorie B. Troeh and Eileen M. Terrill. Independence, Missouri: Herald Publishing House, 1988: 192–201.

_____. "Defenders of the Faith: Varieties of RLDS Dissent." *Sunstone* (June 1990): 14–19.

_____. "Grant McMurray and the Succession Crisis in the Community of Christ." *Dialogue* (Winter 2006): 27–57.

_____. "History and the Mormon Scriptures." *Journal of Mormon History* (1983): 53–63.

_____. "Ordaining Women and the Transformation from Sect to Denomination." *Dialogue* (Fall 2003): 61–64.

_____. "The Last Smith Presidents and the Transformation of the RLDS Church." *Journal of Mormon History* (Summer 2008): 46–84.

_____. "The LDS Church and the Community of Christ: Clearer Differences, Closer Friends." *Dialogue* (Winter 2003): 177–90.

_____. "The Remnant Church: An RLDS Schismatic Group Finds a Prophet of Joseph's Seed." *Dialogue* (Fall 2005): 75–106.

Russell, William Dean, ed. *Homosexual Saints: The Community of Christ Experience.* Ann Arbor, Michigan: John Whitmer Books, 2008.

Scherer, Mark A. "Answering Questions No Longer Asked." *Sunstone* (July 2002): 28–32.

Scott, Richard G. "Receive the Temple Blessings." *Ensign* (May 1999): 25–27.

_____. "Truth Restored." *Ensign* (November 2005): 78–81.

Sheehy, Howard S., Jr. "The Church: Structure, Function, and Unity." In *Restoration Studies III*, edited by Maurice L. Draper and Debra Combs. Independence, Missouri: Herald Publishing House, 1986: 13–20.

Shields, Andrew, ed. *Claimed by Christ's Vision.* Independence, Missouri: Community of Christ, 2008.

Shields, Steven L. *Divergent Paths of the Restoration.* 3rd ed. Bountiful, Utah: Steven L. Shields, 1982.

_____. *Latter Day Beliefs: A Comparison Between the RLDS Church and the LDS Church.* Independence, Missouri: Herald Publishing House, 1986.

_____. "The Latter Day Saints and the Restoration: An Exploration of Some Basic Themes." In *Restoration Studies VII*, edited by Joni Wilson and Ruth Ann Wood. Independence, Missouri: Herald Publishing House, 1998: 119–31.

Skoor, Susan. "'It Was Like Coming Home' My Call to the Ministry." *Sunstone* (October 2007): 59–64.

Smith, Elbert A. *Differences That Persist Between the RLDS and LDS Churches*, 2007 ed. Independence, Missouri: Price Publishing Company, 2007.

Smith, Joseph. *Lectures on Faith.* Salt Lake City: Deseret Book, 1985.

_____. *Teachings of the Prophet Joseph Smith,* selected by Joseph Fielding Smith. Salt Lake City: Deseret Book, 1976.

Smith, Joseph F. *LDS Conference Reports* (April 1904), 1–5. Photo Reprint. Salt Lake City: Hawkes Publishing.

Smith, Joseph Fielding. *Essentials in Church History.* 24th ed. Salt Lake City: Deseret Book, 1971.

_____. *Origin of the Reorganized Church and Question of Succession.* Salt Lake City: Deseret News, 1909.

Sowers, Kenneth D., Jr. "Growing Pains." In *Restoration Studies III*, edited by Maurice L. Draper and Debra Combs. Independence, Missouri: Herald Publishing House, 1986: 54–60.

Spencer, Geoffrey F. "Revelation and the Restoration Principle." In *Restoration Studies II*, edited by Maurice L. Draper and A. Bruce Lindgren. Independence, Missouri: Herald Publishing House, 1983: 186–92.

Spillman, W. B. "Adjustment or Apostasy? The Reorganized Church in the Late Twentieth Century." *Journal of Mormon History* (Fall 1994): 1–15.

Tanner, N. Eldon. "The Debate is Over." *Ensign* (August 1979): 2–3.

"The Family: A Proclamation to the World." *Ensign* (November 1995): 102.

Times and Seasons. 6 vols. Nauvoo, Illinois, November 1839–February 1846.

Trask, Paul. *Part Way to Utah: The Forgotten Mormons.* 2d ed. Independence, Missouri: Refiner's Fire Ministries, 2005.

True to the Faith: A Gospel Reference. Salt Lake City: The Church of Jesus Christ of Latter-day Saints, 2004.

Tyree Alan D. "Diving Calling in Human History." In *Restoration Studies III*, edited by Maurice L. Draper and Debra Combs. Independence, Missouri: Herald Publishing House, 1986: 86–96.

Veazey, Stephen M. "Doctrine and Covenants 163: My Testimony." *Herald* (July 2007): 12–14.

_____. "Perspectives on Church History." *Herald* (October 2008): 10–12.

_____. "Up Front." *Herald* (August 2006): 5.

Vlahos, Clare D. "Joseph Smith Jr.'s Conception of Revelation." In *Restoration Studies II*, edited by Maurice L. Draper and A. Bruce Lindgren. Independence, Missouri: Herald Publishing House, 1983: 63–74.

_____. "Mormonism and the Limits of Grace." In *Restoration Studies III*, edited by Maurice L. Draper and Debra Combs. Independence, Missouri: Herald Publishing House, 1986: 204–9.

Walking with Jesus: A Member's Guide in the Community of Christ. Independence, Missouri: Community of Christ, 2004.

Walton, George N. "Statistical Trends in the RLDS Church: 1940–1997." In *Restoration Studies VIII*, edited by Joni Wilson. Independence, Missouri: Herald Publishing House, 2000: 26–38.

We Share: Identity, Mission, Message, and Beliefs. Independence, Missouri: Community of Christ, 2009.

Welch, John W., ed. *Opening the Heavens: Accounts of Divine Manifestations, 1820–1844.* Provo, Utah: Brigham Young University Press, 2005.

Weldon, Lynn. "Seven Questions into the Future." In *Restoration Studies II*, edited by Maurice L. Draper and A. Bruce Lindgren. Independence, Missouri: Herald Publishing House, 1983:133–41.

Whitney, Orson F. *Life of Heber C. Kimball.* 6th ed. Salt Lake City: Bookcraft, 1975.

Wight, John S. "The Sacraments: Baptism." *Herald* (November 2006): 20–21.

Williams, Clyde J., ed. *Teachings of Howard W. Hunter.* Salt Lake City: Bookcraft, 1997.

Wirthlin, Joseph B. "Christians in Belief and Action." *Ensign* (November 1996): 70–73.

_____. "The Time to Prepare." *Ensign* (May 1998): 14–17.

Woodford, Robert J. "The Historical Development of the Doctrine and Covenants." 3 vols. Unpublished dissertation. Provo, Utah: Brigham Young University, 1974.

Worthington, Galen. "Crises in the RLDS Tradition: New Grasps of Essential/Instrumental Faith." In *Restoration Studies III*, edited by Maurice L. Draper and Debra Combs. Independence, Missouri: Herald Publishing House, 1986: 32–43.

Young, Brigham. *Discourses of Brigham Young*, selected and arranged by John A. Widtsoe. Salt Lake City: Deseret Book, 1969.

Young, Brigham. *The Essential Brigham Young.* Salt Lake City: Signature Books, 1992.

About the Author

Richard G. Moore grew up in Salem, Utah. After serving a mission in Japan, he graduated from Brigham Young University with a bachelor's degree in American History. Richard also received his master's degree in history from BYU and his doctorate in educational administration from the University of the Pacific. He has taught for more than thirty years in the LDS Church Educational System, and he is currently a religion instructor at BYU. Richard is the author of two previous books: 12 Keys to Developing Spiritual Maturity: Achieving Our Divine Potential and Strange Roads and Forbidden Paths: Avoiding Apostasy in the Latter Days. He is married to the former Lani Mousley, and they have three children: Adam, Travis, and Asia.

OTHER TITLES IN THE
KNOW YOUR RELIGIONS SERIES

MORMONISM AND CATHOLICISM

MORMONISM AND ASIAN RELIGIONS

MORMONISM AND ISLAM

MORMONISM AND PROTESTANTISM

MORMONISM AND JUDAISM

MORMONISM AND JEHOVAH'S WITNESSES

LOOK FOR MORE TITLES IN THE KNOW YOUR RELIGIONS SERIES

Note From the Author
[aka: The Plight of the Writer]

As this chapter in Raz's story comes to a close, I cannot accurately portray exactly how much your support and enjoyment of this book means to me, as there are no words grand enough to paint the picture. *The Wings of War* is a labor of love, a commitment to the creation of a story that will entertain, enthrall, and inspire, as so many other tales have done for me before. Your appreciation and enjoyment of my writing is a massive portion of the rewards of being an author.

It is with this note that I move on to a more personal plea, a cry for assistance from all of you who got to the end of the book and were even just a little bit sad it didn't continue on:

Please, *please,* consider rating and reviewing *The Warring Son* on one or two major bookselling or book group sites.

Even better, *please* consider supporting me directly on Patreon, and get early access to chapters and books, art, cool stuff, and much more. Find me at:
patreon.com/bryceoconnor

Many people don't know that there are thousands of books published every day, most of those in the USA alone. Over the course of a year, a quarter of a million authors will vie for a small place in the massive world of print and publishing. We fight to get even the tiniest traction, fight to climb upward one inch at a time towards the bright light of bestsellers, publishing contracts, and busy book signings.

Thing is, we need all the help we can get.

Your positive input into that world, whether it's a review, a follow on social media, or financially supporting your favorite authors, makes the climb just a little bit easier. Rating and reviewing books you enjoy and following a writer's journey gives your favorite authors a boost upward.

With that all out of the way, thank you again so much for picking up *The Warring Son.* If you'd like to give me feedback directly, have a question about Raz and his adventures, or just want to chat, drop me a message any time on Facebook, or on my website.

It has been a pleasure entertaining you, and I vigorously hope you continue to follow *The Wings of War* series to see what becomes of Raz i'Syul Arro.

Bryce O'Connor

Made in the USA
San Bernardino, CA
19 January 2020